What People Are Saying About

What Our Children Do Not Tell Us

This compelling book captures the depth of children's spiritual reflections and experiences, revealing the richness of their inner lives which too often go unnoticed. Through vivid narratives, grounded in rigorous research, the author brings their voices to the fore, while thoughtfully challenging our understanding of silence and its place in their lives. This is an invaluable, engaging text, not only for educators who embrace holistic approaches, but also for other adults seeking insight into children's spiritual worlds. A timely and powerful read.
Professor Kate Adams PhD, author of *Unseen Worlds: Looking through the Lens of Childhood* and co-author of *The Spiritual Dimension of Childhood*.

In setting out to discover whether silence, or lack of it, impacts on children's spirituality, Duffy-Cross skilfully uses the voices of children themselves to show how they experience spirituality outside the binary of 'sound' and 'non-sound', and how children's contexts and experiences correlate with concepts such as liminality, *communitas* and flow. This is a fascinating read, and an essential addition to the bookshelves of both scholars and practitioners who seek to nurture children's spirituality and thereby their wellbeing.
Dr Brendan Hyde, Deakin University, author of *Children and Spirituality: Searching for Meaning and Connectedness*.

Spiritual experiences are often difficult to articulate and are reluctantly shared. But Valerie Duffy-Cross's gentle open-ended questions enabled children aged 12–13 years old to express their feelings about life and death. Her proposed study of silence as

offering the opportunity for spiritual reflection, grew into a wide-ranging study of the liminal space in which children are able to experience openings into other dimensions. Enriched by her scholarly analysis, this book opens up the world of childhood spirituality.
Marianne Rankin PhD, author of *A Quiet Day at Home* and *An Introduction to Religious and Spiritual Experience.*

So valuable to see rigorous academic attention being paid to the hugely important (and neglected) dimension of children's spirituality, however that is experienced and expressed, and its relevance to their mental health and well-being. The result is a feast of insights – for the children themselves as they verbalise their experiences, and for the resulting findings. Most importantly it makes the case for incorporating this awareness into our provision for their mental health.

Just as we have found in the peace education programmes – that children, if given the space, confidence and assurance of being listened to with respect, will come up with revelatory statements, this research has offered that opportunity for children to verbalise their most profound feelings about their spiritual life.
Helen Porter, Co-ordinator, Mid-Wales Peaceful Schools Project.

Valerie Duffy-Cross is the teacher I wish I had had when I was a pupil; an indefatigable advocate for the right of children to a healthy, meaningful upbringing and an inventive ally when it comes to young people discovering who they are, and who they could become.

This could be a hugely important book. In November 2024, half a million children in the UK were in touch with Mental Health services, a combination of individual tragedy and societal shame: How could we allow this to happen? Rather than engage – like most of us – in finding someone to blame,

Duffy-Cross offers a different route towards salutogenesis: recognising that spirituality in children reflects a natural disposition, she explores ways in which their adult environment can provide spaces for tranquil, restorative reflection. She sees silence as a meaningful form of communication, especially with one's Self and the non-verbal parts of one's environment.

The children she interviews are often tongue-tied, and she replicates their words so accurately that one can almost hear them speak. The authenticity of their struggle to do justice to their feelings and convictions, in a language that they have inherited but don't fully possess, is more powerful than even the most carefully chosen academic research. As a result, the reader's heart opens alongside their minds.

In an educational system – and for many children this includes their homes – that supervises and compartmentalises their lives, exposing them to high expectations in cognitive, social and leisure activities, young people need opportunities for non-structured time, regular moments when they are not *accountable*. The natural fluidity of a child's consciousness is an asset worth protecting; it allows them to acknowledge and enter liminal spaces that exist but can't be known, that can be loved without being understood and accepted without proof. This book offers powerful arguments for creating environments that support this.

Valerie Duffy-Cross, in this much anticipated book, has brought years of study and contextual experience to a field that all of us would do well to cultivate. It is to be hoped that, through inspired educators, thousands of children may benefit from her work.

Sven Saar, *International Teacher Education and Development*: www.modernteacher.org.

This book is a very significant contribution to the debates around the mental health of contemporary young people. In its exploration of children's spiritual experiencing, it enters insightfully into many theories in this area and their relationship to the demands of contemporary society, in particular those in education. By listening extensively to young people, the author provides a detailed exploration of the importance of the liminal/spiritual space and how it can be approached. All parents, teachers and education policy makers need to engage with the contents of this book.

The Rev Professor June Boyce-Tillman MBE, author of *Experiencing Music – Restoring the Spiritual: Music as Wellbeing; Spirituality and Music Education: Perspectives from Three Continents; Freedom Song: Faith, Abuse, Music and Spirituality: A Lived Experience of Celebration*.

I first encountered Valerie's work some years ago when she got in touch, having read a discussion paper I wrote about the inclusion of spiritual well-being in the South Australian education department's learner wellbeing framework. I sensed a kindred spirit in our sensibilities – spiritual, emotional, academic and ethical. I wrote then that her work was 'beautifully written, with nuance, sensitivity, high-level ethical orientation and with respect for young people'. It was a delight to revisit her work in the form of this fine book. As I read, I felt as though we were continuing our conversation, respectfully traversing the scholarship of so many authors with whom we are both familiar and then contributing something unique in the form of children's voices and insights. I love the focus on the feeling and embodied dimensions so skilfully elicited through Valerie's subtle questioning. This is so needed in these times when emotions and bodies are so often seen as something to be controlled, kept in check. I myself experienced a significant 'out of body' event as a child, resulting from a near drowning. I would have benefitted greatly from being able to describe that experience to Valerie, who I can imagine sitting kindly, exuding a calm, loving and non-judgemental presence as I recounted my experience of a great energy of love and light, then soaring up to meet it, only to find myself back in a cold, lonely body. There was no Valerie for me, no space for sharing. So, I chose not to tell anyone about it until much later, when, as an adult, I found a spiritual mentor. I think there is an important, healing and witnessing dimension to the authentic listening space she has provided to the children she 'interviewed', that we can partake of, vicariously – a wonderful additional outcome of her study. I feel that a deep reading of this book has the potential to reconnect us with the liminal space of childhood that seems to slip from our grasp as we develop the dominant way of knowing in our culture, that of cognition. In this way, we may become more whole.

Dr Leigh Burows, Flinders University, author of *Empowering Mindfulness for Women; Safeguarding Mindfulness in Schools and Higher Education: A Holistic and Inclusive Approach.*

What Our Children Do Not Tell Us

Silence, Spirituality and Liminality

Our children's quiet plea for understanding
in a pressured world

What Our Children Do Not Tell Us

Silence, Spirituality and Liminality

Our children's quiet plea for understanding in a pressured world

Valerie Duffy-Cross

Essentia

London, UK
Washington, DC, USA

CollectiveInk

First published by Essentia Books, 2026
Essentia Books is an imprint of Collective Ink Ltd.,
Unit 11, Shepperton House, 89 Shepperton Road, London, N1 3DF
office@collectiveinkbooks.com
www.collectiveinkbooks.com
www.essentia-books.com

For distributor details and how to order, please visit the 'Ordering' section on our website.

ISBN: 978 1 80341 947 3
978 1 917991 51 3 (ebook)
Library of Congress Control Number: 2025945232

A CIP catalogue record for this book is available from the British Library.

Design: Lapiz Digital Services

UK: Printed and bound by CPI Group (UK) Ltd, Croydon, CR0 4YY
Printed in North America by CPI GPS partners

The manufacturer's authorised representative in the EU for product safety is:
eucomply OÜ - Pärnu mnt 139b-14, 11317 Tallinn, Estonia, hello@eucompliancepartner.com,
www.eucompliancepartner.com

Contents

To Donald, Alice and Mya

There was a time when meadow, grove and stream,
The earth, and every common sight,
To me did seem
Apparelled in celestial light,
The glory and freshness of a dream.
It is not now as it hath been of yore;
Turn wheresoe'er I may,
By night or day.
The things which I have seen I now can see no more.

From: William Wordsworth.
Intimations of Immortality from Recollections of Early Childhood. 1804

Preface

A casual visitor to the school gymnasium during lunchtime in the mid 1980s might have been alarmed to see a large number of uniformed teenagers lying on the floor, apparently asleep. They were not. Instead, in an English school, in the Midlands, they were listening to a teacher guiding them through differential relaxation and encouraging them to imagine they were on a beach in the sunshine, with all the pleasure that this might evoke. Had the visitor arrived earlier she would likely have heard the teenagers discuss their fear of the impending examinations, and their distress. Lack of sleep, digestive ailments, mood swings, depression and eating disorders were only some of the problems that they raised, and nearly all expressed their relief that they now knew they were not alone with these, often incapacitating, feelings.

This range of anxieties was a very new challenge for schools and parents and there were no resources or guidance available to help.

During the same period an equally alarming phenomenon was being noted in many schools. An increasing number of much younger pupils was manifesting a range of mental health problems, well beyond the support capacity of the usually effective, pastoral care systems. There was, however, no easy possibility of onward referral to mental health professionals for a child. Children were not, by and large, expected to manifest such problems. After all, weren't the lives of the majority of them free from adult cares and pressures? Alerting a local Member of the UK Parliament to the developing crisis eventually resulted in the very first child psychiatrist being appointed to the local hospital in our town of 60,000 inhabitants.

Sadly, over forty years later, there is rarely adult surprise at the surging number of children expressing problematic levels of distress and anxiety in the UK and other 'Western' nations. There is, however, consternation, and it is within this context that the research forming the basis of this book and its findings are situated.

A number of recent studies have explored the positive effects of spirituality and spiritual experience on the mental health of children, and the importance of its recognition and support. This book presents a unique understanding of children's spirituality based on (frank and frequently surprising) extensive one-to-one conversations with children aged 12–13 over a period of eight years. These took place across England and in a range of secondary schools from secular to Catholic, Steiner to Quaker. The conversations particularly explored how children's access to silence or non-sound, affected any spirituality.

Using the children's voices extensively, the book illustrates the range of types of spirituality expressed by them and goes on to identify the when and where of these experiences. They occur in nature, listening to music, engaging in artistic pursuits, in moments of joy and wonder, alone or with others, in silence and in mayhem. They often result in the children questioning the meaning of their lives and their purpose on Earth.

I have worked with children (11–18 years old) as a secondary school teacher and headteacher for 38 years and have seen major changes, many detrimental, over time in their daily lives. I was driven to discover whether the digital noise, lack of silence and apparently pressured lifestyles of the children I was seeing, were having a negative effect on any spirituality and hence well-being. Yet the expected high level of importance of silence to support spirituality (as traditionally emphasised by religious groups, philosophers, meditators and school movements such as Montessori) was not evident in these conversations. I was further confounded when the children explained to me that though silence (as non-sound) might be important for some, for many it was unwelcome and even irrelevant as they entered their own unique spaces and altered states of awareness – unsought states from which they often returned refreshed, renewed and often with a different sense of self. These periods were cherished, vividly remembered, regarded as transformative, and hardly ever discussed with others. The children feared being labelled as 'odd' or even as liars – certainly, they were wary of being misunderstood by their peers and particularly by adults.

Such states have been described as 'liminal' states, and the book examines and finds correspondences between the children's experiences and those described by folklorists and anthropologists following extensive international fieldwork.

Using this completely different way of understanding child spirituality as a springboard, the question is then asked: How can we best support and nurture the spirituality of our children, the better to promote their well-being? The 'we' includes all of us who care for, educate, or bring up children. Amongst other implications for the research (social and educational) it is suggested here, and with urgency, that we listen to them with 'the ears of peers'. Furthermore, as they have much to teach us, we should respect their allowing us into their private world, worlds that they frequently describe as 'weird', pre-empting potential ridicule.

Navigating the content: A guide to the chapters

Because I believe that it is important to reach as wide a readership as possible, I have used the first three chapters to set out the research rationale and methodology, including an exploration of silence in religion, education and philosophy. Readers wishing to focus solely on what the children have said may prefer to skip these chapters and start at Chapter 4.

Chapter 1: Children in Distress

I outline my personal impetus and sense of urgency for the work. The deterioration in the mental health of children over the past thirty years is charted. Evidence is shown for the potential improvement in well-being that is linked to the support and recognition of child spirituality. The chapter examines general definitions of spirituality and ways of identifying child spirituality suggested by a range of writers and researchers. The question is raised as to whether silence, in all its forms, is of any importance to child spirituality.

Chapter 2: Letting the Children Speak

Here we see an explanation of the decisions made regarding who, where and how to have conversations with children and the problems of the adult 'getting out of the way' in the process.

Chapter 3: Looking at Silence

Most world religions and several educational movements, including Steiner (Waldorf) and Montessori schools place a high value on silence, frequently regarded as a trigger for spirituality and spiritual experience. The chapter explores the meaning of silence for children and for their spirituality, as well as giving a brief overview of those movements where silence is regarded as important.

Chapter 4: 'It's Weird, Miss': Children Speak of Their Spirituality

There has been much debate during the last fifty years about whether children are spiritual beings, or whether any such spirituality only develops with maturity. Therefore, before looking at any *contexts* for child spirituality, the case has to be made that it actually exists. Selected definitions of spirituality are presented here for clarification. In this chapter children speak freely and passionately of their spirituality and spiritual experiences, usually without labelling them as such.

Chapter 5: 'It Can Happen Anywhere': Spirituality Arising

One of the most surprising discoveries from the research was that the children described experiencing moments of spirituality in a very broad range of contexts: whilst in nature; whilst absorbed; during laughter and imaginative pursuits; in groups or alone; in silence and in noise; during extreme emotion and during physical exertion. There was no common catalyst for the moments, nor were they sought. They came unexpectedly and largely pleasurably. This chapter presents examples of the 'when and where' of child spirituality and their reactions to it.

Chapter 6: 'Only When I Sleep': Children's Time Poverty

Despite these many situations where spirituality arose or was expressed. A large number of the children spoke of their pressured and highly structured lives, the emphasis on achievement (academic and otherwise), their tiredness, and of their 'to-do lists'. This chapter creates space for their voices and their frequent anguish to be heard.

Chapter 7: 'And Then I Come Back In': Children speak of Silence

Following a discussion of the range of understanding of 'silence', the children's varied experiences of, and attitudes towards, silence as non-sound are presented. Some speak of their dislike of imposed silence and of the association of silence with bereavement and aloneness. Some talk of their enjoyment of being silent – 'it's your best friend'. Gradually, from their comments, we see that, whatever their feeling about silence, they often appear to be entering a special place, one that is powerful and causes them to emerge changed.

Chapter 8: 'You Come from One Dimension to Another': A Sacred Space

Such a space has been spoken of by a range of writers. It has been referred to as 'the crack between worlds', as liminality, where a person can be 'fashioned anew'.[1] The children describe this space vividly in this chapter, and here I propose that the entering of this 'liminal' space is a new and important way of understanding children's spirituality. Though the expression and context of their spirituality may vary, there is an underlying thread that is related to, but is not, silence.

Chapter 9: From Negation to Nurture

Chapter 9 reinforces the importance of listening to and acknowledging accounts of children's spiritual experience, in order to enhance their well-being and mental health. Here it is emphasised that such spirituality *can* be nurtured and that providing an accommodating environment for this, whether in the family home, in educational, therapeutic, or in more general settings, is a responsibility that falls on all who encounter children. It asks that we reexamine our educational system that sidelines more creative and imaginative subjects, and that we also reflect on our society that prizes achievement and busyness above imagination and stillness.

This book, though incubated over a lifetime and researched over nearly a decade, has a sense of urgency. Yet the conclusions and suggestions here are not offered as a messianic panacea for the alarming problems we are currently seeing amongst our youth. The causes and the solutions for these are many-layered and challenging, even if and when identified. The book is offered as a part of the contribution to support our children, and, as it derives from their unfiltered voices, it is hoped it might reach the very 'heart' of the matter.

Foreword

Spirituality is big business. One only has to type the word into an internet search engine, browse social media sites, or scour physical and virtual bookshelves to see that it is a multi-billion-pound industry. Spirituality is also, of course, much more than a money-making machine. It is a field of academic study, and most importantly of all, it is a way of life for vast numbers of people across the planet, through which they find meaning and purpose, navigate difficult situations, and attain positive well-being. And yet, across all these varied and sometimes conflicting domains, there is a significant group of people who are under-represented: children and young people.

I have been researching different aspects of children's spirituality for over a quarter of a century and have seen little substantive change in this situation. I remain perplexed as to why there is not more interest in young people's inner lives in many western countries.

Like Valerie, I had also enjoyed a career in teaching, albeit with younger children, who regularly offered inspirational insights into philosophical issues. Over the years, many teachers and other adults have expressed their belief to me that children, especially those from non-religious backgrounds 'do not have the language to talk about spiritual or religious ideas'. While recognising that words are not always adequate to convey the intangible, and notwithstanding the immense value of other creative methods of expression, I have always challenged their claims. My own research, alongside that of others, and innumerable encounters with children in daily life, illustrates how effectively they can describe their ideas and experiences. The children quoted in this book offer further evidence to support that contestation.

Reading their words, exactly as they were related to the author, makes for moving moments, not least because they illustrate children's capacities for profound reflection on life. However, the emotion is even more acute when they are considered in their cultural context, as they describe it: a fast-paced, noisy, outcome-orientated and demanding world which does not pause for breath. Their descriptions of 'time poverty' are unsettling. Their anxiety is palpable.

The pressures on children are concerning, particularly those imposed by England's school system which, as in many other countries, is driven by government agendas to achieve ever higher test and exam scores. There is a strong, ongoing backlash against such education systems from a myriad of stakeholders. I too have experienced and witnessed the stresses placed upon pupils and teachers generated by policies which value measurable outcomes over holistic approaches. The former diminish the importance of the inner life, of the connection to self, others, animals, nature and for some the transcendent, which are essential for positive well-being. Performative education systems tend to privilege future careers and economic outputs as their primary goals, which both mirror and reinforce wider cultural narratives. The search for meaning and purpose, which can be a lifetime's endeavour, can suffer from being reduced to the discourse of 'what do you want to do when you grow up?'. Yes, this is an important question, as paid and voluntary work can be powerful ways of securing a fulfilling life. Yet many people also find their calling in other ways, which are not catered for sufficiently in schools, colleges and universities. Crucially, it is during childhood that we begin to explore such ideas, embarking on the quest to discover who we are, as well as what we might become. Sometimes, intuitive approaches to finding answers are used, while processing others' views of us. The philosophical question 'who am I?' goes much deeper than deciding what job to do when we are older, as it raises so many questions about the nature of self, 'reality', and different states of consciousness. Many children report experiences related to these themes, and dialogue with others about them can be nourishing. However, many children report not having anyone with whom they can share this type of meaningful conversation.

Of course, in economically advanced societies many adults from all walks of life struggle to find sufficient quality time to listen to young people. Some do not even have the time to rest, recuperate or reflect themselves. Being overburdened, combined with a lack of awareness of young people's spirituality, is an unhealthy situation for society, and also a complex one for which there are no simple answers. Research has shown that spirituality can support positive well-being but, of course, as well as those who embrace the spiritual in its myriad of forms, many other adults have never even thought about it. They may be unclear about what it is. Indeed, academics and practitioners have long engaged in international debates about what is meant by the term 'spirituality', and even whether it is possible to define it. People might be uncomfortable with the word and use alternative phrases, while others do not deem it relevant to their own lives. So where does this leave children? Education has immense potential to support pupils' flourishing, and England occupies a particularly interesting position in this area.

When I began researching, I remember describing the English school curriculum to a colleague from the US. She was envious to learn that the promotion of children's 'spiritual development' has been enshrined in education legislation in some form since the 1944 Education Act. Today, schools are mandated to promote it alongside moral, social and cultural development, and to do so across the curriculum. My colleague was in awe, but unfortunately I had to disappoint her. I explained that despite guidance from various bodies on how to navigate this area, including from the schools' inspectorate, there were swathes of teachers who were unaware of this requirement, or misunderstood it, wrongly equating it only with Religious Education. With little to no time to address the theme in initial teacher training programmes, which had become increasingly prescriptive, I suggested that one way forward is to share children's experiences and ponderings with adults. Surely, I reasoned, adults would be impressed by what they would hear and come to see young people in different ways, even if 'spirituality' did not resonate with them personally.

In retrospect, as a new academic at the time, perhaps I had been a little naïve. I soon came to realise that many other factors mitigate against us *really* listening to children, despite there being countless advocates for them across the globe. We have witnessed an elevation in the importance of the 'child's voice' internationally over the last few decades. Academics working primarily in the new sociology of childhood pioneered its theoretical development, and the concept has been enshrined in legislation through various declarations of human rights, most recently in the United Nations Convention of the Rights of the Child in 1989. While signatories have made provisions for their voice in education, health and social care policies amongst others, its applications to practice have often been considered tokenistic.

Children in this book echo views of peers in different studies of feeling unheard in general, and particularly so in relation to their spiritual voices. Regrettably, that is not unsurprising, given that many western cultures trivialise the spiritual, despite it being 'everywhere' in the monetised and virtual worlds, in faith communities and in secular homes. At the same time, adults also tend to view children (often unconsciously) as what they will become, rather than appreciating them as beings in the present, who carry inner wisdom. Their thoughts are often dismissed as imagination or attention-seeking. These views are further compounded by the imposition of adult lenses onto what they say, which mitigates against really understanding what they are trying to communicate. However, I remain convinced that one of the best ways forward to raise awareness of children's spirituality and to nurture it, is to help adults understand their worlds more effectively, from their perspectives.

Therefore, every new, well-thought-out publication on children's spirituality such as this one is a welcome addition to the increasing body of informed literature on the topic. Through texts of this kind, as well as other forms of sharing research and ideas, we can collectively rethink and reshape how we perceive young people's inner lives and nurture them accordingly. In this book you will be presented with new ideas from the author and rich narratives from children which call on us to truly hear what they have to say, even if it challenges how we think about young people. In fact, I propose that their views *should* challenge our thinking. In so doing, the book conveys messages for all adults, which are as relevant to parents, grandparents, carers, relatives and all professionals who work with children, as they are for teachers themselves.

I leave you in the very capable hands of Valerie Duffy-Cross, who will take you on her journey alongside the young people who walked with her. As she says, if we are humble enough to learn from children, we can make great strides in supporting them in their spiritual lives and their well-being. We might also learn something about ourselves in the process.

Professor Kate Adams, PhD
Leeds Trinity University, UK
July 2025

Acknowledgements

This is the book that my friend and tutor Dr Maya Warrier (1970 – 2021) saw coming, and actually in her quiet way insisted on one day being written. She would, I think, have taken great delight in it and, I hope, would have seen the fruits of our many conversations and of her introduction to me of anthropology and the Turners. Her generosity of spirit and her gentle, luminous intelligence have cast a mantle over the whole of it.

Some of the most important contributions to the book have necessarily to be anonymous. I would like to thank all the children who gave up their time and their secrets to a complete stranger and who made me both laugh and cry as they did so. It was an honour to be the recipient of the stories of their thoughts and lives. I am aware of the extra burden placed on school staff in accommodating my needs during visits and, though the schools cannot be named, I will always remember the staff there for their helpfulness and enthusiasm.

Before any research in schools, I was given generous help and support by several individuals and organisations: I am very thankful to Anna Lubelska and Helen Porter from the Peaceful Schools Movement; Mel Cook and Isabel Cartwright from Quakers in Britain: Miriam Gosling from Peace and Global Studies; David O'Dell and David Donaldson who are involved in the Steiner movement.

I benefitted from and am grateful for pivotal, inspiring conversations with Professor June Boyce-Tillman (UK) and Dr Leigh Burrows (Australia). Their encouragement and validation were of a value more than they probably realise. Dr Alasdair Richardson ensured (and with kindly rigour) that the research was methodologically as well as ethically sound.

Thank you so much to the readers of the early manuscripts (pressganged and otherwise) who provided such helpful and constructive criticism and also much support. I thank the constant Richard Moore for his insightful, detailed feedback; the educationalist Susan Crisp, who read it through the lens of a love of children and their welfare always in mind; eagle-eyed and highly meticulous Alice McCallum, and Donald McCallum whose patience, willingness to discuss, psychological and practical support and forensic critiques were beyond what might be expected from anyone.

Professor Kate Adams believed in the importance of this book from the start. Freely giving her time and her very extensive, internationally renowned, expertise to support it, she embodies the epitome of real academic collaboration and the selfless championing of others in the interest of truth. I am fortunate to call her my friend, and am grateful to her for her humour, calm, and incisive intellect and wisdom.

Chapter 1

Children in Distress

What you are about to read is largely the voices of children. They are speaking to us in the middle of a period of intense concern about child well-being – in particular, an international concern about perceived problems of adolescent alienation and mental health issues. Yet this is a hopeful book, and our children are showing us the way.

I was determined to try to discover more about their experiences and issues by speaking with children, and at a greater length than the usual adult-child interactions. I did not come to this process as a blank slate, and I would like to confess all my biases. I have already described in the preface my interest in child mental health over four decades. During the same period, I had become interested in meditation of all types including transcendental meditation (TM) and started to host a (still-continuing) Julian of Norwich meditation group.[2] I was thus interested in the value of silence for well-being as well as for spiritual engagement.

At one point in my working life, I moved as headteacher to a school that included a slightly younger age group than I was used to, 11–16 rather than 13–18 years.

I had here several formative experiences. At times, and though not a Religious Education (RE) teacher, I would take an RE class for absent staff where the work had been pre-set. I started to chat to the pupils, encountering, I thought, a familiar trope of a child's love of distraction in lesson times. It was, however, more than this. In the midst of drawing artefacts of various religions, the children started to ask me, as an 'omniscient adult': Why are we here? What happens when we die? What is love? Is there a spirit world? and many other questions to which I could only reply that I didn't know. There followed on many occasions a vigorous debate engaging the whole class and also the adult classroom assistants who participated on an equal basis, having the same questions to ask. Children clearly wanted to discuss and explore the big questions, and they wanted to be heard. Yet I knew that the time to allow such 'off the curriculum' discussions could not often be found.

During the same period, in a shared observation of a geography lesson (with an inspector from the UK Office for Standards in Education, Ofsted), taken by an excellent and Ofsted-guideline-adhering teacher, the children were hurried, stop-watch fashion, through a range of tasks involving, for example, group work (five minutes), writing (five minutes) and exposition. The speed of this left me, and clearly them, confused. The inspector declared this to be 'an outstanding lesson with exemplary pace'. Such an emphasis on speed with little reflection time seemed to me to be symptomatic of a modern child's life and educational experience.

We then introduced, in the school, on an annual basis, a carpeted and cushioned geodesic inflatable dome in the school gymnasium. Children (and staff) were able to come and sit for half-hour sessions in silence. Many children wrote in the guest book of a feeling of peace and calm, others slept, some said they had never had the experience of silence in their whole lives. Some were afraid, and one declared, tongue in cheek (as he later admitted), an experience of transcendence. For some children (and several staff) this opportunity was welcome, and, for many, a rare event.

Their deep, yet tentative questions, their harried and often stressful lives and their lack of quiet and silence, created a picture of children that seemed to suggest that something needed to be done for them, and urgently. This was not a localised phenomenon.

Should we be concerned?

Nearly a decade ago, 20,000 young people (15–21-year-olds) were surveyed globally, and the results were published in the *Varkey Report*. The UK was placed nineteenth out of twenty countries for mental well-being, with respondents expressing concern about insufficient rest and little time for reflection in their lives.[3] These comments were repeated across the twenty participating countries. Gradually, over subsequent years, public attention in the UK started to be drawn to what was deemed to be an 'unfolding crisis': in the national press, by children's charities such as the NSPCC,[4] by teachers and medical professionals, and, eventually, by the National Health Service.[5]

Schoolteachers had corroborated these findings as early as 2018 with 78 per cent of teachers in a survey undertaken by STEM4 (a charity supporting teenage mental health) having seen a pupil struggle with mental health during the previous year, largely with anxiety.

The onset of the Covid-19 pandemic (approximately early 2020) is believed to have compounded the problems. The medical journal *The Lancet* (May 2021) highlighted a rise in mental health problems in 5–15-year-olds in England from 10.8% in 2017 to 16% by mid-2020.

The Children's Society charity's annual report 'The Good Childhood' for 2021 also indicated 'an alarming state of decline' in child well-being with 7% of 10–15-year-olds being unhappy with their lives (306,000), almost double that of ten years before.

The UK National Health Service reported in 2024 that 1 in 5 children and young people (age 8–25) had a probable mental disorder: over 2 million. This represents a rise from the 400,000 young people under nineteen treated in 2018 (up 3% from the preceding year) with 50,000 children and young people referred every month for treatment in that year.

In May 2024, The National Society for the Prevention of Cruelty to Children reported that over half of children's counselling sessions in the UK related to mental or emotional health and well-being.

Similarly, the UK children's charity Action for Children, whose remit is to 'protect and support children and to improve their lives', reported in 2024 that 1 in 6 children (aged 5–16) in the UK is likely to have a mental health problem. The figure had risen in the previous three years by 50%.

Many reasons have been attributed to what has been described as an 'alarming state of decline' of children's sense of well-being in the UK. Increasing poverty, unrealistic expectations of wealth and fame, academic pressures, diet, family disintegration and the onset of the Covid-19 pandemic have all been named, amongst other reasons, as contributing factors. Studies in the US have also reported the rising rates of mental problems and emotional distress among even relatively affluent children and adolescents. One such report, *Hardwired to Connect*, as early as 2010, suggested fundamental social change was needed.[6] This included a shift from a pharmacological model of treatment, focussed on remedies for individual pathology or dysfunction, to a radical shift in thinking that might, according to the report, affect an entire generation. Citing research on the biochemistry of connection, the study asserted the profound influence that religiosity and spirituality can have on the young, enhancing their well-being to a significant level.

This was not a new idea. Janet Seden, in the Faculty of Health and Social Care at the Open University UK, had long suggested that neglecting children's sense of truth, justice or mystery may leave them expressing their terror and pain in ways which society might find unacceptable, and that it is important to respect their spiritual values.[7] Psychologists and educational psychologists were also finding the positive effect of spirituality during the general recovery from trauma and illness and on coping with stress and depression. In 2009 Australian educationalist John Fisher was particularly blunt. In his suggestions for enhanced health care, he proposed that an accurate assessment of human spirituality was needed in order to restore spiritual health for 'the survival of the whole human race'.[8] This is spirituality seen as a counter-apocalyptic and therapeutic tool, alleviating the *terror and pain* identified by Janet Seden.

Others took up the baton with a sense of urgency. UK educationalists David Hay and Rebecca Nye (2006) sought to identify and name key aspects of children's spirituality. Coining the phrase 'relational consciousness', they suggested that this was a major and core aspect of children's spirituality, denoting a sense of particularly powerful relationships with people, animals and places.[9] Once again, we are warned, that following the development of extreme individualism, especially in Western nations, there has been a 'forgetting' of this relational consciousness.

To underline all of this, in 2014 a group of researchers led by US developmental psychologist Peter Scales undertook a global study of 12–23-year-olds.[10] They found a positive correlation between higher scores on a Youth Spiritual Development Index and well-being. So, in the new millennium, we see children's spirituality afforded not only some recognition but also valorisation.

Spirituality examined

I was convinced that, if given sufficient time and space, children would eventually provide some ideas as to how they might be supported in their spirituality. And quietly, I felt sure that somehow silence might provide some kind of solution to this. I needed to talk to them. When I did so, it seemed necessary to find out whether it was reasonable to say that children were indeed spiritual beings. After all, since philosopher and political theorist John Locke (1689) spoke of children entering the world as *tabulae rasae*, others from a range of disciplines, for example, educationalist Piaget (1926) and transpersonal psychologist Ken Wilber (2007) had maintained that the majority of children 'grew into' becoming spiritual beings, in a set of recognisable stages.[11] In other words, there was no fully formed spirituality that could be discerned; it was still developing.

Edward Robinson's challenge to this, as early as 1977, after a range of extensive interviews with children, did not find a foothold in its time.[12] Nor did the powerful evidence presented by psychiatrist Robert Coles, also in 1977, and drawn from a lifetime's international psychologically therapeutic work with children, hold sway. Noticing the frequency of references to religious and/or spiritual topics raised by the children he had interviewed, whom Coles met up to 25 times, and directly influenced by conversations with British psychoanalyst Anna Freud (youngest child of Sigmund Freud and Martha Bernays and often regarded as the first child psychoanalyst), he sought to re-examine his data using a different lens – that of spirituality. Describing children as 'seekers', his wife and co-researcher, Jane Hallowell, concluded that the children were clearly 'pilgrims, travellers, on a road with some purpose in mind'.[13] As will be seen, it was not until the turn of the millennium that this new optic fully affected the questions and approaches that any researchers adopted with children.

But what was actually meant by spirituality? Are there different definitions for child spirituality? These are such problematic questions that many working on children's spirituality simply do not venture to define this term. As a solution, it has been suggested that we should not seek to find a consensus on *one* generally acceptable definition, but should instead, use whatever is most helpful to our own work and focus. We are cautioned, however, by Hyde that the concept of spirituality is in danger of being about almost anything.[14]

Noting this caveat, I, nevertheless, found the following definitions to be the most helpful for this investigation, and they are to be regarded as overlapping. They are consistent with the view that children's spirituality might best be identified in their everyday lives.[15]

a. Spirituality refers to everyone's natural connection with the wonder and energy of life and the instinct to explore that experience and its meaning.[16]
b. Spirituality exists wherever we struggle with the issue of how our lives fit into the greater scheme of things. We encounter spirituality every time we wonder where the universe comes from, why we are here and what happens when we die, or when we are moved by values such as beauty, love or creativity that seem to reveal a meaning beyond our visible world.[17]
c. Spirituality is the way individuals seek and express meaning and purpose. It is the way they express their connectedness to the moment, to self, to others, to nature, and to the significant or sacred.[18]

When examining the literature on spirituality and, specifically, children's spirituality, we see the terms 'spiritual experience', 'religious experience' and 'spirituality' used almost interchangeably. They are difficult terms to separate.

I adopted the framework suggested by Marianne Rankin who describes *spiritual* experience 'as an experience which points beyond normal everyday life' giving 'an indication of a greater reality underlying the physical world of the senses'.[19] Rankin distinguishes this from '*religious* experience' that additionally confirms, or conforms to, the tenets of a particular religious tradition. These two terms imply an *event* that may be remembered, something time-bound, with an often-lasting impact, whether positive or negative. Spirituality, in contrast to spiritual experience, might be viewed as a condition, or a state of being, but one that is not always perceived by individuals, particularly children, to be worthy of note, and which they often may not identify as 'spirituality' at all.

Children's spirituality more closely defined

Towards the end of the twentieth century there was noticeable growth in interest in children's spirituality. Gradually there arose the conviction that it is only through *their* voices that we can truly learn about it. In 1994, Clive and Jane Erricker founded *The International Journal for Children's Spirituality* with a strong recommendation that future researchers should listen to children with 'an open ear'. Unsurprisingly, there began at the end of the millennium a steep rise in studies based on interviews with children. One such study led by David Hay and Rebecca Nye proposed that spirituality was a biological inheritance, transcending culture and even religion. During their interviews with children, Hay and Nye noted a meta-cognition and an awareness of themselves as subject. As we have seen, 'relational consciousness' was also deemed to be of key relevance, and this was unrelated to cognitive development. In a challenging assertion, they suggested that children might be the model for adult spirituality, rather than the reverse, and that spirituality in its widest range was entirely natural, growing out of a predisposition, which could potentially be enhanced or diminished by cultural influences.

This work catalysed the development of new lenses through which those interested could ascertain and analyse the spirituality of children, and it heralded the move away from the religious vocabulary and the largely Christian assumptions of earlier research. There was now a new focus on the responses of children to everyday and ordinary activities and a flurry of attempts to categorise, name, group and contain the many forms of spirituality that appeared to be shown. Some of these forms include:

1. **The Felt sense**: incorporating the idea of flow and an integration of the person with the experience (Hyde)
2. **Integrating Awareness**: the transcending of an activity and a second emerging level of consciousness (Hyde)
3. **Weaving the Threads of Meaning**: incorporating a sense of wonder and the creation of a world view and a meaning (Eaude,[20] Hyde)
4. **Value Sensing**: the search for ultimate meaning and purpose (Hay and Nye)
5. **Spiritual Questing**: moral sensitivity gauged in terms of the child's response to the question 'I wonder what you think really, really matters?'(Hyde)
6. **Sensitive**: the perception of the world through the senses and an awareness of being-in-the-world (Champagne[21])
7. **Awareness sensing**: heightened awareness, flow (or full engagement and immersion in an activity) and focus, including a 'felt sense' (Hay and Nye)
8. **Relational**: a sense of being in relation to others, a filiation, rendering oneself open to love (Champagne)/ Relational Consciousness (Hay and Nye)
9. **Mystery Sensing**: with a stress on the importance of the imagination (Hay and Nye)
10. **Existential**: a sense of being in time and space and, for children, of the 'here and now' manifested in the child's imagination, games and symbols (Champagne)

The collations and interpretations often overlapped, varied in number and emphasis and would be later critiqued as either dismantling that which should better be regarded holistically or focussing too narrowly on the factual 'what' of spirituality rather than examining *how* it is experienced.

Less complex frameworks were exemplified by British educationalist Eaude, who succinctly identified child spirituality as 'a universal search for meaning and identity', stressing the importance of awe and wonder. He suggested that 'unfolding', implying the manifestation of an already-existing potential, would be a more apposite way of understanding their spirituality.[22]

Did these definitions help when talking to children?

Briefly – to an extent. As I have said, I felt that my first task would be to confirm whether the children I interviewed were actually expressing spirituality. After all, if they were not, then there would be little point in trying to find out whether silence had any significance for such spirituality. To do this, I drafted questions for them that might elicit responses corresponding to some of the headings created by interviewers and researchers before me, for example, 'What do you think really matters in life?'. The headings proved useful as a starting point both in my meetings with children and in examining their words afterwards. My instincts, however, warned me to keep an open mind. A similar mind had to be adopted when considering silence, as we shall see later in this book.

I now needed to talk to children, and the most natural place for me to do this was in schools. And so, armed and somewhat burdened with definitions, and ideas for questions, I set forth to see whether schools could be found that would welcome me to interview their children. This proved not to be as easy as I had hoped.

Chapter 2

Letting the Children Speak

This was the period of decisions and clarification and came not without some apprehension. After all, any opportunities I had to reach children and to talk to them would probably be singular, unrepeatable events. The challenges and questions included: what was I seeking to discover; which age group of children did I want to speak with; how many conversations and for how long could I reasonably manage alone as a single researcher (and whether that number was deemed by the academic community as sufficient from which to draw some general conclusions); should the conversations be one-to-one, in groups or a mixture; should I in fact, as I had assumed, undertake the work in schools or elsewhere; should the conversations be question-led and, if so, which questions would help the process.

As you have read in Chapter 1, I was curious about whether a lack of silence and solitude in children's lives adversely affected their experience and/or expression of spirituality. I decided to pursue this with young people aged 12–13 years, simply because so few others had researched with this age group. There is already some significant research on the spiritual experiences of adolescents[23] though most studies have focussed on primary age children (5–11 years).[24] There was also research evidence to show that the children in the age group that I had selected were potentially in early puberty and possibly less inhibited than a post-pubescent child.[25] I quickly decided that school-based work was time-efficient and, I thought, easily organised. This age group, not yet approaching the GCSE examination at the age of 15–16, was less likely to be affected if they missed an hour or two of timetabled lessons, and the children are often organised in mixed-ability groups, which meant a varied sample was more likely to be available.

Approaching schools

I then selected four school types in which I wanted to meet the children: a secular comprehensive (non-selective); a Catholic school; a Steiner (Waldorf) school and a Quaker school. They offered varied and contrasting opportunities for silence and solitude during the school day, and they represented a range of pedagogic and philosophical approaches to silence and also to spirituality. (I had understandably considered researching in a Montessori school, where, as you will read, silence is regarded as of critical importance. With, however, only one school in the United Kingdom with children of my selected age, confidentiality would have been problematic.)

My breezy assumption that setting up meetings with key people in all these schools to explain my venture would be simple – after all, I was a fellow teacher and wasn't my work thrilling – was quickly baffled. The secular and Catholic schools were known to me and I to them, and I was quickly and warmly welcomed. Establishing links with a Steiner school proved exceptionally difficult. Early attempts to contact such schools by email and phone failed. Unofficially, I was given to understand by a contact that previous negative experiences with researchers, the press, and even, apparently, the schools' inspection body Ofsted, may have led to wariness on their part. This suggestion was to some extent later confirmed: in July 2019, a public letter to Amanda Spielman (Chief Inspector of Education in the UK) signed by Steiner educationalists, the Former Archbishop of Canterbury, Rowan Williams, and senior educationalists, requested a more nuanced understanding of Steiner pedagogy by Ofsted inspectors, who had often been strongly critical.

So, all attempts over eight months to make effective contact with a Steiner school were met with politeness, but were fruitless, and I was tempted to abandon the idea of including them. Eventually, however, and via a long chain of personal contacts, I was able to contact the Chair of Governors of a Steiner school, who identified very wholeheartedly with the project. This led to the confidence to write to a class teacher, one with international standing in the Waldorf (Steiner) movement, who invited me for a visit, and who declared my research 'imperative and socially valuable'. Thus validated, I was galvanised.

Obtaining contact with a Quaker school was also a lengthy process and was initiated through a series of approaches to the Religious Society of Friends in London. Given the fundamental emphasis on silence in their movement, my work was greeted with warmth. Eventually I was invited to visit a school to meet with the governing body, the headteacher and a 'Peace Studies' coordinator.

Approaching schools through a third party or through already established contacts was an important factor in gaining access. Generally, many requests are made to schools for visits, and several echelons of decision-making bodies may have to be approached or involved. Additionally, school leaders are understandably aware of the many demands on staff and student time, on the limitations of space for interviews, on child safeguarding issues, on the importance of maintaining a positive public profile, and of parental/guardian sensitivities. Some external reassurance from a third party was, therefore, vital. Beyond this, even after initial permission to visit a school has been given, it was important to engage in a lengthy meeting, on site, with the school contact (appointed by the headteacher) to explain the philosophy of the work and how I hoped to conduct it. This followed a common format with a checklist and included aspects such as noting any child vulnerability[26] and child protection issues, distributing and collating documentation and permissions, making other staff aware of the project, ensuring confidentiality and agreeing dates – checked against an always very full school calendar.

Without exception these meetings were energising, immensely supportive and often moving, and the school contacts became key collaborators who sometimes at the lunch table engaged other colleagues in debate around the key questions and who looked forward keenly to the outcomes. Doubtless the slow process of the research was frustrating for them. For several, the dissemination, years later, involved a careful tracking down to any new school posts.

Meeting the children

The work took place in three stages. Permissions and letters distributed and returned, I met a whole class in each school selected by the school contact of 24–28 children. I discussed the details of the research with them, explaining *my* understanding of the word 'spirituality' and how I believed that if they took part in this work, they were all part of something that could help other children in the future. Secondly, I handed out questionnaires and based on the responses to these, I then selected ten students for two later 30-minute interviews held months apart. Thirdly, I commenced the interviews. In all, 39 children were interviewed. Interviews with ten children per day in each of the four schools was the maximum I felt able to achieve.

The initial class meeting and the researcher's dilemma

Decades of teaching experience were of little help meeting these classes. Quite the opposite. I was not meeting them as a teacher but as a visitor and a stranger, wanting to talk to them about sensitive and personal experiences that had, seemingly, nothing to do with school lessons. How should I present myself? There were conflicting requirements in this respect. The school needed to be reassured that I was a professional researcher, with appropriate formality and gravitas and the children needed to feel that I would be a safe and trustworthy recipient of their stories and answers. As well as this, if they were to spend an hour in my company, they would need to see a more relaxed side and some humour. Some time was spent, therefore, reflecting on clothing and demeanour prior to each visit to support the child's view that what they said would not be heard 'too clinically'.[27]

Why a questionnaire?

Questionnaires are often used for research when a large number of responses are needed and they have been used when examining various aspects of children's spirituality, for example, spiritual well-being and sensitivity[28]; happiness and spirituality[29] and altruism and sensitivity.[30] This particular research was not quantitative but qualitative and yet the questionnaire was valuable and necessary.

It provided a non-threatening introduction to both the research and to me for the 95 children involved – box filling is not out of the ordinary for classes with the advantage that, as I assured them, it is confidential (not even their names were on the papers, just numbers) and seen only by one person. They provided a great deal of preliminary general information, as well as specific background information, that could be used to smooth the initial 'getting to know you' phase at a first interview. Importantly, they also potentially captured the views and experiences of those who were more reticent and who, at least initially, might want to present information non-verbally. They also provided opportunities for the triangulation of results[31] and helped with the selection of children to be interviewed, giving the children the chance to 'opt out' of the whole process unobtrusively.

The questionnaires were carefully introduced in the classroom and supported throughout. The vocabulary in them was discussed as the children proceeded and the children were encouraged to ask questions of me or their teacher. It was important to walk around the classroom comfortingly, even reading questions out loud for slower readers as they filled them in, and to create a relaxed and informal environment. Despite the box filling, even this was not a quantitative exercise but a scaffold for future work.

Some students treated the questionnaire as a speed-test, hurrying to finish ahead of others. I had to encourage them gently to think more deeply about the questions and perhaps think about readdressing them. Sometimes, I quietly gave extra prompts to help them expand on their answers, as in: *What do you mean by that?* Some found the questions boring and distracted themselves doodling or chatting with friends; others were tentative and needed encouragement; yet others used the session as an opportunity to share pre-teen secrets with a stranger researcher. Many were strongly influenced by their peers, and students who were sitting in close proximity to one another often showed similar levels of enthusiasm or lack of interest.

As the initial focus of the research was on silence and solitude, many of the questions, using accessible language, were connected with daily activities and opportunities for quiet and whether silence had ever been particularly important for them. It moved on to asking whether they would describe themselves as a spiritual or religious person. There were spaces for the children to write or draw anything they felt they might want to add, and several did draw pictures of the experiences they had had whilst in silence.[32] Finally, they were asked whether they would be willing to be interviewed. The responses to this varied from 'please, please pick me!' to the bald 'I would be very unhappy being interviewed'.

Selecting the interviewees

On the basis of these responses, I selected a group of ten students from each school. In choosing interviewees, I included those indicating a willingness or a desire to be interviewed and, using the information the children gave regarding their time in silence and also their free time, I sought to balance those who said they had little such silent time and those who claimed to have more. More girls than boys declared themselves willing to be interviewed and it was tempting to select mainly the articulate and enthusiastic. I aimed, however, to include those perhaps less confident or shyer children, who did not specifically indicate their desire to be interviewed, yet whose responses showed that, with some encouragement, they might be willing to participate.[33] It was not always feasible to pick a sample that was representative of the group's diversity in terms of gender, ethnicity, religious affiliation and family size, though that had been an early intention. Finally, once a list had been determined the class teachers were consulted as to whether they deemed it appropriate for me to interview those students.

Interviewing children

Thus, ten students from each school were invited for two in-depth, voice-recorded, one-to-one interviews of approximately 30 minutes' duration. I did consider the option of holding whole group or small group interviews but responded to the cautions given by other researchers and my own classroom experience that, in such situations, children fear teasing from their peers and also ridicule.[34] In this way privacy was ensured with no fear of peer pressure. As importantly, such interviews gave me the opportunity to establish a more personal relationship with each student and to respond with an open mind to any spiritual experiences they might recount. My hopes that this would have advantageous implications for their well-being and sense of security were frequently borne out.[35] As will be seen in further chapters, many of the narratives were given tentatively, sometimes tearfully, and very often spoken of for the first time.

I do not believe that such conversations would have taken place had there been another person in the room.

To hold two interviews, separated by some months (giving time for transcription – a slow process – and analysis – even slower) provided both me and my interviewee time to reflect on the questions and responses and to deepen the engagement, as well as an opportunity to refine the question set for the second interview.

The interviews

The method of the interviews, semi-structured, flexible and voice-recorded was influenced by other researchers[36] and, as indicated, some of the first questions asked were derived from responses to the questionnaire, a hopefully comfortable ground for the interviewees. Following this informal chat, which included asking about the shape of an average day, there was a fuller enquiry into opportunities for solitude and silence.[37] Using the practice of 'funnelling', subjects such as spirituality and emotions were raised towards the *end* of the interview.[38]

The second interviews took place several months after the first (in one case due to staff changes and a sudden school closure due to deep snow, a year later). I lit a candle for this second interview and allowed silence to pervade the room, with the aim of creating a space for deeper reflection, in an atmosphere unlike that of a classroom. This was not an original idea, Coles (1977) in his work with thousands of children internationally had stressed the importance of a permitting and prompting silence and Hart (2003) had regarded candlelight as having a positive impact. In truth, and possibly due to the inevitable school noise and occasional interruptions affecting the interview rooms, the candle and the silence did not seem to effect any discernible change from the first set of interviews. Nevertheless, a relationship had been established with the children, and I started each session with a useful short recapitulation of our earlier conversations. I also presented them with photographs of children sitting alone looking at nature as a stimulus for a conversation. The pictures were rarely well-received. Many of the children understandably remarked that being alone in that way, away from the security of adults or friends, would be intimidating.

The questions

As can be seen from Appendix 1, the interview questions necessarily related to the initial research question: whether opportunities for silence and solitude affected a child's spirituality, and were specifically created for this purpose. In trying to establish whether the children exhibited any forms of spirituality, I 'borrowed' a direct question – I wonder what you think really matters?[39] – presented by me as a sentence completion exercise. Similarly, the children were asked to complete the sentence, 'I believe the world exists because...'. Both were an exploration of the value-sensing, meaning-making and sense of mystery identified as aspects of child spirituality by other researchers.[40] A question on happiness was prompted by research on the importance of positive emotions and spirituality[41] and, similarly, later questions on absorption, flow and transcendence.[42] The second interview set of questions also probed the *feeling* of an event and built on the work of those researchers for whom the 'felt sense' was a key aspect of child spirituality.[43] Other questions were redolent of the 'Hardy Question', though adapted for this context with children.[44] These interviews were not a verbal questionnaire, and the questions were merely a supportive framework for a conversation that would be influenced by the questions but not constrained by them.

On some occasions the conversations were shaped by the research of Claire Petitmengin (2014) who describes a deep form of questioning which might require, for example, 30 minutes of questions to probe one or two seconds of experience. She describes how the evoking of a past event, involving passive memory, might be stimulated by the use of a series of questions, each determining the next. This could help uncover things that were possibly unknown or unnoticed at the point of experience. She describes this process as loosening our grasp on the 'what' in order to let the 'how' appear – enabling an 'invisible microgenesis' and an 'underground universe' to become visible.[45] This process, however, undertaken with young people and with a potential power disparity, required sensitivity and a willingness to abandon the process where there was resistance. There were obvious time limitations, and this technique was sparingly but fruitfully employed.

Entering the unknown space

One of the greatest challenges of the interviews, after a professional lifetime of largely controlling interactions with young people, was, as Ogden would say, 'getting out of the way'.[46] I tried to seek between myself and the child, as so many have before me, Gadamer's 'fusion of horizons' and a shared space to support my understanding of each child's perceptions.[47] Paediatrician and psychoanalyst Donald Winnicott describes this in terms of a metaphoric 'holding', allowing the child (or patient in his case) to be known, and this being 'a state of coming together in one place'.[48] Thus, the underpinning of the research saw an emphasis on understanding, interpretation and the search for a common language.[49]

Given my cultural distance from the interviewees by virtue of age and history, life situation and inevitable personal bias, I made a deliberate attempt during the interviews to meet the students on their terms, not mine. This meant, on occasion, allowing lengthy child-led digressions, the better to create a relaxed atmosphere and a confidence in the child that what they had to say mattered. Such attempts were not always successful, and my failures were painfully highlighted during the transcribing, when I winced at hearing my own interruptions.

I sometimes explained to the interviewees, when they faltered, that I too would struggle to answer some of the questions I was asking. This was truthful and also strategic, with the aim of creating a context that allowed us both to enter an as yet unknown space. This might lead to the emergence of something else, or something new – defined by Gadamer as *Die Sache* or thing, and which is an understanding between two people, reached by language, about something they both understand. Breaking what he calls 'the spell of our own presuppositions', indeed 'the tyranny of our prejudices', became vital for the research, both during the interviews and, critically, when reviewing the contents of the first interviews.

A change of direction

There followed a period of four months transcribing the recordings from the first interviews and annotating them in terms of body language, from memory and also from notes taken during and after the event, Doing this myself, though intense, was immensely valuable for several reasons: the facility to describe a tone of voice and a reminder of the personality of the interviewee; a prompting of the memory of particularly affective moments; the value of revisiting an interview and being able to annotate aspects of nuanced utterances (where the speech alone did not convey meaning) and also body language. It also meant I was able mentally to record, link and synthesise aspects, perhaps on a subliminal level, that I later sought to analyse more formally.

From the conversations it became evident that children in *all* the schools were manifesting those aspects of child spirituality already identified by key researchers.[50]A brief summary of these will be found in later chapters. These appeared to be precipitated by conditions and contexts other than silence or even solitude (in the sense of non-sound). So, one of my initial hunches that the expression of children's spirituality would be adversely affected if they lacked solitude or silence in their lives was confounded early on in the research. Some were *entering* a form of silence rather than being deliberately choosing to be *within* it (a point I will elaborate on in the following chapters). It became clear that my original hypothesis was flawed, or at least incomplete, and a more nuanced approach was needed.

I now had to keep an open mind, return to an even more extensive literature trawl and to deepen my analysis of the transcriptions. Eventually, I also felt I had to reappraise my questions for interview two.

Analysing the interviews

A preliminary analysis took place immediately after the transcriptions of the first interview. I took a tiered, scaffolded approach. Firstly, it was necessary to review those aspects of child spirituality already determined by previous scholars. These included flow, joy and laughter, moral sensitivity, peak experiences, connection with nature and people, seeing life as a mystery and a belief in higher powers, awe and wonder, having a purpose in life, asking 'who am I?'.[51] These were annotated using open coding by hand, using coloured symbols,[52] against paragraphs and sections. The themes above were later expanded on, using *in vivo* codes[53] and, as will be seen, new ground was broken. This initial confirmation of the existence of children's spirituality in the interviews was the first foundational step, prior to looking at contexts. Further, I found the slow reading of the transcripts, with the growing familiarity that accompanied it, to be superior to an analysis by means of a computer package.

After extensive comparison, I was able to see patterns emerging of the contexts and situations in which spirituality and spiritual experience arose. The second stage of analysis, therefore, was that of searching for these contexts and there followed a process of axial coding that noted the *conditions* which gave rise to such experiences.[54] I noted that the chief contexts were during positive emotions, such as wonder and joy; a loss of self/absorption and flow; silence; in an experience of nature and the natural world; during out of the ordinary and/or peak experience; during physical catalysts (dancing etc.) and during periods of imagination or laughter.

As was now becoming clearer, silence as a context rarely arose and the research was now evolving into a hypothesis-seeking process. Throughout the first tranche of interviews there was an apparently common contextual (and also experiential) strand that was resonant with the concept of liminality as developed by anthropologists Edith and Victor Turner.[55] On the basis of the new literature research, the second set of interview questions was extended to include questions on paradox, ludic events (expressing disorder), transgression and joy. All of these might be, according to the Turners, prompts or indicators for the exploration of liminal states that might have led to, or act as, a spiritual experience. Now during the interview process I became alert to any evidence of liminal states and explored this more deeply, allowing the research findings to shape the interpretation and analysis. From this point there was an approach akin to 'grounded theory'.[56]

The additional questions, however, proved less helpful than the existing more open-ended questions and took up time better spent on a more discursive process. Such a process was exemplified in some interviews where there was a complete suspension of previously determined lines of questioning, and was characterised by the spontaneous pursuit, at some length, of issues and events raised at the time – effectively reconfiguring the whole session. More than this, slowing down the interview process to match a student's mood, allowing an incubating silence, or even wholly digressing to create a more relaxed atmosphere, are just some examples of how the interviews were shaped by the children.

Following completion of the two interviews and after open and axial coding, I collected a list of 34 aspects of liminality and *communitas* identified from the extended literature and returned to the transcripts for analysis based on these new categories. And through these means, new theories, as we will see, emerged.

Talking to children and respect

The work in schools was founded squarely on the effective development of relationships with the children, and I was aware that the advantage I had, by virtue of experience, in accessing schools was also a potential disadvantage when trying to establish relationships with those children. Care had to be given to self-presentation and personal style. There were dangers that the children might just 'aim to please' a professional-looking adult outsider, and that was a challenge not always overcome. Additionally, over a period of, in some cases, 14 months I was aware of the importance of nurturing and developing these school relationships. I found Graham Harvey's analysis of 'guesthood, colonialism and anthropological research' and the importance of developing increased proximity to those under review, particularly insightful.[57] His emphasis on the moral responsibility of a researcher to be a respectful and patient guest, who is aware of the history and habits of the community being observed, and is also respectful of their right to withhold or divulge information, was a useful touchstone throughout the work.

In the same way I was aware of Brendan Hyde's warning of the danger of 'colonising' children – seeing them merely as intriguing objects of study.[58] Throughout, therefore, I tried to be critically aware of any power imbalance and there was the pervading need to emphasise that I, the researcher, did not know 'the right answers' and that only our coming together might help us achieve the intended goals. At times, particularly when asking children about (usually mildly) transgressive acts,

I deliberately sought to enter *their* space in order to understand their amusement, delight or ambivalence at what I might have regarded in a former role as instances of poor behaviour!

During some of the interviews there arose, accidentally at first and with some sense of guilt, some self-disclosure on my part. This arose naturally as the interviews had a conversational style. This was not consciously instigated to access information or 'rich data', but rather to create a crucible of openness, and a reduction of the power differential through a preparedness to show vulnerability. There was also a sense of the 'giving back' to a child who needed validation, or to digress in a suspension of my agenda for theirs.

There were other ethical problems to confront. I was aware of the children's general, sometimes acute vulnerability during the interview process, and, in many cases, as I have said, their anxiety to please, to be helpful. When they recalled sometimes distressing life-events, or when they were unsure or expressed confusion caused by unusual experiences, I felt it my duty to reassure them, and with their permission to refer particularly troubling issues (such as bullying, grief, even physical pain) to a relevant member of staff. This placed me in a more overt 'problem-solving' power position, shifting the dynamic of the interview. In this situation, I had simply to use my experience to make a judgement, and the validating feedback I got, sometimes years later, seemed to justify the interventions. Human first, researcher second.

Beyond this, I tried to validate any frightening or confusing experiences as being within the normal range of human experience (even, as you will read, a 'Near Death Experience'). At the end of the interviews, I understood that the children needed (as any adult might) verbal reassurance and affirmation. It was not a matter of perfunctory courtesy when I informed the children that they had given an interesting, useful or thought-provoking interview – it was important feedback affecting their self-esteem and their future feelings about their, often hitherto private, revelations. I felt a bi-lateral duty – to the research objectives *and* to the children, who were, in effect, my research partners. In other words, there was to be a mutual benefit, not just any putative social benefit derived from its completion and possible publication, but *during* the process itself – a simple giving back.[59]

It was important to 'give voice' as much as possible to these young people, to listen fully to them and to empower what is often regarded as a group that is disempowered. It was also important to be alert to the dangers of 'ventriloquy', of using the voices of the participants to say what I wanted them to say, whether through the formatting of the questions, or in my, often unconscious responses (verbal and visual) to their contributions.

Having outlined in this chapter the rationale for the selection of interviewees and venues, my approaches to them and the methodology and methods used in my work, including its design, data gathering, analysis, and its ethical base, we can now move on. Before doing so, and with the intention of clarifying why silence was the pivot for this work, the following brief chapter investigates its importance in religious and educational institutions and movements and delves more deeply into the meanings of silence and its potentialities.

Chapter 3

Looking at Silence

So why does this book centre on silence and even more apparently paradoxically, children and silence? As I have explained, I own to a personal valorisation of silence, to meditation, to early Catholic prayer and to growing up in an age when even the television (all two channels) fell silent at the appropriate hour. I could not help but be aware that things were different for our young people, and felt that maybe, somehow, this 'lack' of space and silence was important. Fortunately, I was not alone in this thinking. This chapter ranges over the problems of definitions and understanding about silence from a variety of thinkers and fields and is also a brief investigation of educational and religious movements for which silence was deemed to be fundamental.

Understandings of silence

As an educationalist concerned about children's access to silence, I understood such silence to be non-sound or quiet. After all, that is what I, in my adult life have looked for, whether for meditation or relaxation. This simple understanding was, however, soon confounded, both by the children and following deeper examination.

I soon had to ask whether silence, in the way I had understood it, actually existed.

When in 2003 the Cambridge astronomer Andrew Fabian and his team discovered a black hole in the Perseus cluster of galaxies 250 million light years away from Earth, they detected the emission of a humming, the lowest sound ever heard by humans, in B-flat, albeit 57 octaves below Middle C.[60] Even in space, where total 'silence' might be expected, there is still sound. Yet silence is still variously defined as 'an absence of sound'[61] and 'a period without any sound; complete quiet, a state of not speaking'.[62] It is also often associated with stillness, and is defined for most part in terms of a lack or absence of something. Yet this common understanding is challenged by some who suggest that silence is, rather, an ontological reality and, indeed, a potentially productive one.

The idea of silence as an active force, subsisting in and through itself, existing before all else, is seen in the work of the philosopher Max Picard (1888–1965). Picard insists that silence is not just simply 'something that happens when we stop talking'; it is more than the simple renunciation of language. In fact, for him, 'when language ceases, silence begins' and is an 'autonomous phenomenon', an independent, creative whole.[63] He laments that:

> Today words no longer arise out of silence, through a creative act of the spirit which gives meaning to language and to the silence, but from other words, from the noise of other words. Neither do they return to the silence but into the noise of other words, to become immersed therein.

This is a silence with a positive value, a catalysing force. British theologian Maggie Ross also sees silence as an ever-present core environment, a natural habitat within which we live, and which irrupts into our everyday life, giving us access to new knowledge, not hitherto self-consciously learned.[64]

We see this view endorsed further by the Italian philosopher Michele Federico Sciacca (1908–1975), who suggests that silence is itself a meaningful form of communication,[65] and by the American philosopher Bernard Dauenhauer, who describes the deep silence that is at play in all human performances (which he describes as 'utterances'), whether in speech, art or music.[66] Silence for him is not first and foremost a cancellation of sound, but a naturally occurring phenomenon. This 'silence of the to-be-said', according to Dauenhauer, is an active performance, a yielding which binds and joins, before some power which is beyond one's control. Perhaps this is the space, deliberately, actively, created by us within which something as yet unknown may arise. He finds in silence an opening for what he describes as hope and what Picard describes as faith. In similar vein, we are also prompted by Gemma Fiumara, Italian philosopher and psychoanalyst, to recognise 'the utility of what is not', evoking Lao Tze's description in poetry of the critical power of the gap between the spokes of a wheel.[67]

In these ideas we see the understanding of silence as having an important and positive purpose, and, notably, existing as a *potentialising* context rather than being an 'absence' of sound. Such an understanding was particularly interesting when interviewing children, whose access to what is generally deemed to be silence might be limited. This also affected the process of the interviews (the tolerance of pauses; a deliberate period of quiet before beginning the second of the two interviews) and impacted on the analysis of the children's contributions. Nevertheless, as with spirituality, the concept of silence, lacks definitional consensus and I had to be open to the broad range of interpretations alluded to here, and the possibility that silence might be non-binary – being both the absence of sound (insofar as this is possible) and a *space* from which phenomena may arise.

This nuanced understanding of silence can be seen reflected in the three key movements to follow. Coming from different philosophical and religious origins, each, nevertheless, holds silence to be fertile and fundamental.

The Religious Society of Friends (Quaker) education and George Fox

George Fox (1624–1691) abandoned his family's devout (Anglican/Puritan) religious practice at an early age and became convinced of the idea of an 'inner light' in each person. The possibility of a direct connection and revelation of the divine existing in each person was reinforced by his own personal and pivotal spiritual experience on Pendle Hill in Lancashire in 1652. He contested the idea that the religious was in any way a special dimension of life – indeed it was available to all who could access the 'inner light of Christ'. He began to support an inward-looking process, facilitated by silence in a group context. This became a fundamental of what became known as 'Quaker' life and continues to be so, as demonstrated in the injunction to 'Take heed dear friends to the promptings of love and truth in your hearts. Trust them as the leadings of God'.[68] Quaker worship, now known as 'meeting for worship', lasts about an hour with no set song or prayers. The aim is simply to seek a connection with others' and one's deepest self, and with God, thus helping to contribute to the world. Early 'brethren' were encouraged to be guided not by 'the letter' or liturgies (because this 'killeth'), but by the light.[69]

The schools set up by the Quakers are of particular relevance. Fox privately established the first Quaker schools in 1668 to educate the children of Quaker families. These became partly absorbed into the state sector following the introduction of universal public primary schools in England in 1870. There are currently ten independent Quaker schools in the British Isles[70] with schools distributed throughout the world in over 17 countries[71] and all the children participate in Quaker worship and reflective silence.

This experience of silence is an important aspect of Quaker education. Children and adults gather together in communal worship, so that they can 'experience the benefits and powers of silence', 'opening ourselves ... making ourselves ready to listen to others and to that of God within us'.[72] This is, therefore, a purposeful silence – an active silence. We are told that this will help us to see things more clearly and that 'a light within us will enable us to see ourselves and what we are doing'. If we are receptive enough, we might see that it is the 'self' that gets in the way. Such a self might manifest itself in the intellect, and this should be put aside to see the light within. Quakers are advised: 'Now you must die in the silence, die from the wisdom, die from the knowledge, die from the reason, and die from the understanding.'[73] It is believed that through silence we are brought back to our true selves. Silence for the Quakers is not passive, it is entirely active, and it is not something that is done to us; rather, it is something that we do.[74]

Quakerism is a movement from which schools arose, based on that movement's principles. It was not and is not a pedagogy and its focus is not on children. This is unsurprising as the gradual development of educational theories up to the eighteenth century saw scant attention paid to any need for, or love of, silence and solitude among children. The nineteenth and twentieth centuries saw, however, two educational pioneers for whom silence *was* an important facet of, and a factor in, child development and spirituality – pioneers whose work still has international influence.

The silencing of the self: Rudolf Steiner and Waldorf schools

Austrian social reformer, philosopher and esotericist Rudolf Steiner (1861–1925), from a Catholic background, established a movement that was to have an impact on education internationally and which set much store on silence.[75] Steiner was concerned, particularly following what he described as his clairvoyant experiences, to unite spirituality and science, seeking a long-lost bridge between the material world and the spiritual.[76] Encouraging us to gain the ability to see what ordinarily is invisible, he was convinced that 'though we carry body, soul and spirit about us, we are conscious only of the body'.[77] He did not, however, suggest that we diminish the importance of the body. Instead, he believed that the physical body was 'the expression of far greater powers of wisdom than any that can be grasped by an individual ego-consciousness',[78] and that knowing could be accessed through the body as lived experience. We will read in later chapters of the relevance and importance of this belief in *body-knowing* to children's spirituality.

Speaking in his series of key talks in 1923, known as *The Dornach lectures*, Steiner explained his view that modern science impacted negatively on the human soul, leading human beings to be alienated from themselves. Our physical nature, he said, is but a reflection of the soul and a young child is an 'ensouled sense organ'. Thus, in this way, the religious element (called by some spiritual) was *inborn in each child* and simply part of a child's being.[79] All students of anthroposophy (his own system of beliefs) should, he believed, withdraw themselves for fifteen minutes a day to meditate, and he advocated the 'silencing of our own self to meet other, both human and spiritual, realities around us'.[80] During this beneficial silencing we would, he said, be helped to merge with the being, the very soul, of that other.

It is the emphasis on the spiritual nature of all children and the necessity of honouring, even revering, this, that is most striking in Steiner's view of education. It was, for him, the unchanging, deepest part of a child, which meant that they could feel at home wherever they went.[81] It was the divine in children's souls that enables them to actually see the divine in their surroundings, and it was, for him, in silence and solitude that we saw the world differently, 'In these quiet moments every flower, every animal, and every action will disclose mysteries undreamed of.'[82]

After founding his first school in 1919 at the Waldorf Astoria cigar factory, his philosophy persists in the twenty-first century in more than 1,100 Waldorf (Steiner) schools worldwide. He was not alone in his thoughts about silence. During a similar period and on the same continent another passionate educationalist drew similar conclusions.

The child: A spiritual embryo. Maria Montessori

Italian physician and educator Maria Montessori (1870–1952), also from a Roman Catholic background, based many of her ideas on the close observation of children, particularly those socially disadvantaged in terms of cognitive or physical disability, or poverty.[83] Her successful early work establishing a small school (*Casa dei Bambini*) for culturally, socially and financially impoverished children, in a tenement in Rome in 1907, resulted in national, eventually international, recognition and the creation by 2025 of over 22,000 Montessori schools in 140 countries.

Like Steiner, she underlined the value of the sensual and movement in education and placed strong emphasis on responding to the needs of each individual child. She also identified 'an inner teacher that dictates within'... 'responding to a severe inner syllabus which has been imposed by nature'.[84] In other words, education is not simply what the teacher imparts.

Two key aspects of her work are significant for this book's exploration into children and silence. First, she asserted that the child, 'this spiritual embryo' requires a 'life-giving environment of calm and peace'.[85] Once provided, she believed that she didn't need to teach anything to the child – rather it was the child who taught *her* – revealing their spiritual secrets, as long as their souls had not been deformed.[86] She believed it was necessary to 'deprogramme' the wearing of an adult mask by the child, effected only when the child can choose tasks for herself and can become absorbed, resulting in what she called 'normalisation'. This was, for her, like a healthy plant that had been neither thwarted nor forced. She explained that a key characteristic of a 'normalised' child was a love of silence and working alone and this psychological isolation was not solitude but the outcome of utter concentration. She recognised, from her close observations with children, the importance of joy, a 'crowning characteristic ... and a deep and mysterious emotion ... which comes in obedience to the laws of our nature'.[87]

In her view (and one that will be reflected by many of the interviewees in this book), traditional forms of imposed silence in Italian schools, as a form of discipline, led nowhere. In contrast, she sought to teach silence to primary age children during an event that she described as 'the silence game', the better to achieve discipline of the self, leading to spiritual development. Montessori described the origins of the silence game as coming from an experience in the classroom she had had whilst holding a four-month-old baby girl. The baby was very still. This impressed Montessori, who suggested to the schoolchildren present that none of them could do so well, could breathe so silently, whereupon the children became totally still and sat as if meditating – and gradually, stillness was regarded by Montessori as a precursor of silence. During this event the smallest sounds of nature could be heard. The children seemed to have a deep desire for silence and later even refused her proffered sweets as rewards. This 'silence game' was later incorporated into lessons and children's names would be very gently whispered by the teacher, calling, Montessori said, on their very souls, with the children rising proudly upon hearing them.[88] This was said to allow the children to know their own soul and involved the drawing of attention to every part of the body and a quietening down. Through an effort of will, the mind was almost isolated from outside voices.[89] This allowed the children to actually '*feel* the quiet', acting as a preparation of the nervous system to receive new stimuli.[90]

This state of hyper-concentration was believed by Montessori to lead to a psychologically healthy state. It achieved also an outcome of extended focus, facilitated by the availability of up to 3-hour sessions of self-focussed work, leading to exceptional spiritual qualities. Montessori also noted that children loved silence to an 'extraordinary degree', but further, that it was in silence when movements are so ordered that the inner sensitivity – the religious or spiritual sense – might be developed.

Children found in the *casa* that listening was privileged over other activities, with a particular higher order appreciation of sound, an encouragement of the inhibition of impulses that might interfere with achieving quiet and that there was a collective effort to gain silence.[91] This non-doing was not about an emptying out, but, rather, about creating the space for inner experiences.[92] This was an important facet of Montessori's educational philosophy and consistent with her view that children were spiritual beings, psychic entities, with an inner natural drive. It was vital to allow the children to access their true selves as a 'world power' in order to serve society. This was extraordinary. Instead of we, the adults, guiding and informing the children, we were to honour *their* role and allow *their* light to shine. We should, she believed, support our children to release their psychic energies to create a world of harmony.

Though this philosophy reflected a strong reconstruction narrative after World War II, its message resonates today. The idea that this seed, in each child, would bloom naturally under the right conditions was revolutionary, and silence paid a key part, whether sensory silence or the inner silence found in total focus. From this, children came like 'individuals who had rested' and resembling those who had experienced the great joy that is part of human inheritance.

It is also worth noting here that joy was a recurring motif in Montessori's pedagogy. For Montessori this arises when a child, allowed to determine the form and speed of her own activities, achieves spontaneous success – this could be, for example, in writing. It is Edwin Standing who suggests this is due to the fact that the child has acted in accordance with the laws of her nature, unrestrained by teacher-determined timetables of her work.[93] Though this reference to joy and the constraint of timetables may seem tangential to this section on silence, we will see their importance in future chapters.

These three key movements influenced my motivation in examining silence as being relevant and important in supporting children's spirituality. Yet I was aware that others argue that such generalised assumptions about the beneficial impact of silence and solitude, and the assertion that children actively seek these states, are flawed. They point out that whilst some may indeed benefit from and enjoy, for example, mindfulness and silence, others are intimidated by, or even afraid of, such experiences.[94] Nevertheless, there were many *individuals* working with children who viewed silence and solitude as critical for their well-being.

The provision of silence

American psychologist Tobin Hart, whose self-description interestingly lists 'father' as his key role in life, used his experience of the insights gained when caring for his grandchildren to state categorically that children have a rich inner, spiritual life. It is this quiet voice that he fears is in danger of being lost and, as adults can learn from children, we are all the poorer for it.[95] It is a voice, he says, that is nourished and reinforced by the spaciousness of silence and by adult listening. Australian educationalist Brendan Hyde concurs, advocating giving all children space for silence and solitude during the day, to reflect on those things that are of ultimate meaning.[96]

In the UK, educationalist Julian Stern advocated the creation of 'enstatic' schools – being 'contented in the self alone' as described in the *Bhagavad Gita* and the valuing of solitude as a path to self-realisation.[97]

The weight of those calling out to support children in the enjoyment of their secret inheritance was growing.

An early pioneer in the mid twentieth century, German educationalist Theophil Thun, introduced *Eine regelmaessige Denkstunde* into the primary curriculum at his school (literally 'a regular hour's thinking time').[98] In contrast to Rousseau's belief that children do not have any religious sense at all, Thun argued instead, and as we now see increasingly suggested by others, that many children seek to have a connection with God and that there is a latent religious spontaneity amongst children. Almost, he says, as if they were waiting for the messenger.

It is, however, towards the end of the twentieth and in the early twenty-first century that we see a growth in the number of largely psychologists and educationalists, who stress not just the importance of silence but, as with Thun, the *provision* of silence for the general well-being and spirituality of children. Karen Marie Yust in the US would have agreed with him, albeit using the term *spirituality* rather than religiosity. Working with 5–6-year-olds and in (for some teachers an unprecedented and astonishing) 15 minutes of silence she found that young children not only have the ability to sit in such a silence, but also actively desire it.[99]

We now see work undertaken in this respect internationally including in Australia, China, US and Ireland, and the UK Educationalist Margaret Taplin even embarked on research with children in Mainland China through the practice of 'silent sitting'. This was rooted in the teachings of Indian spiritual teacher Sri Sathya Sai Baba. Almost 60% of those children who took part felt that improved well-being was an outcome (and 97.4% were positive about the experience), though direct discussions were not possible with either teachers or students in this context.[100]

During the same period, Rachael Kessler's extensive work with teachers and on the curriculum in the US through the Passageworks institute stressed the importance of the feeding of the spirit, particularly through the offering of opportunities for silence.[101] She regretted that this is a lost art, once welcomed, and one to which contemporary culture is hostile. Due to lack of habituation, it has become, she says, almost unnerving, alien and strange. Instead, and sadly, we see the prevalence of the over-stimulation of children and, as Elkind warns, 'the never-ending programmed activities of the hurried child'.[102] The introduction of quiet times of silence and stillness and deep listening, prompted by Kessler's work, into the school curriculum, in schools both primary and secondary, saw beneficial changes in behaviour and well-being and even some unanticipated sleep.

We are also seeing a new emphasis on the introduction of various forms of meditation in schools internationally. Positive outcomes have been noted by researchers in Australia, Ireland and in the UK by de Kuyken.[103] De Kuyken's work with his co-researchers involved a large-scale project with 522 school students, looking at the effectiveness of the 'Mindfulness in Schools' programme in the UK. Their findings showed that the programme led to a reduction in depressive symptoms, greater well-being and less stress.

Nevertheless, there are caveats and some of those working with children did note and warn of the dangers of the irruption of thoughts and memories for some pupils during these quiet periods and that it was important for those with responsibility for children to be aware of that. Moreover, you will read of the variety of children's attitudes towards silence in all its forms later in this book and of the implications of these variances for any adult 'interventions', however well-intentioned.

Moving to the children's voices

We have now seen the issues involved in defining silence overall and the variety of ways of understanding it, assuming such a concept exists at all. The range of movements both religious and educational that place value on silence has been examined. We have moved on to explore more individual research that advocates and introduces opportunities *for* silence and the outcomes of these. But these are just the foothills – necessary, but not the goal of the journey. They explain the reasons for the expedition itself. Now we return to the initial problem: does the lack of silence and solitude in our children's lives affect their spirituality – assuming (and we cannot) that such spirituality exists. And so, we must now first listen carefully to the children and decide whether they are indeed, as others have said, spiritual beings.

Chapter 4

'It's Weird, Miss': Children Speak of their Spirituality

And now, at last, the children's voices are allowed a space and a hearing.[104]

As I have indicated, the first step towards looking at the relevance of silence to children's spirituality was to establish whether the children with whom I spoke showed any evidence of this. This is not such a mystery, as if they had not, then clearly this book would not exist. Holding an awareness of the very extensive definitions and categories of children's spirituality already given, I nevertheless felt (instinctively and practically) that the addition of a more inclusionary, overarching framework would be beneficial. I found American psychiatrist Lisa Miller's work particularly helpful. She suggests that there are surges, a crescendo, of spirituality in adolescence, biologically and genetically driven, the core of which is a transcendent relationship – a dynamic sense of connection with a higher power – and a sense that we are capable of going beyond the limits of our physical or ordinary self, as a unitive part of a greater universe.[105] Fellow American and psychiatrist George Vaillant emphasised the *expression* of such transcendence through positive emotions including love, awe, trust and gratitude and these provided useful markers when examining the children's words.[106] Such ephemeral moments, often hesitantly and tentatively articulated by the children, are included here, giving rise, as they do, to what Australian educationalist Best describes as an 'unexpected, unpredictable affect'.

These three further views gave me a necessarily broad analytical 'crucible' and yet, as will be seen, this chapter will also include examples of those more specific aspects already referred to.

And yes, I was reminded throughout of the primary influence of personality, asserted so strongly by Hay and Nye. How could I not be? Each child came into the room so vibrantly and vibratingly different, each reflecting a unique context, background and approach to the world. For each child clearly expresses spirituality in a different way. Some of the children articulate their spirituality using the vocabulary of the religious traditions with which they are familiar – unsurprisingly given that one cohort was from a Catholic school. Others speak more generally, simply describing beliefs in higher powers. Several speak passionately about their sense of environmental connectivity and express concerns about its derogation, showing a pained empathy and awareness of the world's problems, all of which can be placed under the wide span of Miller's concept of feeling part of something larger.[107]

As we move to the children's examples, it will be seen that they are grouped under specific headings. I will admit that this was both a challenge and a paradox for me. On the one hand, they provide an opportunity to synchronise with frameworks already accepted by an academic community, providing some credibility; yet on the other, many of the extracts selected here not only straddled a range of definitions and delineations, but also, by the nature of their *being* extracted from a larger view of a particular child's unique spirituality, they can present a fractured and etiolated picture of the individual's worldview.

It is with this in mind that I have tried, by way of lengthier unexpurgated extracts, to present fuller, more balanced passages from the interviews, to present a more holistic picture of a child. The division of this chapter into very broad sections of identification, therefore, is presented with misgivings and yet with a wry shrug.

Transcendence: The mystery of life and death

That life was about more than could be seen, was a recurring theme during the interviews and the children were often eager to discuss their beliefs in higher powers, death and whether their lives had purpose.[108] Many of the children felt strongly that they had a particular path to tread in their lives and that this path was somehow determined or supported by unseen powers. For some this was expressed as general assistance in one's life.

Catholic Millie, for example, from a secular school, had experienced many hospitalisations, and her belief in God had helped her through some hard days. She seemed very much older than her years and spoke clearly and seriously:

> I try and pray most nights like, mainly about bad things. I ask, like, God to help. I think of him as a he. And like he can, he helps people; he helps his people, and he protects them. And he also helps those who are not necessarily *his* people. So, people who aren't necessarily Christians. As in, he'll help someone going through life and lead them to like where they're meant to be.

Millie commented later in the interview that it was necessary to be selfless and kind in life, helping friends as much as possible 'because other people are as important as you are'. She felt passionately that her life had a distinct function and that she had a role to play in 'making my generation more aware of disabled people ... and more ... that they might know more about the fact that we are still human'. Asked about how that made her feel, she grew exceedingly quiet, and in a fervent whisper she explained, 'It's almost an honour ... 'cos every person's special and the way that they share that with the world ... yeah ... it's almost like ... it's *their* way of doing it'. In Hyde's words she was 'weaving the threads of meaning',[109] and we see her trying to make sense of her role in the world and then taking pleasure and comfort from it.[110] Musing on death, and counter to the tenets of her religion, she had clear ideas about the process of life:

> I think we ... I thought it was really silly; I thought about it yesterday quite a lot. I think what we do is – we go to a place that no one can ever speak of, because when we ... I believe we are reincarnated into something new, and we can't describe it, because we are obviously a new person that hasn't died ... if you understand [...] we pass away and go to this amazing place, and then we are born again and can't ever know that place. I think we join our loved ones and then we go on to something even better and start a new life to become an even better person.

The idea of reincarnation was a common theme amongst the children of religious faith or none. Kamal, from a Sikh family, arrived at his first session in physical pain and was often tearful, though insistent on continuing the interview. He believed that when we die our thoughts are still in the atmosphere, to the particular advantage of our immediate family, who might be helped by us. His football-loving classmate Sam shyly stressed that reincarnation would be almost immediate after death, whether as an animal or in a human life:

> When we die, we obviously can't feel anything, once we're fully, officially, dead. So, our soul and stuff will be taken away from the earth and our mind ... Yeah! So, our souls and mind will be taken away from the earth and we'll just be reborn without any knowledge of our past life or future, into another body and a different mind ... feeling different things. [I feel] ... a little more ... I don't know how to put it ... er, kind of safe, but in a weird way. So, I feel that once I've died, if it's like old age or

> something, I have this feeling in my mind that we'll be reborn or something. So, it's a bit weird!! But I just feel like a bit of reassurance that I'll like still live, but I won't feel anything ... about my past life. Your soul is taken away and stuff and it's like replaced in your body when you're reborn. You get a completely different soul and a different mind once you've been reborn. That's what I think.

Isaac, Arianna and Lucy, all from Catholic backgrounds, felt strongly that God helped them grow and that God looked after us in life. Outdoorsy and sporty Lucy, who described herself as spiritual, was very moved by this thought and declared that we should never give up on things in life, because some things were simply *meant* to happen – views also held by Catholic Kaitlyn who saw multiple path choices ahead of us, to be selected only when it felt right. Kaitlyn was very often alone and had been in several different schools in the UK and abroad. Though she clearly very much wanted to be interviewed, she spoke in short sentences and in a nervous reflective manner. Her sense of life-purpose was well illustrated in her descriptions of taking food and books to less fortunate children and how this filled her with happiness. This was an example of 'doing things right' lest she 'betrayed God'. Such sense of connectedness and its 'implied compassion and awareness' is regarded as a core motif of spirituality.

Bubbly Alyssa, who happily explained that she just liked talking, also felt that we were helped by God with life decisions, though she expressed disappointment in never having heard 'a voice', not even at her first *Holy Communion,* a situation that led her to complain plaintively: 'So what chance will *I* have in life?'. This disappointment was perhaps ameliorated by her surprised awareness that she was able to predict things, a skill of which she was very wary, 'as people gamble on things like that and it's very dangerous'. As so many other researchers have discovered, this sense of the universe being mysterious and full of wonder, so apparent throughout her discourse, is also a common indicator of children's spirituality.[111]

Josh, who was very keen to be interviewed, sometimes needed silence at the end of a long school day, say ten minutes, just to relax. He was adamant that he was neither religious nor spiritual:

> I believe that there is *something*, but I don't believe it's a person or anything like that. I don't know what it is. It's kind of hard. Kind of like a light or something. A glowy beam or something. A glowy beam but just like a ball of light. Just kind of in the atmosphere. I don't know ... it kind of ... I think it kind of ... just like controls people ... I dunno ... just controls people and tells them their feelings and tells them ... I dunno ... knows what they're thinking. And everything like that.

You might remember his concept of a glowy beam when we meet Josh again in a future chapter, following a momentous event in his life that occurred during the gap between the two interviews.

In contrast, Ravi (who in typical for him rather courtly fashion, declared that he would feel honoured to be interviewed) described himself as a religious person and a 'person of spirituality', praying each day in the morning and at night, particularly when he felt he needed help. He was often alone, frequently doing homework. He presented almost as professorial as he explained that God had created the universe through a 'pre-determined algorithm' because he wanted to 'find a variation in the dark and void of space'. He then mused with bafflement on a potentially life-impacting football injury that he had experienced, that had, after praying he said, resulted in a minor scratch. This outcome he described as 'bewildering', 'confusing' and 'inexplicable', echoing the *mystery sensing* category already identified by Hay and Nye. Though he generally only prayed to God for help with test results –'work, productivity and being successful in life' being key to his happiness – he later prayed for a good outcome to an operation and felt that this had been productive, though he expressed this almost reluctantly and, once again, with some surprise.

A similar, slightly conflicted view was held by non-theist but 'spiritual' Charlie who explained in his questionnaire that he often asked himself what happens when we die, or how the world was created. Asked whether he thought there was a reason why we were here on Earth, he replied categorically that there was no particular reason. He later amended this to 'I feel like there is something' and went on to describe his confusion about the experiences of 'weird' *déjà vu*, descriptions of which arose frequently among the children and often gave pause for conjecture during the whole series of interviews.[112]

Some children were more adamant about there being a meaning to life. Christina described herself as spiritual, but only following her father's death, as she liked to think that 'everything happens for a reason and that there is some form of life after death'. In her interview she rejected the idea of a God or superior power on the grounds that such a power would not let good people die. With puzzlement she explained that, nevertheless, she believed that if you did something good, there was a reward, 'So, I feel that somebody might have something to do with that'. After her father had died, she was given a memorial cushion covered with his photographs:

> Erm, I think, yeah, one time I was speaking to the cushion, and I was like, erm, I wish you were still here, and then I put on some music, and it was his favourite song on the radio, and I was like 'Whoah!! That was crazy!' [**Small**

> **laugh**] And then the song after that was a song that was like our holiday song 'cos it always got played when we went on holiday, and I was like 'That's crazy!!' [**Laughs**] I was just a bit ... I didn't believe that it had happened and then I was like 'What!' I told my mum, and she was like 'That's crazy!' as well. I felt like he was giving me a sign and that he was listening and watching us.

Christina's comments exemplify what became a trope throughout the interviews – that of making personal sense of the world, rejecting previous 'givens', holding a paradox, and creating original spiritual pathways that reflected their particular sense of a meaning to life.[113] Also trying to make sense of her world and 'trying to follow God' was Catholic Hannah, an enthusiastic daydreamer, who was highly intent on being interviewed. She explained in her questionnaire that she had many questions about spiritual matters, which were not taken seriously by her parents, or that they answered them 'weirdly'. Children such as Hannah, often holding views running sometimes uncomfortably counter to their religious or family upbringing, manage the challenges by operating parallel paradigms, adopting personal, sometimes highly original belief systems alongside traditional religiosity. These, often private, models emerged quietly, often tentatively, during the interviews, and were often connected with a child's understanding of the mystery of death and the 'afterlife'. Hannah prayed to her deceased grandfather and spoke to him offering hope that he had regained use of his damaged legs in heaven. She had a very original idea of God:

> For me God is ... it's really weird ... is kind of a flame. A little fire. Flying a bit everywhere. And like, it's really funny ... and like ... it's just with us and inside us and ... like I think that when we are warm, or when we have fever it's because we feel very bad inside, so God is going to help us.

One of the most fruitful questions, drawing enthusiastic responses, was 'What do you think happens when we die?'. The topics of death and dying more often arose, however, in the context of questions about silence or when asked about things they couldn't explain. Many of the children eagerly described their own or others' continued sense of connection with those they had known. Isobel who by her own admission spent many hours daydreaming (a comment that was substantiated when she arrived very late for her interview because she 'forgot about it') mused on what happens after death:

> I think everyone is here for a purpose, but they don't know what, until, like, the end of their lives ... [I] think you get all happy memories. Like you see your life in front of your eyes, and then you go ... I don't think you go somewhere, but I think like you're aware of things happening, but you can't interfere with them ... it's your personality, the way you think. Just like your heart's feelings really. I think you're peaceful. You're like ... it's just like sleeping. But instead of dreaming, you're more aware. And you can see things. Like the family, or if someone's doing something that you wanted to do, but you couldn't. Like, say, if you wanted to start a charity or something, but you died before then, and someone had made the beginnings of a charity that you wanted to make, even if you didn't know them, you're sort of aware that that's happening. And it makes you more peaceful!

Asked whether she had ever had direct experience of this, she responded, 'I think at least once in a lifetime something will happen. Like someone's trying to reach out to you?'. She explained that she meant a deceased person. Kaitlyn, explained in her questionnaire that she wondered what 'the true religion is'. In a lengthy conversation about heaven, hell and purgatory, she described the continuance after death of a soul 'that has been with you your whole life' and which could never disappear after death as it's non-physical:

> Like you don't have any needs. You don't feel like you're missing anything. Even though you're not with your family, you feel like everyone's your family. You don't really have to do anything. You just have to, like, be in heaven. But you don't ever get bored. You're just there.
>
> Because you're with God. That's all I can think of ... [**Laughs**]. You just stay there and help everyone on Earth. So, if like a family member prays to you, then you can give them guidance. I don't know ... just like show them that you're there by sending a robin or a feather or something down ... When my grandad died ... well, he always used to feed this robin who always came every single day. And whenever we, like, prayed to him, the robin would be there. I think that was like him showing that he's there for us.

We see such beliefs with self-confessed 'under-confident' but 'curious about life' Alana, trying to fit into a new school, shedding her former 'tough girl' persona in a new, regarded as 'softer', school environment, as she talked confidingly about a recently deceased cousin who had been very important in her life:

> Say if I'm having trouble with the girls and that, I'd ask him to like help me or something. Like for him to ... like if something was happening, to make sure I was alright and look over me or something. Like random little signs. Like before I was thinking in my head like ... 'Cos I sometimes ask the question, whether he could, whether

> he was actually there, like, listening. And I'd be thinking. He used to be like a fencer. And there used to be, like these 50p coins, like Olympic sports and my mum came in and she was, like, I've got the fencing coin for you or something. And I was, like, I wonder whether that's a coincidence or not … there's loads of, like, coincidences that, like, I notice. Like, round Christmas time, my aunt passed away, and then, like, in the garden where she'd always sit, like, randomly, a load of smoke was coming from, like, the ground! [**Small laugh**] It was really confusing! But my grandad had recorded it and sent it to me. I was, like, it could actually be a sign that she was still, like, even though we think she's gone, there still, like, she's still here.

Such conjecturing was common amongst the children and ranged from the tentative, as with Alana, to the more forcefully articulated. Some proposed a variety of possible rationales for human existence. Gracie, yet another daydreamer, who felt that in silence everything seemed to make sense, wanted to talk about her views about life in both her interviews:

> I think that when people daydream they're not just like … I feel that there is something else. You know like when people say when you die no one knows where you go, I feel like you can't just like … die! You can't just like die and rot and everything just goes. All those memories, all those things you discovered just go! You just like […]. Well, you know the spirit … you know, the body stays but the spirit goes up. It's see-through. Erm, but it's kind of, it doesn't stay up and go, it kind of goes, you know it just goes into the world. But up. 'Cos I always imagined that it went up.

Sophia, who found silence with her cat 'cleansing', also felt that there was a force inside her that was hard to explain:

> So, like, I think that we, kind of subconsciously make things happen? Because something ... knows that that's the right thing. It's like ... on another level. But we don't realise it at the time.
>
> I feel like there probably is a life before this one, like a thousand more above, and I feel like when you daydream you might go into one of those, you know like, lives, and be somewhere else and maybe the one before was a worse one and maybe the one before was better, you know ... the life like. So, I dunno, I just feel like when you're daydream [*sic*] and not just sat there thinking, you're somewhere else because otherwise how do you think all those thoughts that you don't normally think?

Jacob who had very little free time in his life was worried that he might get tired in the interview as he often did in life. He believed that all nature was alive and, therefore, important and thus he never felt alone in the world:

> I don't really believe exactly like there is a God or anything like that, but I do kind of believe that there is such things as spirits that look over you sometimes. I just kind of feel that when I am alone, I just don't feel alone? I don't ... I just feel like ... I just don't feel like I'm alone. I just feel like I have company. Even though there's nobody else around. It's usually comforting. Not like a vibration, more like a ... yeah. Like a feeling, just like an inside feeling.

Nature-loving Katarina, who also had very little time alone, though loved the woods and sitting by the stream listening to birdsong, often sang to herself. She felt that she was quite religious, just as her family was, though she explained in her questionnaire that she was loath to tell this to her friends in case they 'said something'. She was definitely a 'spiritual person', with a phobia about death, and really wanted to believe that 'there is something out there that will listen to me'. She expressed her feelings that her grandfather watched over the family. Describing the sensation of sitting outdoors, she confidently and very warmly explained her hopes:

> I think like 'cos everyth(ing) ... like every beast is like free around there and you feel free, and you think you're closer and you just kind of hope. I might pray for my grandad because he's now dead and I might like to imagine he's a bird or something and he's like happy or something. Yeah, he could be anything. He could be ... even like a being ... just watching over you like ... just his soul. Like his being. Some people say that you're just a lump of flesh in a grave, or something, like that. But I think that's just really depressing. I just don't think, I don't believe that. I believe that you could become anything. Like my little sister loves elephants. She's obsessed with them. We say she might have been an elephant in her past life. Because she's ... she knows everything about them.

For Katarina, Alana, Kaitlyn and then Kay, who described her pleasure at her uncle seeing his deceased wife in a cloud, this is a world of possibilities and mysteries, that brings them into contact with something larger than themselves. This, for them, is a universe that is caring, loving and transcendent.[114]

Karla, who sometimes sought solitude from her busy and 'noisy' family and her sometimes overwhelming life, mirrored this sense of mystery, of unanswered questions. Her questionnaire contained a passionate (and unnecessarily apologetic) critique of all religion, feeling that it 'holds you back', and she enjoyed wondering and imagining what happens after death. Tarot cards and a belief in helpful angels were part of her everyday family life:

K: Well, I guess I kind of believe there must be something like when you die or something, you must go somewhere else, like go on, or something. Like your soul doesn't like just disappear ... kind of comes out of your body, that goes, I don't know where. 'Cos no one can really prove it. But erm, yeah, I guess I kind of believe in like good karma and stuff, like if I do, you know, something really bad, then you're not as happy really are you?

V: You said something about soul. What's soul?

K: Like your spirit. You know, like your personality, your spirit. I think that like it's in your body but your body's just like the carrier. And when you die your spirit leaves your body and it could go into another body, or it could go on ... somewhere else ... but I think it lives more than one lifetime.

Trying to clarify her beliefs in an external power, she conjectured:

> Well, perhaps there is a God, but it's not like an old man with a beard or something. It might just be ... It wouldn't really have a gender, because that would be unfair. So, it would probably be, I don't know ... it wouldn't be like human. I'm not sure. And perhaps there is like, you know, forces out there that we don't know about that are looking down on us ... 'cos you know like Mother Nature or something, something like that. 'Cos if you think about the world, it's just so amazing how it's made. I don't know if that could happen by coincidence. Like all the amazing stuff it has.

Such delight and awe in a 'hidden' world is palpable amongst most of the children, whether the daydreaming, fast-speaking Gracie who described herself as 'loud and out there' and who felt strongly that there was 'a bigger picture' and that the world is not just there to look pretty, or Fazia, whose powerful, almost disconcerting, imagination involved ghosts (we will meet her in later chapters); or Katarina, who, as we know, hides her religiosity from her peers and who rejoices in the colours of flowers, believing (against her family's views) that her time sitting on a hill was more spiritual than any experience in churches. For her there is power in everything:

> Well, people say God, but I don't think it should be God ... it could be anything. It could be ... whatever. I just don't believe it's something. I believe everything's ... powerful ... erm ... [**Small laugh**]. Everything ... I don't believe that there's one thing that's powerful. [**Slight pause**] Yeah, I don't know how to explain it ... there's more than just God. There's ... Like I said when we were on that hill ... that everything's like ... erm ... I dunno ... helping me, if there's something that you've done wrong, or something. You can just go up on that hill. It will soak it all out of you and put nice images in your mind. Or something like that.

These children are saturated in wonderment, brimming with questions, open to transcendence and carry the feeling that there is more to be understood about the world than is generally discussed. It is the space identified by Brendan Hyde as being beyond logic and into 'the space of mystery'.[115] Other researchers have already noted that children are capable of meta-cognition, a standing outside themselves, seeing themselves as objects and capable of reflection on their experiences.[116] We have seen Hannah's concept of being imbued by a flame that is an all-pervading God, and Sophie's sense of the possibility of expanding beyond this existence to another, possibly former, life during daydreams. We have read of Katarina's belief of there being power in *everything*, rendering the sitting on top of a hill a transcendent experience, beyond herself, beyond this world. Such descriptions and beliefs are often outside everyday consciousness, surpassing it, and they correspond to some of the positive emotions of which Vaillant speaks when he describes 'natural spirituality': awe, gratitude and hope.[117] It is of another such emotion, love, that the children speak with the greatest eloquence, as we will now discover.

Love and relationship

During the course of the interviews the children were asked 'What do you think really matters in life?'. This echoes a question posed by Hyde as a means to examine children's values and what they deemed to be of utmost importance to them.[118] Unsurprisingly, in their replies, the word 'family' arose with great frequency, as did 'friendship' and helping others. Many of the children distilled this into a broader concept – that of 'love' – a word that prompted some embarrassment in some, who, though they did use the word, apologised lest I should deem it 'cringey' or 'corny'.[119] Naturally I reassured them that I certainly did not. Such expressions of love, kindness and connection have long been recognised as important aspects of child spirituality.[120] When the children use the word 'love', I asked them to define it, making sure to reassure them that even the wisest of adults would find this challenging.

Jasmine, lover of song and dance, and who described herself in the questionnaire as neither spiritual nor religious, pondered, nevertheless, on the meaning of spirituality and explained that it was important to be able to love and also to hate (the only child to mention the latter). She burst into laughter when asked to explain the word 'love':

> Loving is ... to feel like really close to someone, but ... 'cos you can love people in different ways, can't you? You can love them as a family. You can love them as friends. You can love them as like a husband and wife or something. But like there's ... I don't really know ... feeling connected to someone in a way that can't be explained. You just know that you love them. [...]
>
> 'Cos if you don't connect, then you're sort of a bit like, I guess like two magnets going opposite ways. Whereas if you connect you can stay close and become, get closer ... So, if there's no connection, you repel each other, I guess. Like opposites.

I asked Waldorf-school educated Martin, always prepared to explain his thoughts in detail, what mattered in life:

> Probably I'd be like ... this is going to sound cringey ... but I'd be like love or ... [**Laughs**] or like lots of people the dearest thing they have is like money and stuff.

When I asked him to explain the meaning of love for him, he sought to clarify a range of meanings, though ended with a single, unitive idea:

> It's ... It's just like [**Squeezing this out with real effort**] ... it's kind of like an element. You can't ... it's just part of life. You can't get rid of it. It's always going to be there, unless like, well unless everyone dies [**Laughs**], but you can't ... I don't think the planet would be able to live without love though.

In his second interview he explained that fate determined romantic love before we were even born, a vibration that was felt in the body. Yet this vibration was not limited to love between human beings, but extended to love of animals, sport or art, the job one chose – everything in fact. He had no idea how it worked but he felt strongly that there was a natural, almost magnetic, force pulling us towards people or situations. For him this was obvious, and he shrugged as he insouciantly explained it all.

Best once described a special time dancing with his beloved granddaughter and how there was a palpable 'affect' that signified a special and highly significant moment of spirituality, or in the words of Coles 'moments of edifying wordlessness'.[121] Such moments arose in the interviews. They were unexpected, often born of silent waiting, and had a strong effect on the emotions of either the child, me, or both of us, leading even, on memorable occasions, to our tears. There was at such times a tacit understanding that we had both shared something significant, that the hidden had become, as it were, manifest. Such a moment occurred during an interview with Kay. Reflective and self-described 'shy' Kay, who valued silence enormously, though experienced very little of it according to her questionnaire, discussed the recent loss of her grandmother and was then posed the same question about the most important thing in the world. She replied, as so many others had, 'love and happiness'. When asked what 'love' meant to her, she replied:

> Something that, something that makes something inside of you ... come out ... in a way ... like if you ... if there's love, you can't be like really ... upset, in a way. Like ... like ... sometimes you might just want to like scream that you love someone like ... it makes you just emotional and ... happy [**Small voice**] ... I don't know ... [**Very long silence**]. Erm, it's like ... **it's kind of like the truth**. And when it comes out, you ... it like goes straight like ... it's like ... aw. I don't know ... [**Long pause**] I don't know.

This was then followed by both of us bursting into laughter and then, on my part, a tear. It was the laughter of incredulousness about sharing something special – something important to Kay, who had expressed her desire to be interviewed as she wondered what she might say. The atmosphere had shifted quite noticeably during this conversation, and she had gone very inward before finally linking the concepts of love and truth – probably unbeknown to her, an ancient pairing.[122]

Similarly, Katarina stressed love, and, for her, its corollary – happiness, as being what really mattered in life, and indicated its practical expression in her life, as well as joy in its reciprocity. Love is, as far as she is concerned, a *sine qua non* for everybody, including those who have transgressed:

> For everything. For *everyone*. Who's having a hard time. Who's maybe killed someone. For everyone, because they need the love. Because if everyone is like 'We hate, we hate, we hate', then that makes them be a hateful person and then, even for someone who *is* bad, they need the love, so that they know it's not all ... not everything ... not everyone's against them. Now that they've done something bad they need the love to make them ... I just mean like, you know, in London when they had the terrorist attack. Those people just need love and not hate, to make them feel better and not want to do that again and again.
>
> In the street in T., you smile at strangers. Like I always smile at strangers [...] Like what is the point in not smiling? You don't have to pay or anything. It's all free, like love and happiness! It makes you feel happy, and when someone smiles back it makes you feel even more happy.

Catholic-educated Dominic also equated love with happiness and worked hard to explain his idea of love even to the point of challenging his own religion's teaching on 'hell'. For him love transcended this concept and resided in our very consciousness. Pointing to his chest he tried to show me where it dwelt:

> Yeah. Like ... argh ... like just ... it's hard to explain ... I don't really want to say soul, but ... do you know what I mean? ... I don't know. You know when you get that feeling when you really, really love somebody. Like that feeling on the inside of you. In your heart metaphorically, not in your actual heart ... I ... I don't know ... it's just like ... not your conscience ... just ... your brain? But the thoughts ... I can't say it ... I don't know what to say. [**Dominic later explained that he had meant consciousness**] ... I've been like on and off with Catholic, like on and off for years, and I finally decided I am a Catholic, but I don't believe *everything* that's in the religion. So, it's my own type of Catholic. It ... it follows a lot of the ways 'cos it teaches to love your neighbour and respect everybody right, which I totally believe in. I believe in God, but I don't like the concept of hell. Because I don't think anybody deserves that, no matter how bad they are.

Throughout these conversations we see the importance and impetus of love for the children and also their desire to give it to others, which in turn makes the giver happy, irrespective of the response of the recipient. Such love, they describe as different from, though including, romantic and familial love. They see it as variously: a magnetic force, a connection, electricity, an element that is just part of life, a kind of respect that comes from the 'soul' and consciousness, and as simply 'truth'. For these children, love is the essential condition of existence, without which the world would be a desolate place. It *flows* from them in what Miller would describe as a 'bonfire model', where love begets love.[123] It is for many of the children a form of positive contagion.[124]

Some of the children described not only their valuing of the importance of love, but also revealed a particularly strong, and not always, to them, welcome, personal quality of empathy. Miller describes this spiritual characteristic resonantly as 'heart knowing' and it is an outcome of the partial dissolution of the boundaries between self and others, registered by the brain in what Ramachandran calls 'mirror neurons'.[125] Yet, as we shall see, such empathic connection is not always limited to people but extends to encompass the living world.

Both Gabriel and Alexander expressed strong distress at observing suffering. Gabriel, speaking quietly and with a broken, faltering voice, told me that making others happy and stopping suffering were of key importance for him: 'I just don't like it when people suffer.' It was at this point in the interview that the emotional pain he experienced became palpable and his silence seemed to indicate that it would be inappropriate for me to continue; yet he indicated non-verbally that we should. He seemed to want to share this inner torment. His schoolmate Alexander explained that empathy was just putting yourself in another person's shoes and 'thinking of what it would be like if you were that person'.

I asked Alexander whether this thinking was useful to the world:

> I think it is in some ways. But sometimes I'd be quite happy not to have it because you get really sad [**And he sounds sad now too**] ... Like when I see them alone or sad ... and then, yeah ... that's when ... well ... not ... pain. As such. It's just ... beyond comprehension. Just why ... I don't understand [**Very quiet and broken voice**].

This acute grieving was expressed by both boys, in a whisper, as if they were almost afraid to voice it. Isabel, too, 'picked up' on the emotions of others, and explained with references to her currently frequently arguing parents, and expressing strong powers of analysis, that when 'there is no colour in life' you didn't care how people felt, and focussed on yourself, almost disliking yourself. She wanted, therefore, to help, especially when she was happy, projecting happiness onto others, 'like a cycle', noting poignantly, that others sometimes inadvertently do this in reverse.

This exquisite and affecting view of the world, a selflessness described by Hyde as 'the outward expression of the fire within the soul' is an aspect of child spirituality widely seen by a range of researchers.[126] It extended for many beyond a sensitivity towards other people to a broader sensibility involving the whole Earth.

Love of nature

Sadness about the world and the state of the earth erupted during Megan's interview as she explained that she found even litter upsetting, as it took away 'the earth's natural beauty'. The laugh that followed this comment seemed self-deprecating, as though she had been embarrassed to voice it. Following affirmation, she spoke of her sadness about poverty, climate change, sea pollution, sickness and issues with animal life and she expressed, as the interview was closing, the hope that there would be an end to all these problems. Reflective Gavin felt equally strongly about animal rights, expressing confliction about his love of eating meat and the equality he wished to ascribe to 'every living thing', including 'rivers and trees'. 'After all,' he said, and like Isabel alluding to a chain reaction, 'every little thing affects the world.'

Such powerful empathy with the world produced a quiet rage against the activities of humans, expressed most incisively in Martin's question: 'What has the human done?', a rhetorical question that prompted an articulate railing about the world's ills:

> But if you think about it though, what has the human done? It's kind of destroyed the world. It doesn't have a particular use. It's built houses where, like, trees used to be; it's used trees to build houses; it's made massive factories and stuff; it's killed a lot of the wildlife; people are using chemicals to spray crops which means that the bees and stuff are dying because they can't pollinate or anything, and the melting of the polar caps. Like it's destroying everything.

We see this bafflement again with Karla and Gracie:

> K: 'Cos you know, the world's being kind of messed up with all the, like, pollution and stuff. I mean you think about all the animals and they're all here for a reason. Like the bees, they pollinate the plants and all that. We're supposed to be the intelligent ones and we're here to like look after the planet and to look after everything, but we haven't really done that.

Gracie had no faith in technology helping. When asked whether there was a reason for our existence, she explained:

> Well, there should be because it just seems a bit silly to think we're put here to just live and die. You know, I feel like ... mmm ... I don't know, I just feel like ... mmm ... I feel like we might not discover that because of ... what ... how ... like they're saying the future would be. I just feel like we're moving away from getting into contact with the earth, you know, the actual nature. I

> feel like we're moving away from that because more technology's advancing. The way we used to be, like cave men and stuff, we were more in tune with the earth, but now we're not.

Distress about the despoliation of the planet and their deep connection with it were consistently and movingly expressed by the children. We see in so many of them, in varying degrees, a deep awareness of the suffering of the earth. Many also feel that they have a 'mission' in life to counter unhappiness or the ecological and human destruction that they see, spreading their own happiness where possible, in the hope of a positive transmission. They also exhibit despair, reflected in their vocabulary of sadness, shocked by the carelessness towards others and the environment shown by the adult world. This is not just a descriptive sorrow, it is a 'felt' and empathic sorrow, and the effects were seen in interview moments when the children were unable to speak clearly anymore, their heads down, and often in contrast to earlier manifestations of cheerful personae. De Souza and others remind us that such empathy is a significant element in human relationship and hence in human spirituality, with the potential of freeing 'the self from the self'.[127] We have seen, too, that many would almost prefer not to have these empathic drives or the concomitant pain. This seeing the world from a wider perspective, feeling part of something greater than themselves and in so doing expressing values about the world[128] was vividly described by Miller as the 'direct sense of listening to the heartbeat of the living universe'.[129]

This listening was reflected in the children's love of and resonance with the natural world and grief at its depredation. This betokened not the mere *exploitation* of nature for leisure or well-being, but a regard for nature as a source of wonder, as a 'symbolic world of meaning', reflecting, like a mirror, a higher reality in a world where, for modern people, nature has become desacralized.[130] The importance of such a connection with nature in a child's expression and experience of spirituality has long been recognised. Almost 50 years ago Coles's work with children involved him waiting patiently and with surprise for a child who was staring at a cloud for a long stretch of time, as he noted, with respect, her absorption and fascination. One of his interviewees felt that the mere sight of the ocean brought him 'closer to God'.[131] For many of my interviewees it was time spent, and experiences, in nature that provided their most abiding and numinous experiences. It could be said to be a barometer of spirituality.

Katrina described her love of sitting in trees and the joy she experienced in the colours and shapes of flowers, regarding being in nature as being 'closer to heaven and to God, than being in a church'. It was here, she said, that you 'just kind of hope' ... For her everything around us is powerful, does its part, and she felt that 'Everything's just like ... I dunno, helping me!' She conjectured that, even though water didn't have feelings, there must be something behind the fact that there was an automatic and consistent supply of it and a cycle of birth and death generally.

This seeking of a deeper meaning beyond the apparent, and a sense of trust in the world, was notably evident with Karla in her description of a moment that made her feel 'lucky' and 'amazed', and after which she sought, in vain, an explanation from the adult world. During a walk in the woods alone, a 'massive pack' of ferret-like creatures came near to her feet before running away. The wonder of this and their closeness made her feel very special, and it remained a memorable event for her years later, all the more because she had just had an especially hard day, and she then felt that this event 'probably had meaning'.

Such a narrative highlights the challenges of the fracturing by definition of a child's spirituality. Her story does indeed encompass aspects of several of the maps and overlays provided by other researchers: a sense of mystery and taking her beyond this visible world[132]; taking place in the 'here and now'[133] and a connectedness to the moment.[134] Yet her experience is an amalgam of all these and more. So, despite their usefulness, the definitions cannot fully delineate or capture the multi-faceted topography of a child's spirituality.

Gracie, whom we have already met, had enthusiastically asked in her questionnaire to be interviewed, 'I would love to be interviewed, as what your [*sic*] doing is AMAZING [*sic*] and I would love to be a help with that!' She also wrote vividly about nature in her questionnaire, complete with illustrations, feeling somehow personally supported. Her words tumbled out during the first minute of her interview in her haste to communicate her feelings. Talking of being near a tree by the river, she explained:

> Well. It's just ... you feel like so alone and yet not alone. So, if you're like, I feel like if I lived in a city I'd never be able to fully be just me, like just on my own, because there's always cars or sirens or, you know, whatever. [...] If you were like in nature, not everything, you know not everything ... not ... nature's just so innocent [...] I suppose like when you walk through the town, you don't feel there's any connection. [...] You know you can walk through and it's just buildings. They're not ... you know they don't ... you can't connect with them at all. But if you go into the woods and you feel like you're actually like ... how can I say it ... you're in, you feel like you can just be yourself [...] I think it's (nature) just always there for you, if you need it. [...] There's just, it's just like, you know, all beautiful stuff and the trees they just give off good vibes [...] I wouldn't know how to name what they *are* ... and put it into words, but there is something there, otherwise it would just be weird walking with nothing, with no connection.

Discussing her utter joy about the nurturing to 'health' of a bee in her garden at the age of nine a few years earlier, an event so lastingly meaningful for her that she had included mention of it in her introductory questionnaire, she explained:

> And I can't really remember what happened, like I can't really remember how I found it, but I just remember seeing it and feeling really upset that it looked like so helpless. I felt that I was really upset that something could eat it. So, I went back inside [...] and I got a really flat plate, and it didn't have a rim, so it could climb up onto it, and I put some honey and water and sugar on it [...] I watched it starting to eat all the honey and sugar. So, I left it for a bit and then I went back and just lay with it. Mum says I just lay there for about five hours, just watching it and looking after it. Then it was time for bed, and I was really upset, and I was like 'No, I don't want to leave it'. And it was getting quite dusky. So, I went to bed and the next morning I came back, and all the food was gone, and it just wasn't there anymore. And about a week later, I was lying in the garden, and this bee flew down and I remembered that the bee I'd nurtured back to health had three spots on its back and it was *really* distinctive. [...] It was like black, black, black and had little white things in the middle of it. And it came back, and it was the exact same colouring, and I *swear* it was the same bee that had just come back, like showing me that it was okay, and I was like 'Wow, that's crazy! Of all the bees that could have flown down, it actually like came back into the garden ... just like bizarre!'. [...] I guess I felt like really grateful that it had come back ... it sounds weird ... come back to say ... like 'I'm fine'. Just to tell me that 'You've helped me, and it was the right thing to do'... I was really, like really, like wow really

> happy! [...] But I felt that there was definitely ... I'd just really recognized it and I just kind of felt that wow, that was actually ... it actually came back, and I was really surprised that I'd actually spent that long just trying to ... I don't really do that anymore. As I'm older ... there's a lot of other stuff going on, but that was a time when I had time for that kind of thing and that's just nice to remember that when I was younger, I was able to just lie there for five hours and like just care for something. Because, you know, there's so much going on now that I'm older. There's so much stuff.

This total absorption, where time seems to be irrelevant, is another phenomenon identified as indicative of child spirituality, a special space – and one which will resonate in future chapters.[135] There was a lasting effect for Gracie, and the joy it brought her was combined with some existential amazement at her unexpected connection with the bee. Her story also exemplifies an experience of flow, or the 'single pointedness' identified by psychologist Margaret Donaldson and deemed by others also to be universally available to children.[136]

Though there was a sense of mourning here for a lost connection with nature, Gracie added later, laughing, that she felt this, 'her best friend' was always there for you if you needed it. Jacob, a non-theist but karma-accepting classmate, explained to me at length that we are all part of nature, all animals and all plants, and that we are all part of one thing, all alive, sharing something with everything else – a fact, he said, forgotten by those who just live 'with technology'. The thoughts, values and experiences of these last three children undoubtedly reflect their attendance at a rural school, and such contexts will be examined more closely in the next chapter.

Many children experienced a sense of safety in nature, not just connection but a feeling of comfort and a sense of freedom, just to be themselves with no societal pressures. A variety of senses were engaged in this enjoyment. For Isaac, who spoke with amazement of the belief that 'God made all this, just for us!', it was the *sound* of birds' flapping wings and 'just being in the moment' that was important – a pleasure that was stressed both in his questionnaire and in his interview. For Dominic, burdened with 'loads of homework', there were many special moments: for example, the sight of Koi carp and a massive blossom tree in a botanical garden. He confided at the end of his questionnaire, in the space at the end for any additional information or comments, that when he visited a certain deserted harbour on holiday he was 'really moved by the beauty of it' and, he said, it made him question many things and described it as 'a magical moment', unsullied as it was by human life:

> It was just weird really because I'd never been anywhere like that before. And everywhere you can just see where other humans had been. 'Cos like litter, pavements or like signs. There, there was [*sic*] literally no signs of human life, other than the jetty. Literally like it had been untouched. And I found that really weird. And fascinating. Just because it … You couldn't hear anything or see anything to do with humans. It was just nature – it was silent; it was just the sounds of nature – like the birds and like the waves and that sort of stuff.

Engaging all his senses, Adam told of a moment of joy at the top of a mountain, when all sound ceased, affording, he said, searching for the right word, 'solace'. Speaking as others had of the wonders of colours in contrast to the greys of his urban environment and his unease with the 'vibrancy' of it, he spoke of 'the fresh air and the sounds', a compensation for the artificial grass in his own back garden. Adam was Catholic-educated, though non-theist, believing God to be, however, 'a good role-model' and saw meaning in a gust of wind at a funeral, choosing to comment on this in his questionnaire.

Though not *all* children were similarly captivated (Alyssa, for example, listed her reasons for hating the outdoors: slugs, worms, flies and above all snails and spiders), the majority of the children, rural and urban, expressed their joy in nature. The awe they felt when seeing trees, mountains, bees or even ferrets, and the relishing of sound, sight and colour, reflect unspoken spirituality, once commonplace, where one could note, in the words of the Origenist Basil of Caesarea 'the efficacy of a single blade of grass to occupy the whole mind regarding the skill that had produced it'.[137] This 'supreme fascination', connectivity, relationship with nature and awe in its presence, also parallels the *mysterium tremendum* described by Rudolph Otto.[138] Yet the children did not usually define such experiences as spiritual. They were for them, rather, special times of deep appreciation. Despite this, it is clear that for some of the children at least, the sacred is still beheld in nature and the memory of it is stored and is ready to be shared with a listening adult.

Many of the children were also very ready to discuss their ideas about the meaning of their lives and their purpose on Earth and how they found any *raison d'etre* to be a comforting and energising force.

Who am I?

I was not surprised to find such a willingness to explore their role in the world. Australian researcher Moriarty[139] had suggested, following her work with primary age children at the beginning of the millennium, that they often sought a roadmap or vision of their lives and its purpose, and an extensive range of researchers from varying backgrounds indicated likewise.[140] Indeed, we have already read of the children in this book doing exactly this. We met Millie, who had a strong sense of being in the world to make a difference, arriving from 'somewhere' with a specific purpose.

Lively Harriet, who bounced into the interview room, full of enthusiasm, energy and life, had a strong sense of being formed through the personality traits of our ancestors, and that we should absolutely not change ourselves to make others happy. When in 'her comfort zone' usually when dancing, she was in a place of 'total self-expression', defined by her simply as 'I'm there!' She described, with some intensity and trepidation, an unusual experience she had had when on stage. Dancing dressed as a warrior, she described how she suddenly '*became* the warrior' and felt things around her that 'weren't there', although she knew they really *were* there – a fact she found 'confusing to think about'. Isaac conjectured about the motives of God, feeling that life was like a test, and in a moment of absolute specificity, said he was 'hoping to change the lives of ten other people in his own lifetime', helping them to have a good life.

Earnest and ambitious Ravi tried to clarify the context of his existence:

> The one thing that irritates me a lot, and really shouldn't, because it's bad to, is that people keep on saying that God does everything directly. To me that makes zero per cent reasoning whatsoever [*sic*]. Because take for instance, this is the easiest way to explain it, if a person makes every single line of code themselves, 01, 01, so much effort needs to be put into it. But if they just create a script to make the [**Inaudible**] ... for them, it makes so much more sense. If everything was written in a script, then that means that everything was made prior. Meaning ... erm ... everything comes in a predetermined pattern, as it were. So, it's not everything is done directly by God, everything is done indirectly.

He went on later to exhibit a metacognitive and almost rueful critique of his own life:

R: Erm. I'm saying that we rush things a bit. Not appreciating the little things. Not appreciating the work that you need to apply to get to where you want to go ... I feel like I'm a living contradiction. Which I should elaborate on. A lot. Erm ... great, I've lost my train of thought!

V: [...] You were saying that slowing down helps you achieve more.

R: Yeah. I'm a living contradiction because I don't *do* that! Because I guess it's kind of trained into me at birth. As you know already, I study a lot. I work hard and so forth. Don't do terribly at school I would say. But I am a contradiction because I do exactly what I say I don't want to. As in – I don't take the time to think through. I don't take the time to slow down and think upon what I should do. What I should be enjoying and what ... I should be grateful for, I guess.

V: And how does that feel, to be in that contradiction?

R: Currently ... ergh ... I would say disappointed, but I'm too confused to say which part I should be disappointed with myself in. But mainly confusion. I can't find the time anyway.

Such musings on the self and a purpose in life were commonplace during the interviews. That there was little time for such inner reflection, as explained by Ravi, is an important issue and one to which we shall return. Nevertheless, the majority of the children interviewed felt that their existence had meaning within and beyond this present life, and they wanted to talk about it, whether Adam who believed we are born to 'use our time wisely' or Kyra who felt there was a not-to-be-revealed-until-after-death 'purpose for each person'. Both would have agreed that there was more to their lives and personalities than was obvious. Many spoke during these attempts to find a meaning or mission in their lives, of their 'being' something beyond the body, a metacognition. Such discussions were deepened during our conversations about the self during moments of flow and the deep absorption experienced at times by nearly every child.

The spirituality of flow, absorption and peak experiences

The state of *flow*[141] has been regarded by many researchers as a state that can precipitate (whilst not being of itself) a spiritual experience.[142] There was a high number of these states described by the children and it was a dominant trope throughout, readily recalled and universally regarded as pleasurable and meaningful. The examples presented here, however, go beyond the usual centring of attention and loss of ego characterised by Csikszentmihalyi in 1975, they are unbidden and involuntary.

Katarina was able to access this pleasant feeling of flow through art:

> It's kind of like when I'm drawing. I go back to that kind of ... thought. Like calm. Like peace. Just like, yeah, every time you paint or something. You're just feeling calm. Unless it's like really loud around you and that's quite hard ... When it's over, it's not like sudden 'Whoosh!', you know, but it's like – I'm not doing that anymore, so it's kind of ... and then the real world comes back. You know, it's like ... stopped. But then, you know, I can always go back to it.

Art also prompted Noah's flow experience where he 'zoned out', achieving such heightened senses that he could hear the pencil scratching on the paper. He didn't feel that he was 'actually there' during this very calming experience. He described returning from this:

> It's like waking up in the morning [and time] ... and it goes really ... well, it goes slow. It feels like it goes slow. But I think that it kind of speeds up. Like if I'm doing something in the lesson, it'll make the lesson feel really short, but at the time it felt really slow. But looking back on it. It goes really...

Many children referred to returning from this state as 'coming back to life', as if they had indeed been, as we will eventually see Kamal suggest, in a different dimension. Christina suggested that this place is 'here, but not quite here', and that she is aware but also simultaneously in 'her own place'. The main pleasure for her in this state is that she absolutely cannot be disturbed, because no one else would be there and she becomes unreachable. It is a state that the children find hard to describe, but Christina, seeing it being experienced by others in her family, tried hard to convey the sense of it:

> Well, I think my little sisters have it as well, because my little sister says that sometimes she's in her room and she's like talking to herself. And she says that she's playing with dolls but ... she's like ... she's not holding dolls sort of thing. I'm like 'who are you talking to' and she was like – 'Er, nobody'. And when she was younger she used to say she was talking in 'my language', even though it was English. And I was like –'Okay' [**Doubtfully**]. And it was like, you know that you're like ... there, but it ... aw I don't know how to say it ... it's like ... you just ... I don't know [**Laughs**].

Alyssa describes such a situation as a 'nice-odd' feeling, and this is consistent with the pleasure told of by many of the other children. The loss of self-consciousness, without worries of failure, one-pointedness of mind, extreme joy (and more of that later) without apparent reason and an autotelic integrated consciousness after which we feel more 'together' are all outcomes of 'flow' identified by Csikszentmihalyi. The self loses its boundaries, he tells us, expands, and is enriched and becomes more complex than it has been. Time also expands and diminishes, and there is sometimes a feeling of union with the environment. Activities (particularly artistic or sporting) and achievements seem to occur by themselves.[143] Trousdale accurately describes these as 'peak experiences', where the use of kinaesthetic vocabulary, an 'embodied knowing' may provide signposts of sudden insights and moments of awe – a sense of transcendence.[144]

Interestingly, though many of the children experienced flow in the midst of endeavours or activities, many, too, as we have read, encountered flow without having any particular activity, focus or intention.[145] For them it is an enjoyable state of consciousness, easily entered, sometimes at will, and, although flow is not in itself automatically spiritual, it is potentially so. It is possible, as Csikszentmihalyi tells us, to experience major breakthroughs in its midst, and it seems that for many of my interviewees there was a realisation that they have accessed, and might access again, states of consciousness beyond the everyday. When describing this they are expressing their connectedness to a particular moment and with the wonder and energy of life – both aspects identified in the definitions of spirituality in Chapter 1.

So, did they express spirituality?

If they had not, then this book would clearly be rendered irrelevant. So, yes, they did, and even to me the extent and clarity of the expressions of these were surprising. In particular, there was a plethora of examples of positive emotions expressing transcendence, including gratitude, love, trust and awe[146]; deep connections, sometimes empathy with the natural world and other people combined with a deep moral sensitivity[147]; a sense of there being a meaning to life; joy and perplexity in the experience of boundarylessness; metacognition and transcendence; a belief in a higher power, both theist and non-theist; and, as so many researchers have identified, a general sense of there being mysteries in life and wonders to be discovered.

Once again, I will state the difficulty of the acutely felt artificiality and tendentiousness of placing these children's extracts under particular headings. After all, many of them were multi-aspected and defied simplistic categorisation.[148] Yet, analytical expediency is a powerful driver and helps to underline emphatically the point that the children with whom I spoke are, beyond doubt, spiritual beings. The examples of this spirituality given here are extensive, yet only by presenting these quite fully am I able to establish the ground on which I was then able to ask the question: what are the conditions and contexts that give rise to them.

And yet more. If we *are* to use categories, we can see here a broadening, a critical widening of existing categories for the defining of children's spirituality. We can see how for some of the children there is an apparent, sometimes painful intensification, an acuteness, even urgency, of aspects of spirituality relating to empathy. What is new here is the general, almost pitiful distress voiced by them and the preponderance of a *depth* of awareness (sometimes born of a problematic empathy) of the current suffering of other beings, human and animal, and nature in all its forms. This moves beyond the 'relational consciousness' asserted by Hay and Nye to a deeper sense of identification with *all* existence, and an assumption of shared responsibility for its welfare. It is a manifestation of a form of spirituality that is a synthesis, a melding, of many of the categories shown here: an awareness of the mystery of the earth, a sense of one's place within it and of the passionate seeking of a meaning and purpose for each human life, catalysing powerful, highly affective and somatic experiences of transcendence and love.

The key question now to be asked concerned the contexts within which the children experienced their spirituality, and whether silence was at all relevant. Though each child's individual personality *did* act as one of the determinants of their experiences and their expressions,[149] the more important agency of the cultural, educational, social and environmental situations in which they found themselves will be seen to provide a much broader set of ingredients for understanding variances and similarities between the children. It is to these ingredients that we now turn. As for the relevance of silence – this proved not to be a straightforward question … at all.

Chapter 5

'It Can Happen Anywhere': Spirituality Arising

The spiritual experiences and spirituality shown in the previous chapter are broad-ranging, and each expression of them was, perhaps unsurprisingly, unique to each child. What is of particular interest to those who care for children, however, is that the *catalysts* for them, the contexts within which they occur, seem to coalesce under significant headings: being in nature; being engaged in creative or imaginative acts; during laughter (!) and positive emotions; during periods of sensory sensitivity and embodiment; experiencing 'out-of-the-ordinary' situations; in deep thought and flow and in silence or quiet. Of course, these occasionally overlap, but these situations and contexts often acted as a springboard for memorable, frequently ineffable, spiritual events.

Being in nature and 'out-of-the-ordinary' experiences

We have already read many examples of children's love of the world and their grief at its depredation. This reflected a particular sensitivity towards and a resonance with nature. This is certainly not a newly defined area of spirituality (many indigenous communities would testify to that), but it does underline the sense that children have of being deeply part of the earth, in relationship with it, and hence their great distress about any ecological problems that arise. Such sensibility could be said to be a barometer of spirituality.

Nature also provided, for many of the children, a stepping stone into their most abiding and numinous events.

This sense of being personally supported by nature was powerfully conveyed by Gracie, who wrote vividly about nature in her questionnaire, complete with illustrations. Her words tumbled out during the first minute of her interview in her haste to communicate her feelings. Talking of being by a tree near a river, she explained:

> You know all the animals, they don't do anything wrong in life, they're just there. Do you know what I mean? It's like nice to be with things that are just like natural and don't like, you know, will just like be with you. You know like we have this tame blackbird who just comes and feeds from our hand and stuff. It's just nice, you know, just let everything go and just be with stuff like that ... it's just happy. [...]
>
> I think it's (nature) just always there for you if you need it. Like, whenever I go like to the woods, I never feel that I bring my troubles with me. It's a kind of place where you can leave everything else behind and just be like happy and you can just ...'cos nothing judges you there, nothing gives you bad thoughts, just like all good things. There's good vibes there. There's like no horrible vibes. [...] There's just, it's just like, you know, all beautiful stuff, and the trees they just give off good vibes.

The natural peaceful sounds of nature, and the relationship the children sometimes felt with it, were powerful backdrops to many of the children's spiritual and numinous experiences. When something out-of-the-ordinary occurred to them, such events became for them especially precious and often momentous. We have already read of Karla's sense of being awestruck when confronted at such close hand by a business of ferrets, an event remembered years later and after asking adults, in vain, for an explanation. This, to her, was a wonder, all the more intense after she had had 'a hard day' and she felt that such a meeting 'probably had meaning'. Prior to this she had been discontented with her life, and this mystery had a transformative and positive impact on her.

This sometimes sudden connection with animals and insects provided a gateway for several of the children. Jack was rendered speechless and full of gratitude after his encounter with a shark during a holiday:

> You *see* a whale shark bump into your boat, and you think … whoah! … Actually, *doing* it leaves you speechless …'cos … I don't really know how to describe it!! … I … I just … I don't know really … it was one of those experiences that I'll never forget, and I can't really describe why. I know in my head why, but I wouldn't be able to describe it … but I'll never forget it. [**Very long pause**] … Awe … and complete and utter amazement … and I guess it also like puts into perspective like, we as humans think that we're amazing and that we have all the power, but it gives you the realisation that there's bigger things out there.

Here and in future chapters we read of other children who found themselves in unfamiliar, occasionally startling situations, that pierced the boundaries of their expectations, emerging changed, questioning and, as Jack forcefully tells us, awed. Such awe, often merged with the concept 'wonder' is an extraordinarily powerful emotion and regarded as a principal source and a 'defining element', a catalyst even, of spirituality.[150]

Awe, wonder and positive emotions

Wonder is largely associated in English with the idea of surprise or amazement. A little wider examination shows that other languages hint at an even deeper interpretation. German *Wunder* suggest more of a sense of miracle, whilst in Sanskrit *Adbhuta* includes, after extraordinary and marvellous, a sense of the supernatural. The etymology of the word may derive from the Greek verb *thaumazein* emphasising not only surprise but also transcendence. In his excellent 2006 book *Spirituality in the Flesh,* Robert Fuller suggests that we see 'wonder' as an emotion that 'invites us to entertain belief in the existence [...] of an order of reality that lies beyond our sensory experience'.[151] For him, it is an emotion of perplexity or bewildered curiosity. So, wonder leads us somewhere; it prompts, energises and is developmental. It is also a highly functional emotion and was the most frequent effectuating emotion voiced by the children, when describing the arising of a spiritual state or event, often accompanied by joy and awe.[152]

When Katarina tried to explain, in a tentative yet emphatic manner, that she believed there was power in everything and that nature in particular was somehow helping her, this was beyond the rational.[153] She did not understand how this might work but felt that the mind was involved in a way she could not explain. In a similar way we have read of Jacob's inchoate sensing of spirits, through an 'inside feeling' that he was not alone, and that led him to feel that there was something below the surface of life that was inexplicable and wondrous. Similarly, Gracie's nurturing of a bee for over five hours at the age of nine, a bee that appeared to be communicating with her and then returned to 'thank her', seemed to her bizarre and meaningful and never to be forgotten by her current 12-year-old self, who rued the way that such an event couldn't happen for her now in her time-pressured world. For her this was wonder saturated with joy.

As we have read, events in nature kindling the emotion of wonder were common, yet other circumstances also provided such frameworks. For Kay, wonder occurred in a dance performance. Loath to recount this experience lest it be seen as 'stupid' and speaking in a slow, musing and deliberate manner, she described her feelings of this transformative event:

> When I think about it, it's not necessarily ... it's kind of like in that moment, everything like freezes and like, you feel like, I don't know [...] It's like everything freezes and you get overwhelmed by something. Like, say, a *new* feeling.
>
> [**Very quiet voice and seemed to be filled with wonder**] Yeah! Maybe like, at that moment, you're considering something ... like bad ... you can say like ... not conquer your fears but because you've got the sense that you just did that, so you were scared of doing that, and now it's like giving you pleasure, you could like do *anything*!

Such events often leave the children confused, even perplexed, and though they voice the fear of their own weak articulacy, the events are, nevertheless, frequently lucidly described. When Jack recounted his meeting with a shark, it was evident that this was a special time for him. He went on later to use this as an example of really being 'in the moment' and repeatedly stressed that it was surreal, that he felt 'privileged' and that he regarded it as a 'whoah!' moment. Speaking hesitantly, quietly and slowly – in the manner that I grew to recognise to be a signifier of an event of great import – he told me that it left him speechless.

For these children it seemed to be vital to explain to an adult that the events described were portentous and laden with unfathomable meaning. When the highly sensitive Arianne told of three white butterflies following her around in the garden, she explained tearfully that this was a time of a series of three deaths in the family. A book that her grandfather offered her from his bookshelf following his wife's death and that held a poem 'Do not Weep at My Grave' rendered her 'confused'. Both situations seemed to be important and wondrous, yet she didn't know exactly why.

Butterflies were significant for Alana also, who felt that one recently represented the return of a deceased cousin and that the many coincidences in her life had hidden meaning. This included a memory of smoke rising from the garden in the spot that was her aunt's favourite place, a fact holding mysteries that she could not fathom. For Alana, as for many of the children, these revelations of the promptings of wonder occurred in the first minutes of the interview and had usually been undisclosed to adults. As Alana explained:

> They wouldn't think much of it. They'd be 'Aw, it's just a coincidence'. But I would think maybe it *is* a sign of something.

We have already read of classmate and keen fisherman Dominic, who was eager to share his experience of an extraordinary moment when he came across an 'unknown-to-tourists', abandoned harbour in Scotland with crystal clear water and beautiful fish. Such sights moved him and catalysed spiritual stirrings effected by feelings of wonder, that sometimes lead in the words of Csikszentmihalyi to 'rich epiphanies', where we 'make something happen and expand ourselves'.[154]

D: You know when you just see things … like I went to this other place near X, and you just saw this cliff and the sea. And you know when you just see beautiful views that take your breath away? They just make me question like everything.
V: Do they?
D: Yes. It's just really nice.
V: What goes through your mind when you see something beautiful?
D: I dunno. 'Cos I'm Catholic, it makes me think about my religion and my grandad and all that sort of stuff.

V: What about your grandad then?

D: Well, I don't know. He died of cancer, a couple of months before I was born, and I just think about him.

Ravi ponders on a possible meaning or an external force following his unexpected well-being after a potentially life-diminishing injury, after having been asked in the interview to expand on his understanding of 'miraculous'. He had also used the word to describe his brother's sudden recovery from illness. Asked how it made him feel, he replied that he was grateful but also confused, bewildered and perplexed. The events were for him inexplicable. Both boys acknowledged the feeling that there was something 'more' to be known. This is precisely the perplexity and bewildered curiosity, born of wonder, indicated by Fuller.[155] They are drawn to conjecture about and question a world not immediately available to their senses or mind, and, in wonder and awe, they look for meaning.

We see this particularly in Isabel's sense of a hidden moral force guiding us. Jack and Gracie's expression of wonder at the shark and the bee reflected a respect for and appreciative reverence for the natural world, sensing that there was something unseen behind it all. Dominic's description of a harbour's pristine beauty as taking his 'breath away' was redolent of William James's similar commentary on the outcomes of similar spiritual states of awareness.[156] For each child the context and propulsion may have been different, yet the outcome, born of, or accompanied by, wonder and also awe, triggered a lasting, respectful sense of the numinous.

During the telling of these occasions there was a reflective slowing down of their speech as they tried to recall the feeling of the event. There were extensive and relishing pauses, hesitancy and inarticulacy, as they tried to explain the inexpressible, with breathlessness, even struggle. All this was combined with postures and body language that indicated an earnest desire to communicate what was for them momentous. Ultimately, however, it was not their *words* that bore the meaning, it was the silence between the words, and the enabling within this silence of a new understanding.[157] This created, without exception, a clear reverberation, and a mutually appreciated awareness that something important had occurred for the child both at the time of the precipitating event of wonder, and within the interview itself.

Hope and trust, combined with wonder, fostered Millie's spirituality. After a lifetime of extensive periods in hospital for operations and her efforts to 'put a brave face on things', she expressed a certainty that God helped, protected and led people. She was inspired to seek an intrinsic cause for her previous life experiences:

> Well. Like definitely all my hospital experiences [have helped] because without them I wouldn't be like brave and sympathetic towards others who are going through something similar. And I wouldn't be as accepting.

Similarly affected was the highly empathic Alexander, who described how his compassion for a new and apparently lonely fellow pupil led him to befriend him, with positive results. Alexander's moral sense leads him, however, into confusion when he sees that not everyone has the same response to certain predicaments:

A: 'Cos when I see homeless people, I feel like empathetic towards them [**Broken voice**].
V: I know [**Quietly**]. You have this very strong empathic aspect to you, don't you? Which is painful.
A: Mm. [**Very quiet**]
V: Do you wish you could get rid of your empathy?
A: Well, sometimes ... but sometimes not. [**Very slowly**] Because sometimes I don't *want* to be empathetic, because

it feels like really – it doesn't feel good. But then, it's something good to have. Because you can feel what other people are feeling and you can help them. Kind of.

V: You said sometimes you don't want it. In what way does it not feel good?

A: I don't know. I just feel like I've done something *wrong*.

V: Why? In what way?

A: I don't know. Er, 'cos ... ergh ... I'm not sure. I just ... er, I want to be able to help them [**Very cracked voice**], I suppose. I want to be able to help them ... but I know that it's really hard and just me, and I'm probably not going to be able to do anything ... about it.

V: And that makes you feel bad? Does it make you feel weak?

A: Yeah!! Because I walk round with my family in the cities, and they don't, really ... give a second glance [**Very sad voice**], really. But I feel like, I feel that they didn't get bothered by it ... and I *do*.

This sometimes distressing bewilderment arising from his compassion gave Alexander and others a nuanced vision of the world and society. It shows another beautiful example of a move towards the explicit moral conduct suggested by researchers as often arising from a positive emotion.[158]

In this example such an emotion can certainly be seen to be socially positive, even if not without challenges. Positive emotions were seen in the interviews to be commonly instrumental in the development and expression of a child's spirituality and should be regarded as worthy of the recognition of their value. This is not easy in a prevailing culture of emotional cool and a frequent encouragement to subordinate and manage emotions. All of us dealing with young people should now consider that continued recognition, even elevation, of positive emotions, such as wonder, joy and awe *inter alia* provide valuable spiritual catalysts, critical for children's well-being. The children's rueful comments that such experiences, particularly joy, occur less frequently as they get older, may suggest their associating these with an immaturity best forsaken. We can surely find a response to this.

Physical catalysts: Creativity and flow

Very many of the children described out-of-the-ordinary experiences in the midst of physical activities that seemed to shift them to a 'different space'. When music-loving Katarina describes herself singing and really focussing on nothing around her but the notes and 'being in the moment', she explains that this is a peaceful place, and a space that is similar to when she is doing her art, enabling her to reach achievements that she has hitherto only imagined.

Noah, too, told of his heightened senses when doing art and hearing the scratching of the lead on the paper, and 'zoning out' to the extent that he doesn't actually feel *he* is there and that this feeling is 'really weird'. He described, with apparent confusion, that although he is not trying to move, his arms move, nevertheless. For him, at this juncture, the effect on time is paradoxical. *Within* the moment, everything 'goes slow'. At the end of the lesson, though, when he feels as if it is like 'waking up in the morning', the time appears to have speeded up, as the lesson is over so quickly. For him this is daydreaming, yet he is fully aware, and the effect is beautifully calming.

Jasmine haltingly described how she felt that she almost stepped outside her body as an observer when dancing, enabling her to dance with greater energy than normally. This was a sentiment echoed by Christina, who tried to explain that when dancing 'like, I'm aware that I'm still here, but like ... it's here but it's not *quite* here ... do you know what I mean? [...] Like I'm aware that I'm still there, but it's like my own place at the same time, so it's different'. This is a calm 'place' to which she deliberately returns, feeling she cannot be disturbed there. Christina spent some time trying to convey to me that the reason she was unreachable in this state was because, as she repeated, she was in a different place from everyone else. Then there was a long pause, almost of satisfaction, at the end of this section of the conversation. It was a pause of mutual recognition that she had managed to transmit this experience, despite doubts and 'Aw, I just don't know how to say it!' – and that this was a precious, important, and, as she said, a freeing time for her. Once again, such affective instances punctuated many of the interviews and signified a moment of understanding between the child and me, a space entered by both of us, often resulting in our emerging with surprise at such a succinct description of what was a spiritual experience for the child.

It is important to mention again that the children were generally not at all confident that they could articulate such experiences. They hesitated, were sometimes embarrassed, delayed (with long pauses) and then tried to approach the description from different angles, repeating themselves, the better to arrive at some mutually understood precision – a precision and a sharing that was clearly important to them. To do this seemed to provide a validation for them and a gift to me.

We are reminded by Csikszentmihalyi that this accessing of inspiration, prompted by single-mindedness, is an ancient and ambitious role of religions, creating an order in consciousness precipitated by contexts provided in, for example, art, drama, music and dance.[159] I believe it *is* the flow state recognised by many, but more significantly one which provides a shift in perspective and sense of self.

The imagination and laughter

The imagination has been regarded with considerable suspicion in some religious and philosophical thinking, exemplified by Feuerbach's comment that Christianity gave man 'what his imagination desires'.[160] Despite this, the importance of the imagination in spirituality, particularly child spirituality, is now more widely emphasised.[161] We are encouraged to pay attention to the various worlds of the child's imagination, they often being as real to them as the 'adult world' and capable of inspiring wonder, awe and fear. More than this, and especially relevant to coming chapters on liminality, we are told, for example, by Boyce-Tillman that imagination facilitates the removal from 'everyday propositional knowing', shifting us into transitional space and that it is central to the spiritual domain.

Katrina ponders on the power of her imagination, explaining that when she pictures that her grandad is floating in the air, when the family lights a candle during the evening meal, 'It's not necessarily true about when the flame goes up, that there's a spirit in the room, but if that person *feels* that, then that spirit *is* in the room, you know!'

Harriet, also, expressed her amazement at what she saw as power in the imagination:

> Er, well actually, this really minor thing happened, and I had a dream about my headphones. And the next day I discovered it was real. And I thought I did **not** know that the brain could do that ... I have an imagination, and that imagination becomes into a real thing [*sic*]. And it's actually such a small thing ... headphones, like who really cares about headphones and THAT ... and I was thinking 'Oh, maybe you could change the song by clicking on your headphone' and I said (to my sister)'How did you do that?' and she said 'Oh, I'm just changing the song' and I was mind-blown and I thought 'What's going on? This is crazy'. The next day my sister was clicking something on [her headphones changing the track] ... I don't know if I was alive in my dream, playing with my headphones or anything! [**Laughter**] It was the most baffling moment ever.

For her, her mind and her imagination seemed to create an event. Other explanations, including coincidence and precognition were not discussed.

Many of the children spoke of their use of the imagination to inhabit happier worlds, where they had improved skills, fewer stresses, contact with the deceased, or became, what appeared to be a different personality. The majority found it difficult to return from such reverie to the 'real' world and for all of them there was a sense of potentiality. Imagination for them was a Narniaesque doorway into a world made by *them* and suggests both their participation in, and contribution to, the nature of reality, as well as its origination in bodily experience.

Sadly, this avenue of discussion as to whether the imagination facilitates the cocreation of new realities (or whether it helps to access perennial truths) cannot be taken further here. I will just state that I believe, as others do, that the imagination provides an important catalyst for children into a spiritual state, with unique outcomes, and that for many of the children such imagination goes beyond simple fantasising.[162]

And now to laughter. Many children spoke of the powerful propulsion of laughter providing similar effects to the imagination. We will revisit this context in Chapter 8. Adam spoke of 'being lost in laughter', even of 'dying in laughter'; whilst Millie suggested that it just made her body feel lighter. Kay described in some detail that in the middle of really laughing with friends that 'you are just stuck'. Explaining that further, she went on to say:

> ...you're not like, you're not like thinking of anything else, you're just laughing. Yeah ... you're like in that moment completely and you, I guess you kind of like lose the sense of what's around you and like who may be looking at you and who, you know, *anything*. And you're just completely in the moment and not caring about *anything* in the world!

Classmate Isabel agreed. Laughter made her feel alive, made her lose herself, releasing pent-up emotions. Interestingly it was noticeable that, during the interviews, laughter frequently accompanied the description of an unusual spiritual moment for the children; sometimes this was a self-effacing laugh, pre-emptive of any scorn. Significantly, though, they would often laugh after a period of effort whilst trying to describe a momentous event or an indescribable emotion. It was the laughter of relief, wonder and catharsis and also of their recognition that they had, after all, 'got there', and I invariably joined in.

Leaving the self

We have seen several children describe with pleasure the sense of 'leaving themselves' and being without thought or even any awareness of their surroundings. Once again, such experiences were related in a confidential manner with trepidation as something they couldn't explain.

Joshua confided that he sometimes felt a 'bit weird' (such a multi-purpose word for the children) when on his own or even with others. It's almost like going into a different world, though when he 'goes' he can't hear anything, sometimes focussing on a single object, or view, frozen and unaware of time. During such moments he can 'feel like there is silence, a lot of silence' which is strange for him. On 'returning' he cannot think about or remember what has happened, yet he values these times for the inner silence they bring. Harriet also goes into a different world at times. For her it is during dance:

> ...when you're actually doing it, you feel like this energy. It's like a fire almost. I mean it sounds so weird talking about it, but when you're doing it, it's like there's a new you, like whoosh, takes over your body and just does it.
> V: Harriet is just lifting her arms to the sky.

> Yes! I know! It's ... and it's like when I dance at my grandparents when I go over, they're like 'Ooh Harriet, show us some more!'. When I dance it's like, I dunno, sometimes I feel **[Very rapid and excited speech]** sometimes I feel when I dance I connect with my (deceased) gran, and it's really weird because I don't think that my gran's ever danced before. But the music comes to me, a lot of the things I do is like reach out.

Waldorf-educated Fazia, whose account required deep probing and clarification, gave one of the most vivid and unusual descriptions of leaving the body. When asked whether she was ever deeply absorbed, she firmly explained that this happened in her favourite subjects and was similar to when people left their body during an operation:

> Well, my body's still there listening – I'm there. But I think like there's another part of me that really likes those lessons – are just like ab ... well. Absorbed from the outside.

She was happy to clarify this:

> [...] It's like there's another me, above me, watching over and actually being in the lesson, and like doing the stuff that the teacher's talking.
>
> V: So, you feel, let's take Geography as an example, so the teacher's teaching you Geography, so you go out of yourself and there's a ... a different Fazia?
>
> F: Mmm. Yeah!
>
> V: That is more able to absorb it?
>
> F: Yeah!! And like me here ... I'm still in the lesson; it's just taking me a lot of time to process it, the real me. But the one above me doesn't have that problem ... taking a lot of time to absorb things.

She disclosed that she had never spoken about this to anybody, as 'I haven't found the right words to tell anyone'. Asked if she could get into that state at will, she responded 'Sometimes by meditating and sometimes by watching my favourite TV programme, I start to doze off and ... it just happens ... naturally'.

These are graphic descriptions of the transcending of an activity and yet paradoxically being more fully inside one's own body and losing oneself, one's ego. The children express how, as it were, the 're-entering' of their normal selves, from their 'new you', is a confusing feeling. Such self- and time-transcendence, where the children become reflectively aware of themselves as subjects, is recognised as one of Maslow's peak experiences[163] and a key component of child spirituality.[164] And yes, the question as to whether such an event *precipitates* a spiritual experience or indeed *is* it itself, can be asked here, though not answered.

Feeling it

In contrast to these experiences of *leaving* the body are those that are deeply rooted *in* the body, the 'felt experience'. Here we see Catholic Isaac struggling to find words, having been asked whether he had ever had an unusual experience:

> You just feel like someone's with you. But obviously they're not visible [**Struggling, lots of hesitations**]. When you're, when you're on your own, like silent, I don't know what you're doing like, could be reading, or doing a piece of homework, you've got, obviously visibly there's no one with you, but ... you can *feel* something. I don't know what it is. And like, God's always with you, so it's probably God keeping an eye on us [...] it gives you like butterflies. [**Small laugh**] [**Laughs again**] It's really weird. I ... you just feel weird, and you start to change, and it makes you feel happy.

He added that he would remember these occasions 'forever', but would never tell anyone:

> Obviously ... if you ... let's say I told my mum ... she'd be like ... 'No, you're just feeling things'. Or 'Are you feeling alright?' If I told anything like that, Mum, she wouldn't believe it. She'd be like – 'Naw, you're... '[**The sentence was unfinished**].

Struggling in a similar way to find words to describe a deeply felt and memorable experience was another Catholic classmate, Kaitlyn:

> Well, whenever I think about heaven and I think about it going on forever and ever and I just can't imagine that because it obviously doesn't happen now. Then that just makes me feel really weird, and then I feel like ... I don't really feel like I'm out of my body, but I feel like ... I don't really know. It just doesn't feel ... it feels different. And then it just goes back to normal ... [...] Like life. So, I think about heaven and how it goes on for eternity, or it might go on for eternity, I don't know for sure. Then I kind of just go back to normal and it feels really strange, and it feels like going somewhere else when I was thinking about that. [**She was then asked which part of her goes**] I think it's just like me. So, it's not my body. It's just me. Just Kaitlyn.

Both of these children expressed these experiences using religious concepts, 'God', 'heaven' and 'eternity', for these were, for them, surer ground. As we have by now seen so often, there is the halting speech and the vocabulary of confusion: 'weird', 'strange', 'different', typifying the unfamiliar deep-down non-verbal level of awareness, said by Gendlin to be the internal 'aura' that encapsulates a meaningful experience of which we have not consciously thought.[165]

Isabel, from a different school, challenged the religious context within which she had been brought up, and told of her doubts about the God worshipped by so many, including her family, and how he could care for so many people at once. Asked whether she thought there was a greater intelligence in the universe, she replied:

> I think there's something. But I'm not really sure what [...] Like I sort of think, there's like, a sort of like, something senses what you're doing. 'Cos like, I get this thing where I sense that someone's telling me to do something ... so I'm about to do something and there's like a change in the atmosphere, sort of thing [...] Like a click and it sort of ... makes me stop for a bit. And I like consider what I'm about to do.

Asked where she felt this, she explained:

> I: Er, it feels like it's not too close. But it's like, I don't know. Somewhere like where that window is. Somethink there [*sic*].
> V: You see it or feel it?
> I: Feel it.
> V: Where do you feel it?
> I: It's like in ... like ... I sort of imagine it. But I feel like butterflies. [**Pointing to stomach**]
> V: Okay, so it's a stomach thing?
> I: Yeah!

In these accounts we see that the body is the centre of *interpretation* of the meaning of the experience as well as being its provider. In the following narrative we will read of a near-death experience.[166]

It is included here both as a profound spiritual experience as well as a somatic doorway to one. Adamantly non-religious Joshua arrived at his second interview enthusiastically eager to recount his very recent experience of nearly drowning in a swimming pool:

J: Well, it's ... [**inaudible**] ... I feel like I've almost died once. Basically, it was at a swimming pool, and I was swimming under water for a bit and my friend from class, he jumped on me. And I could feel ... Like I could feel myself saying like – three, two, and, and then I got to two and I could kind of not see my body over water, but I could feel my body move slightly. So, my normal body ... my ... yes, this, my body stayed still and my, kind of like spirit, I suppose, kind of like, kind of like slowly just ... [...]. I could feel this kind of vibration around my body, I think [**Pointing around his body**].

V: And where was the vibration? How far out?

J: It was kind of just around ... And then I managed to get back up out of the water and I kind of ... it's like that blur almost, I kind of go back into my body again. Then I started coughing [...]

I don't know what I was thinking ... just kind of like ... light! I don't know ... I dunno. Light for instance.

V: You were thinking light.

J: Yeah [**Slightly doubtfully**] basically. Yeah. [...]

V: Okay. You seemed to be counting? [...] Any reason for the counting or is it just...

J: No, I can kind of *feel* it inside me. And see it at the same time.[...] Yeah! I wasn't counting. I could feel myself counting, but I didn't *want* to count, but I did ... I could feel like a ... I dunno ... like [...] kind of vibration. Of like ... [...] And I could feel like my body like ... not fading ... kind of like just turn ... you know how you like when you break a bone in your leg?

V: And were you observing this? Where were you observing from?

J: Observing from my own eyes.

V: So, from Joshua?

J: Yeah! Yeah!

V: Where were you feeling this, you called it 'spirit'?

J: Kind of like my ... kind of like my body, in this area.

V: So, torso.

J: Yes, torso. Just kind of slowly...

V: Slowly growing, was it? [**Watching and responding to his body language**] Or?

J: Not growing. [**Speech is remarkably rapid and he is tripping over his words**]

Leave ... like yeah ... I was going to say I felt this vibration leave. [...] I was thinking Oh, I'm going to die now.

V: So, you talked about light. Tell me about that. What was that?

J: So, kind of like ... [**Long pause**] ... I dunno, it's just like these ... I dunno. It's really hard to explain actually [...]. I could feel, it's almost like my body like giving out a light almost. I could feel like a light ... , from my body. [...] Yeah, I felt the light and saw the light. ***From*** my body. Like not completely see, but I could see like, I could see the fade [...][**Words tripping**] Everything was not a fade but like a blur. [...] Everything was like ... and I could see this tiny ... well, not tiny ... but like ... this, this ... light ball.

V: Ahead of you?

J: Yeah, let's say I was here, it would be like where that red thing is [**Indicates an object about two feet away**]. [...] But more like, not a ball but more like kind of just like ... a thing. It was kind of glowing [**This was said lightly and matter-of-factly**] [...] It stayed until ... so, basically once that happened I came, I slowly came up the water and I could feel it coming back inside of me.

In his earlier interview Joshua had explained that, despite his avowed non-spirituality, he believed we came back (as a different person) after death to do the thing we were supposed to do the previous time. In the in-between phase, he said, we were 'just saved in the light' until the time came to be 'reformed'.

This fascinating story dramatically underlines the importance of the felt sense or embodiment, or here *dis*embodiment, as a catalyst for spiritual experience. Here Joshua differentiates between his 'normal' body and his 'spirit', and he describes counting, that appeared to be being *done* but not volitionally. He was the observer of his bodily experience, as well as feeling a vibration from and moving beyond his torso. He both felt and saw a light that emanated from him, as well as a 'glowing light' that was before him and which he sensed returning to him. Joshua had mentioned in his earlier interview that his concept of a higher being was that of a 'glowy beam' and we see this reflected in his interpretation of events. During all this, the medium of this intense experience was his body, bypassing cognition. His repetition of words such as 'feel, feeling, vibration and body' place his experience firmly in the 'felt sense', expressing and understanding the incident, as best he might, in physical terms. Joshua was at once the *I* and the *that*, using his body as a portal to non-verbal, non-rational understanding.[167]

He later confided that he felt he now knew what happens when we die, and although he had been confused by the event, he readily accepted it as 'normal'. It was for him embodied knowing.

Preconceptions collapse

As you have read, the whole point of the initial interviews was to examine whether a lack of access to silence and solitude might adversely affect children's spirituality. It became clear, however, that these children experience and attain any spirituality diversely and universally. There were myriad situations expressed here, often overlapping, that offered potent springboards and vehicles – artistic endeavour, imagination and deep thought, nature, through the body and senses, positive emotions, particularly awe and wonder, and even laughter; and yes, for some, even *my* much-valorised silence and solitude. Discovering this unexpected reservoir of potential impulses meant a rethinking of my earlier preconceptions (in any case always dangerous to have). And though for some children silence as non-sound, a binary, was indeed a precipitant, many (though not all) seemed to find their catalysts in situations congruous with a *much broader* understanding of silence.

Before approaching this understanding and the children's attitudes towards silence in all its forms, the following chapter allows us to glimpse the highly pressured, overstructured yet normalised, daily lives of the children – lives that militate against their even finding the space to experience what appears so clearly to be a natural tendency to spirituality.

Chapter 6

'Only When I Sleep': Children's Time Poverty

When a twelve-year-old boy who fell asleep in the 'Silence Dome', mentioned in Chapter 1, returned on subsequent days to do the same, some few members of school staff felt that this was a misuse of its offering and that he should be stopped from visiting. The majority of us, however, perhaps identifying with a level of exhaustion too well known in adult life, advocated his being left to rest. We were, as I now see, only to a limited extent aware of children's tiredness.

So, one of the first things I asked each child as we settled down to the first interview was to tell me about a typical day for them. This was partly to relax them and partly to get a sense of their interests and activities and whether there was any space in their lives for silence. I already had their questionnaires in front of me which gave some indication of their opportunities for quiet time and solitude. A saddening picture emerged of young people, some of whom at that point had not reached their thirteenth birthday, focussed mainly on academic achievement, fearful of disappointing their families and teachers, and whose free time was circumscribed by daily clubs and activities and punctuated by domestic chores and the completion of, or worry about, homework. For a few, the only 'down time' was sleep.

Harriet's busy life illustrates the intensity of activities:

> I wake up in the morning and I just do normal breakfast and then I walk to school, normally on my own all the way. It's like half an hour walk and I listen to music, and ... I love my music. I normally listen to musicals, and then I just get to school and just work, work,

work! And then I do lots of extra curriculum, so … like Mondays I have … actually Mondays are my only free day, and I see my nan and grandad, and Tuesdays I play cricket, and I have band practice. I have my own band on Monday. And then I'm in Junior Jazz […] and then I have that on Thursdays and then I do dance. I actually did it yesterday and I have it today and tomorrow and I have lots of different types of that … so … I've quite a busy schedule most of the time? I have lots of cricket matches as well.

If I don't have a club after school, I do netball and rounders, and I've just finished a drama production. I walk home, like half an hour walk, sometimes I meet my sister. She's in Year 10, doing her mocks at the moment and then we go home, have a snack, go to our bedroom … I do work, have a bit of chill time, maybe listen to music, maybe watch something on my phone, and then … recently I haven't been able to do any drum practice but normally I would.

Clearly Harriet had very little free time, let alone time for silence. It was provided only when walking to school, or as she later said, when standing in a sports field, thinking about the match to come. She showed no indication of regret or concern about this intense schedule, but, rather, appeared to relish it. Her schoolmate Ravi, in similar vein, tried to explain the reasons behind the shape of his daily life:

R: I am more of the 'stay at home do nothing and just get good grades from studying quite frequently' type of person. I don't get out much, as people would say. I just don't walk to the park for no apparent reason. If my friends invite me, then I'll go, because it's rude to turn people down. But if it's just up to me, then I would preferably just stay at home and study, to make sure that I get a better start later on in life. [...] So, my parents aren't pushy as much. They usually just prompt me to take extra curriculum studies, because they want me not to turn out as a washout, basically. And I can see why they do. The more work I do early on, the less I'll have to do later on. Life just seems easier if I do the work now. [...] I don't just read books on science. [...]

V: So, are you ever on your own doing nothing?

R: On my own doing nothing? Thinking about it now, I don't actually think ... doing absolutely nothing. I do that quite rarely. But being more productive means I get more done. If I get more done, then I can do less work later.

Ravi takes his textbooks on holiday, focussing on his end of year 8 (12/13-year-olds) exams and manages to sketch (a pastime that pleases him) if he hasn't any work left to do. Asked whether he is ever silent or contemplative, he explains:

> I think I do that ... quite infrequently ... because, I have done in the past, but that's only when all my other options are basically dried out. Such as if I was on holiday and I didn't have any textbooks, or have no signal **[Laughter from V]** [...] It's important, because the way the school curriculum works is ... it goes test after test after test, and then all the tests are compiled to one final figure, so ... and the last end-of-the-year exams are the biggest test and I can score the most points. If I score the most points, then I can get into the best classes. If I get into the best classes, then I'm going to learn more. If I learn more, then my life just becomes easier.

Ravi also explained that he studies before he leaves for school in the morning:

R: [...] Kind of can't fit in extra curriculum during break and lunch because there's not actually a lot of things to do, because I'm not a fan of reading, which people find is very strange, because of the amount of studying that I do. And then I go home, usually mess around on the computer, as in listen to music and play a couple of video games, like an hour or two back to studying. Then I usually have like swimming or tennis and then I come back, have dinner, do more studying, or, say I'm doing studying and I feel really bored after everything in the day. Then I go to sleep!! Meaning ... my day's quite packed now I think of it.

V: It is, isn't it? There's no real down time, is there?

R: No, if you don't take sleep as down time.

Dominic described his life as simply 'jam-packed'. Jasmine, also, has problems fitting in everything, though she told me that she enjoys everything she undertakes. Getting up at 6.30 a.m. every school day morning, she catches up with homework before arriving at school at 8.10 a.m. In her lunchtime breaks she has maths club on Tuesday, singing on Thursdays, group counselling on Fridays, and preparation for public performance during the other days of the week. After school she has speech and drama on Monday, ballet on Tuesday, hockey on Wednesday, contemporary dance on Thursday and every other week she babysits for her mother on a Friday, using the weekend to catch up on schoolwork. Arriving home from school on a 'good day' and often out late in the evenings at classes, she falls asleep exhausted. Despite her pleasure in these activities, she bemoaned the loss of freedom she had felt as a 'child':

> It's like you can see the world differently if you're a child. But as an adult, it's all about work and like ... lots of adults concentrate on what they have to do. Like

> children don't really care about it. [...] Like if I'm sitting in silence and I've nothing to think about, also I get really stressed because I start to think about all the things that I have to do. And like ... yeah. Especially like, because I have a dance show in about two weeks and I haven't choreographed one of the dances yet, and that stresses me out. And the homework that I have to do. It still makes me really nervous and stuff.

Karla showed some ambivalence about finding again what had clearly been valuable times for her when sitting by a duck pond. Asked whether she would like to do this more often, she explained:

> I dunno. Just not like a priority really. I mean I *would* like to do it, if I could. But it's not like on a list of stuff that I need to get done. If you know what I mean?

Abigail came only for one interview; the first one having been missed due to her illness. She explained that she didn't have many moments of solitude or silence due to her busy life, though she 'didn't mind it'. Asked later to describe a moment of extreme happiness, she became tearful as she started to recall a special moment standing on the peak of a mountain:

> A: [...] It was one of those times when I got lost in the moment. I was just there and not elsewhere, thinking about other things. I was just there with my family, having fun [**Tearful**].
>
> V: And can you remember that? That you were lost in the moment? Why is it moving you so very much?
>
> A: Because there's always people everywhere, and there's always something to distract me. Even if it's just me and my family at home. I'm always talking about my day

> or someone's saying about their work. There's always something else to talk about ... And that day there was nothing else. We were just there. [...] It doesn't happen very often and it's nice not to have to worry about things and just to be there without having to think about anything else. Because nothing could go wrong up there. I didn't have a test up there. I didn't have something to worry about. It was just calming because I knew nothing could happen.

Asked, also, if she had many tests, she recounted the *exact* number for the current and for preceding weeks and she described the pressure she felt:

> A: I try to be organised but sometimes I've just got so much going on that I don't get round to it. And then I just stress that I haven't done enough, and I do get very stressed under pressure.
>
> V: Do you? But if I offered you 10 minutes a day just to sit and be silent, like you were on that mountain [...], what would you say?
>
> A: I don't know [**Sad tone**]. Because sometimes I like it, but if I just tried to sit there for 10 minutes, it would be forced, and I'd just get bored and think about things [**It was clear here that she was referring to school stresses**].

This rueful tone, almost wistful, for past moments of peace, now apparently unattainable, was identifiable in many of the interviews. It is worth reminding ourselves of Gracie, after tending her bee for hours in the garden, telling us...

> ... that's just nice to remember that when I was younger, I was able to just lie there for five hours and like just care for something. Because you know there's so much going on now that I'm older, there's so much stuff.

Getting things done, completing homework, juggling a range of activities, time pressure and the constant awareness of examinations that would be taken in three years' time were themes arising very frequently during discussions about daily life. Asking the children about opportunities for silence and solitude was clearly going to be interesting, and I had to keep reminding myself that they were in fact children and not adults.

Concern about such a relentless programme of activities and tasks for children has already been expressed by other writers. Kessler held that finding solitude was a lost art.[168] Psychologist David Elkind goes yet further and warns us of the potentially dangerous social and psychological effects of rushing our children through childhood in a never-ending programme of activities.[169] Yet perhaps surprisingly, as we have seen, most of the children did not generally complain about this busyness. They accepted this as the norm, as part of their necessary preparation for adult life, and as a template for the life they might expect in the future, often modelled on their parents' time-starved modes of being.

So, returning to the initial impetus for all the conversations with children, it appears that, for many of them, the very *opportunities* for silence, quiet times or solitude, were scarce indeed – even if they *were* being sought. The corollary issue, though, is whether the children actually wanted to find any such silence at all. The next chapter, therefore, takes us into new territory – beyond that of descriptions of their spirituality and the contexts in which they arise, and into their thoughts about silence and solitude and the (to me) surprising unearthing of commonly experienced states of awareness that were akin to silence but not of it.

Chapter 7

'And Then I Come Back In': Children Speak of Silence

Earlier chapters have already introduced a broader range of understanding about silence, beyond the binary, and firstly, in this chapter, we will read of the children's attitudes towards binary silence, particularly any imposed silence. We will go on to discover that, irrespective of their, often negative, approach to non-sound silence, they were frequently entering a singular space. This corresponded to a broader understanding of silence, as already outlined, and this space was the crucible of a spiritual experience or their spirituality. It is this place, this understanding, that provides the rationale for this book, and this chapter is the final stepping stone before the culmination of all the searching.

No-sound silence

For some of the children 'soundlessness' *was* important, both as a precursor to their spiritual experience or spirituality and within the experience itself. When Gracie tended her sick bee, she *entered* a silent state where time seemed to disappear. For her, as we know, silence was the place where 'everything made sense' and where she could be fully herself. Adam's arrival at the top of a mountain, when all sound ceased, left a lasting impression and provided 'solace'. Fazia sought, and was often thwarted in finding, opportunities for silent meditation; and Kay, though experiencing little, valued it greatly. Joshua felt an unsought-for silence when he 'blurred out', entering a dream-like state:

> [...] When I go, I can't hear ... not when I go, but when I like ... walk ... not when I walk along ... when I blur out I can feel like there is silence, a lot of silence. Even when

> people are talking quite loud [*sic*]. It's quite strange ... it just feels nice really. I don't really notice. It's kind of like a blur, like. I don't know how to say it. I just kind of blur out. Then you don't know your surroundings ... exactly ... [...].
>
> It's kind of different because one minute you're kind of somewhere else, one minute you're back. But like when I come back, I don't exactly remember ... Like I can't really think of what actually happens. It's like a dream almost. Basically. It's basically a dream.

These experiences and contexts largely correspond to the understanding of silence as a binary (though certainly Joshua's description here is ambiguous). In three of the four schools visited, examples of such spirituality within contexts like these proved relatively rare, though there were at least *some* children in each who actively sought it. Yet anomalously, and notably, *every* child in one particular school expressed a need and a desire for *some* form of silence, as a respite from the stresses of their lives – a feature that will be explored in some depth later.

The children's attitudes towards silence were clearly central to the investigation. Any negativity towards it would militate against either their seeking it or their accepting any imposition or offering of it. My initial surmise was, as explained, that they simply would not have time for it, both in terms of the social and academic pressures on them and the way they chose to spend their 'leisure time'. This was largely justified. Their attitudes towards it, however, varied, though with a preponderance of negativity. I had expected, then, some causal link between the level of opportunities for silence and spirituality. Additionally, it seemed likely that negative attitudes towards silence might imply a reduction in spiritual experiences or descriptions of spirituality. This was manifestly not the case. It became clear that the concepts of silence did need a reconceptualisation and the children's narratives a re-examination.

The shift of focus

Chapter 3 has hinted at a broad and nuanced understanding of silence, and a series of views on this, showing surprising coherence, arise across a range of disciplines. Maggie Ross provided two of the most influential texts for this work, casting light on this.[170] She suggests that silence exists with an elision or suspension of self-consciousness or *excessus mentis* – a departure of the mind. For her it is even possible to be solitary in one's mind while living in a crowd, in a self-created silence. In such a silence perception can be transmuted or 'transfigured', and this is an 'ever-present silence' that can 'irrupt' into everyday life, creating a suspension of self-consciousness. This has been vividly described by Rowan Williams as 'the quiet before the dawn'.[171]

Philosophers such as Max Picard (1948) see silence as an actual 'catalysing force' – not an emptiness at all, but rather as having a *positive* value, independent and creative, and from which other phenomena may arise. Dauenhauer, Fiumara, and Sciacca provide similar ideas.[172] Dauenhauer identifies silence as a 'fermentatory yeast', the existence of which is abiding and is a state of potentiality.

Educationalists such as Berryman, Hart and Muldoon also convey the sense of silence as a creative element, providing an 'opening for knowledge and the creation of meaning' with Lees suggesting that it is a state of mind, rather than an 'absence of mind'.[173]

Such non-dualistic thinking helps to cast illumination on our understanding of children's spirituality. Yet hitherto there has been an emphasis, largely from educationalists, on the importance of the provision of opportunities for binary silence, sometimes in the forms of mindfulness and meditation, affecting well-being and spirituality.[174] Whilst acknowledging the therapeutic value of such increasingly common developments in, for example, school environments, I believe that it is important to recognise that the accessing of our 'natural habitat' and the state of 'deep mind' identified by Ross,[175] permitting an immersion into a space of potentiality, is more readily available to children than that accessed by techniqued means. I believe this to be critical in our understanding of ways to support child spirituality.[176]

We will see that such forays into this space were often made without the child's intention, or that of others, but, rather, were encountered in the midst of daily activities and events. This resulted variously in wonder, a sense of merging with the environment or, as Ross described it, the loss of the sense of 'distinction between body and matter'.[177] Here the self-conscious mind experienced a hiatus, often simply referred to in the creative process as 'inspiration' – accessed beyond normal consciousness. The children describe entering a singular 'zone' of awareness, a place of unusual stillness that brings peace, expanded powers, freedom and happiness. It is not the quiet of non-sound, as this goes beyond the auditory into the state of 'imperturbability' identified by Evagrius – the eye of the storm as it were.[178]

A great deal of effort was clearly made by the children during the interviews to convey such a sense of going beyond normal reality, and when they strove to do so the atmosphere in the room, as we have seen, often shifted. Speech slowed and their body language indicated deep reflection and recall. This happened frequently and was always extraordinary.

For many others such a transformative space was reached in the midst of sound. We have already read of Katarina sitting in a lesson surrounded by the sounds of others, entering a state of peace and then describing, as Alyssa did, a return from a world that had just 'stopped'. Katarina also entered this space when singing and she declared the two 'spaces' to be very similar in feeling and impact. This ground from which they return, often changed, provides the context for and the experience of spirituality itself. There seems to be a form of silence underneath everyday experience, described by Strawser as 'a fundamental tone'.[179]

We have read of Noah, who spoke of his sense that he, as Noah, during art, had entered a space where time dissolved and then of his returning as if a new day had arrived. Christina, similarly, entered such a space during dance, becoming, to her thinking, 'unreachable', being in a different space from everyone else. We will soon read of Isaac, whose mind goes 'to a different part' of his body, when, in a variety of situations, he is simply deep in thought, and he 'loses' himself. For all these children, such an experience was both enjoyable and bewildering. Yet such interior silence, regarded by Ross as an example of 'returning to the wild' is, she says, available to all of us through ordinary living and is, in fact, a natural spirituality.[180]

The children mentioned here, stumbled, as it were, into a particular type of silence, usually unexpectedly. Notably, another whole school group of the children stood out as actively seeking *some* form of silence and solitude. All enjoyed it in its broader form, even though some expressed antipathy to non-sound. Though the research was not intended in any way to be a comparative study of school types, the outcomes of the narratives from one school were so striking that they merit a diversion.

An appreciation of silence in one school

All of the children from this school spoke of their need for some form of silence and/or of their need for solitude to support their well-being. Joshua, for example, relished those moments when, as he said, he 'left' himself and entered an inner silent space. Asked when he entered such a space, he explained:

J: Yeah, I find like ... I can't remember what was on, but I was listening to a song. And I just like, kind of, went ...

not went into the song, but like ... so let's say if ... let's say there's a good story happening; let's say it's about birds for instance [**Small laugh**] I would like to go there and I would be with the birds perhaps.

V: Where would Joshua be?

J: That's the thing. I don't know. I just see what my eyes see. I don't think of who I am, I don't think around, I just see [...]. I'm not thinking anything. I can't ... I'm not hearing anything ... I'm just focussing on one object and just ... I don't move, so I'm kind of frozen on one ... do you know what I mean? [...] Let's say there's a massive view. I'm just focussed on that one view [...] I'm just staring at something and then I come back in....

Without apparent volition, Joshua relates here a beautiful example of *excessus mentis* and loss of self, occurring naturally, and then returning. This is a 'secret homesickness' according to Ross and latent in us all.

Joshua's friend Katarina describes being taken to a mosque by the school:

K: And we did sit there in silence, but I didn't really ... [**Coughs**] like it wasn't the religion I would have preferred. Like I prefer being out there on a hill with everything around you, instead of like ... being in a building, because you're not open enough to around you [*sic*]. [...] If I wanted peace, I probably wouldn't do that. Like if I was going outside and I couldn't draw, I'd probably go for like a walk with my dog or something. I probably wouldn't do that.

V: So, if the Head of all schools and education was here and you wanted to make a plea, what would you ask for?

K: Peace. For people [to] just be ... calmed down, because I dunno, it's probably personal to the people who are

> loud – they're finding it hard, so they feel that they have to be loud; but it's like, it's easy to be loud in the room with your friends in the class but it's easier for everyone when they're not ... being loud. [...] I would provide a space ... where they could go ... to be peaceful. And yeah ... and just ... yeah.

Whilst some like Sophia stated in her questionnaire that silence was 'cleansing', later expanding this to calming and relaxing, others, such as Madeline, though happy to do yoga and meditation with her mother, had very mixed feelings about it. She preferred to be alone in the woods, breathing the clean air. For her, sitting in silence had no appeal; she would simply get bored. Gracie, though, wanted to convey in her questionnaire and in the interview her feeling that everything made sense in silence:

> I guess you can just piece everything together when you're in silence. Like I guess, if you're in a classroom or whatever, there is always something distracting you, or you can never, like there is always a piece missing. You can never like – if you're confused about a situation and you can't see it from their side – you know you're sitting there and there's always going to be some distraction, and you can never make sense of it. But if you can just go somewhere and sit somewhere in silence, you can kind of piece it all together and make sense of the situation. [...] When you're in nature, you just feel like nothing judges you. You know you can just be yourself and it's nice to be in the silence.

She valued those times when she was alone or with a friend, composing music and allowing the music to come *to* her, rather than *from* her. When asked to say more about this she explained:

> I think I'm more calm and more like focussed and more centred. Like in one space. I guess like if you go downstairs and get your tea and go upstairs and do something, do this, do that. Like you're doing lots of stuff, so it's not going to be like just one sense space [*sic*]. But I feel like if you're just sat there and you know what you want to do and, you know, you're trying to find it, you can just be like in that quiet space and just be open to like whatever's going to come.

We see the confidence that Gracie expresses here in the power of this special space – a space that is accessed in both quiet and also without a cessation of noise or even solitude – to deliver her expectations of inspiration. Here we also see her deliberately seeking it and then allowing herself to be open to what is yet unknown. It is the solitariness and expectant silence that can admit of creative imagination, and, for Gracie, it leads to the writing of music.[181] Returning to Ross, we see here an example of 'gap in the schematising activities of the self-conscious mind', leading to a part of the mind to which we do not normally have direct access.[182] For Ross it cannot be forced, and spiritual experiences arising from this state are entirely fortuitous.

In a very similar vein, yet from another field of endeavour, educationalist Berryman sees silence as an 'opening' and a 'waiting for knowledge', a return to pre-language knowing.[183] Gracie's confidence was not in the certainty of outcomes within the space, but in its *power* to deliver, and in her ability to be open to it. For Christian writer Weil, it is 'a grace that fills an empty space that one can only enter when there is a void to receive it'.[184] Gracie had entered this void and had experienced, through active listening, the creativity and fertility of the silence advocated by theologians, philosophers, religious movements and others.[185]

The children in this particular school were, in many ways, distinct from the other children interviewed. As the school was a rural school, some travelled long distances to get there and came from rural homes with easy access to the countryside. Some were children from households that might be deemed to be 'alternative', placing value on the numinous (for example, in the use of Tarot cards, meditation or use of alternative therapies). Their enrolment at the school was largely 'elective' (rather than it being simply their local school), often chosen because of the specific values held by the Waldorf community of which the school forms a part.

It was difficult, however, to extrapolate from their responses, the relative influence of their rural environment, their familial contexts and their school ethos. The only certainty is that most of these children spoke with unusual fluency and intensity, and at length, about spirituality (though rarely religiosity), with an appreciation for nature and their environment, for quiet and for silence and for the creative arts in general.[186]

From the first minute of his interview Martin described himself as a 'jokester' who enjoyed art, and he was very sporty. He loved walks in the woods which punctuated his very busy days that caused him to fall asleep in the car on the way back from school. Declaring himself non-religious, he then attempted to answer the question as to whether he was spiritual. He then, by way of an answer, repeated that he preferred to go into the woods and just sit, peacefully, with his dog, and where the only sounds were those of wild animals. Only, he laughed, in dry weather! The experience was, for him, like a storm, with everything flowing out of him and without his having to think of anything. He described the effects of this on his body:

> Sometimes, when I'm sitting on my own … I sometimes feel I'm getting a bit like … kind of like the feeling when you're light-headed, like you're going upwards. But it

> feels like you're kind of floating but you're sitting down? It's really weird.
>
> Er, usually if I'm like nervous, or I've been sitting for a really long time, I just start feeling like ... it's like ... you feel like you're on a trampoline. It's like your body's trying to go up. It's like you're coming back down. [**Long pause for thinking**]. It's just like you're getting ... [**Struggling**] [...] It's like I'm trying to explain something, but it's not the right words. [...] Erm ... it's just like you're being pulled upwards. It's like someone's got you and they're trying to pull you up.

These experiences eventuated in quiet, though not entirely sound-free situations and elicited the dramatic simile of a storm (such figurative devices often characterising spiritual experiences) and summarised by that oh-so-familiar word 'weird'. He apologised after the interview for not being able to articulate what he meant and was reassured that some things just cannot be described. He was unable to explain what 'they' referred to, but it was clear that he was referring to some external agent. We can see here the attendant currency of ineffability described by Szakolczai (2009) and the heightened awareness noted by Hay and Nye (2006) both signifiers of spirituality. We also note the intensity of the somatic effects of such an experience and his repeated use of the verb 'to feel' underlining this. He does not say that *he* was trying to go up, but that his *body* was, and it was as if at this point he was observing the actions and desires of another part of himself. On returning from this space, however, he reverts to being fully himself. This space, so important a trope in the conversations with the children, will be revisited in the following chapter.

What is notable is that Martin's interviews exemplified the general facility and intensity of the conversations with children from that particular school when discussing spirituality or the numinous. His classmate Kay often took her time to answer questions while she considered her responses. She regarded silence as 'nice and calming' but went further:

> And it just like ... it goes really quickly because I just think like you can think of anything. And ... it's nice ... and yeah. Like, it's like your best friend because it just listens to you and it doesn't like ... yeah ... it will just listen to you. [...] Erm, well I just think that it like, obviously it's not a person, 'silence'. [...] But you can kind of tell it anything because it's always there, like you can always get to it, and it can never leave and it's like your best friend and it just listens to you.

The extracts presented here are representative of the conversations with *all* the children from this school, though similar narratives were in fact presented across every school. Closer scrutiny is certainly merited, though outside the parameters of this book. It might be reasonable to assume that the Steiner philosophy of fostering that which is spiritual in each child, of the valuing of the wisdom of the physical body and of silence and solitude, the acceptance of the extra-sensory, and the emphasis on magic and imagination, may well be a contributing factor, facilitating a set of interviews that were notably different from those in others schools. It is possible, even likely, that such a background has impacted on their ability to articulate their own spirituality and also their enjoyment of the contexts (often silence in its broader sense) which nurture it. Such contexts, as we have seen, arise naturally and are not prescribed by any external authority. Where silence *is* imposed on the children any such enjoyment is often moot.

Attitudes towards silence

The thinking about silence amongst the children, therefore, was complex and varied. Many, understandably, associated it with death, having sometimes taken part in a public minute's silence. It was, for several, intimidating. Hannah, for instance, loved silence, but only when in sunshine and light and she explained to me that it might not be regarded as 'cool' to own up to wanting it:

H: Because I think I have so much pressure at school and sometimes it can be a good thing to relax in school and show that there isn't any pressure and work.

V: Ah, it's interesting that you should say that. So, you think that part of the important thing is to have it in school, to show that ... as if to say, look ... school is quiet and peace as well as hard work?

H: Yes. [...] But we just don't put it into place because I think sometimes some students think that it's a bit, a shame, to go there [...] Maybe they think it makes them not cool or something.

In similar vein, Fazia described with a small and sad voice, the mockery she faced from classmates when she wanted to meditate. 'Everyone laughed at me and said, "Why are you meditating?" and all this stuff. And I said, "I'm a Christian, this is what we're supposed to do. I need silence." And they just talked over me and all that.'

Those children who lived near open spaces or in the country or who had animals, usually dogs, were most likely to find regular time for solitude and silence, and they described obtaining this during long walks, sitting in the branches of trees or in woods or by water, and in the case of Dominic, particularly when fishing. They did not go into the country or nature specifically to find silence, but this was a by-product of the activity chosen. This was a time much appreciated by them and they regarded it as refreshing, peaceful and helpful. Jacob and Gracie typify this simple pleasure:

> J: I do live near a little wood. Not too far. But I do take the dog out sometimes and I do sometimes stand there for a bit. Just in the silence when I do […] I feel very peaceful.
>
> G: There's a massive field and there's ten fields all in a row and like trees and the River W goes past our house. So, I go out into the woods over there and just sit in the woods on my own for a bit, because it's just nice to have some time.

Christina's approach was even more pragmatic; for her silence would be useful in order to facilitate mental organisation time, to effect the better organisation of her work. For many of the children, whatever their view about silence, consciously seeking it out and fitting it into their daily lives was clearly improbable – their life schedules and the expectations of others precluded it. On the surface, it did appear to me, in the early stages of meeting the children, that this was not an important or valued part of their lives. Some went further and were forthright in their views that silence was not something that they would want or seek.

Apparent antipathy to silence

Kaitlyn, who spent much of her time scanning YouTube and watching the posts of family vloggers, was utterly clear that she didn't like silence at all. She commented that if a silent time were offered to her in school, she would take it up only if it meant she could miss lessons! Though this was said with a laugh, it was evidently a serious stipulation. She found it boring to be alone and only accepted silence when forced upon her, as at a funeral when her grandfather had died. Jack felt exactly the same:

> Silence – I find silence boring. That's one of the reasons I really like my music. So ... silence ... I just don't find it all that ... enticing. For me, when I'm not doing anything and I just want to be left on my own, I just put my earphones on and just listen to some music ... on a certain theme depending on my emotions. I play, yeah, whatever I feel like.

My first impressions following early meetings with children and reading their comments was that silence was generally shunned or at least not sought by them. What became clear in time, though, was that most children were not exactly showing unequivocal antipathy towards silence but, rather, they were expressing fear of the idea of being alone, a dislike of the potential boredom of having nothing to do, a concern about its apparent lack of productiveness, a trepidation about its social acceptability and, as we have seen, a markedly strong dislike of *imposed* silence. This did not mean that when they actually found themselves in solitude or relative silence they disliked it.

Imposed silence

In two of the schools visited, time was set apart for some type of common silence. For children in the Catholic school many of the children attended a church service either in school time or on Sundays. Some lessons, particularly Religious Education lessons, started with a prayer. Such a time was not generally associated with silence in any form, but rather with active prayer – petitioning prayer,[187] prayers of gratitude, or simply 'speaking to God'. This was, for them, a word-filled time and not numinous.

In the Quaker school the whole school community gathers, weekly, for a forty-minute Meeting for Worship (occasionally punctuated by anyone who feels inspired to contribute). No direct questions were asked about this for reasons of ethical sensitivities. Nevertheless, many of the children interviewed expressed irritation with, and a dislike of, a silent period that they felt was an imposition. Kyra expressed this forcefully when asked what silence was like for her:

> I don't know. It depends if it's like forced. If it's like Meeting for Worship, I find that quite boring. Because it's like, in the middle of the day and I'm not really ready to sit down and be quiet.

Kyra later explained that she did in fact love a form of silence when she was outside and in the country, and this was one in which she felt totally free. When I suggested a quiet area in the school to which she might retreat, her friend Isabel, who enjoyed peaceful moments with her violin stipulated firmly:

> If it was outside I might like it ... [**Inaudible**] [...] And I really wouldn't like that [just silence] because I really don't like Meeting for Worship and things like that. And we used to have to do meditation on Mondays [...] but I really don't like it when we're inside. Because you just want to go outside. [...] It's just like, in the summer, it's like got a breeze and it's sunny and there's the grass and like the smells and things. And just being happy.

The introverted and sensitive Gabriel expressed some concerns about the gathering, not because he did not value the silence, but rather because he felt observed and exposed:

> Well, I enjoy spending time alone to think. Because I don't really like doing that around other people because they might be able to tell what I'm thinking by my facial expressions. I just like being alone, when I'm with my thoughts.

Fortunately, Gabriel found time for this when wandering in his local woods, finding great comfort in this. Gavin, in contrast, was unique in expressing an active liking for the sessions, albeit seeing them (as we have seen others do) as opportunities for mental organisation, as he did for the other times he found himself in silence:

> Then we have Meeting for Worship, which is quite nice on a Friday. It's just like a way to relax in a way. [...] I don't mind it at all. I feel like they could change it. Like you could read quietly maybe, instead of, well, like staring off into the distance. But I quite like it, because then you can just stay quiet and just think about what you need to do.

In similar fashion, the personal efficacy of silence was declared by Alexander, whose sensitivity and problems in a previous school meant that he experienced any silence, accidental or otherwise, as a happy period when he was not being 'told off' and, therefore, he said poignantly he 'was not worrying'.

In the three other schools there was no obvious period of 'imposed silence' other than for disciplinary purposes. Some, as we have read, declared that they simply didn't have time for it. It was a distraction from their main aim – of curricular and extra-curricular achievement. Yet, we have seen, for example, with Ravi, how such views often sit uncomfortably with their expressions of joy when they do have an opportunity to be in a silent or quiet space.

A different lens

In general, the children's attitudes did vary from appreciation through ambivalence and contradictory feelings, to, even, antipathy (especially for imposition). Such dislike of silence corresponded to the 'fear (of silence) in the majority of Western hearts' noted by Ross[188] and the frequent conflation of the words 'lonely' and 'alone' noted among children by Wood and Tribe.[189] When the concept of silence is, however, seen differently and is expanded beyond the binary of sound and non-sound, corresponding to the non-dualistic understanding of silence, a new relationship profile to silence emerges.[190] For most of these children, any appreciation of silence was of a silence that arose naturally in their lives and was unsought and unimposed. For many of them, peak and spiritual experiences and expressions arose from the bounty of an unfathomable silence, for example, in nature, in creativity and the arts, in liturgy, in dance and sports or simply when sitting. We see this in Katrina's feeling of great hope and a sense of 'heaven' when outdoors, and also in her loss of self, as with Noah, in art; in Joshua's memorable elation in sand dunes; in Gracie's passion when observing her ailing bee; in Jack's awe on meeting a shark; in Kay's loss of self in laughter; in Harriet's sense of an unusual energy in dance, or, as Isaac said 'It could be any moment, any time' – even, if you are Gabriel, when doing maths! Such moments arose spontaneously and unexpectedly, often with lasting impact. Without their naming this, there appears to be an accessing of the embryonic fluid of an all-encompassing, ever-present silence that enriches the spiritual life of children, and it is valued and appreciated by them. In other words, silence in these situations is not named or defined – what we see are the *fruits* of the accessing of what seems to be an abiding element of silence that they describe with wonder and amazement.

Furthermore, it was a silence of a different order than normally supposed, and it proved necessary to engage with this more nuanced understanding of silence, as, on deeper analysis, the children's apparent superficial attitudes towards silence gave way to a deeper and more complex, multi-aspected, phenomenon.

And so, in a sense, my original suspicions that children's spirituality was being negatively affected by a lack of silence in their lives were confounded. It was certainly true that relatively few were finding or even seeking total silence … and yet … they were almost without exception demonstrating *some* form of spirituality, much of which derived from a space that was not silent, but certainly akin to silence. This took the research into completely new territory, one of anthropology and folklore and the work of van Gennep and Edith and Victor Turner.[191] Their work on liminality and *communitas* resonated so strongly with the children's narratives that deeper analysis was required. We will now move on to this denouement.

Chapter 8

'You Come from One Dimension to Another': A Sacred Space

And so, it became gradually clear, over months of interviews and across all the schools, that the children were relating to me their contact with some form of altered space. In many cases this was silence-like but not actual silence, in which they enjoyed spiritual experiences or states. So many described, as early as the first interviews, their entering what appeared to be a place or arena of ambiguity or potentiality, and then emerging from these conditions positively changed, almost with a sense of having grown. Additionally, I was often hearing children describe moments of spiritual engagement that they said arose during periods of intense social communion. Other such times occurred during play, laughter and joy, or even when the rules of society or the world did not seem to apply or were seemingly suspended. This undermined my expectation that a lack of silence and solitude would negatively affect their spirituality. For me this was at first confusing, and certainly unexpected, but an understanding fell slowly, tentatively, into place – that such states were powerfully redolent of the concepts of liminality and *communitas* introduced by the folklorist van Gennep and later expanded on by anthropologists Edith and Victor Turner.[192] In this chapter we will explore their work and the consonances of it with the children's voices, the way the research took a new turn, and the link between liminality and the experience of 'flow' and loss of ego that was so evident in the children's narratives.

Liminality and *communitas*

Though we will be exploring work largely by anthropologists, it is worth mentioning that the concept of liminality is discussed, as anthropologist Thomassen tells us, within 20 varied disciplines.[193] Sociologist Szakolczai suggests enthusiastically that it is one of *the* most important conceptual tools and that its application is not only wide, it is 'potentially unlimited'.[194]

This notion was first coined by the French folklorist and ethnographer Arnold van Gennep in his seminal work *Les Rites de Passage* (1908). Here he focussed particularly on initiatory rites for young people entering puberty and he coined the word 'liminality', derived from the Latin *limen* or 'threshold', essentially a place of impermanence. He describes the structure of such rites as having three stages: the pre-liminal, the liminal, and the post-liminal. Citing practices in China, India and Africa, he notes that the young are first separated from their communities (the pre-liminal stage), then initiated via a series of formal rites (the stage of liminality and transformation), and then eventually reintegrated into their former communities as persons with a new identity and social status. They had left one world behind and entered a threshold or a liminal stage – where they had left their old selves behind but not yet assumed their new identities – before going through ritual transformation. Interestingly, he noticed that the young people entering liminal spaces often committed what their tribe or community would regard as anti-social acts, including thefts and sexual licentiousness. Yet as liminal beings and effectively outside their society, social norms did not apply. Such threshold states are deemed by van Gennep to be simply part of human life, and there are always new thresholds for us to cross, including that of death, as we act and cease, wait and rest, and then begin acting again, but then in a different way.[195] Having experienced a 'new world', 'magico-religiously and physically', the young people return and are then reincorporated into their former society as changed individuals.[196]

These concepts were then developed by anthropologists Victor and Edith Turner some sixty years later. They noticed during rites, largely in Africa, a social-levelling process, where the normal traditional hierarchies and social order were turned upside down. Once again, they saw that the status of those who were in such a liminal framework was ambiguous; they were located 'betwixt and between' the normal structures of society.[197] Victor Turner later identified liminal spaces, and the powers gained within them, as sacred and full of potential for transformation. For him it was a moment in and out of time, where an underling, whether by age, gender or social ranking, becomes 'uppermost' during a period of status reversal. During this period, he says, they acquire the *sacred power* of the meek, weak and humble. Edith Turner commented that children in puberty are naturally, by virtue of their age, in a liminal, neither-nor position.[198]A person was during this process 'fashioned anew'. When Victor Turner witnessed such a reshaping of people during his work with the *Ndembu* tribe in Zambia, he noted a feeling that such an effect was born of powers felt to be more than human.[199] In the children's narratives, as will be seen, the entering of a liminal space was often transformative, felt by them to be 'other-worldly', and frequently, and by now familiarly, euphemised as 'weird'.

This 'transformation' is an important aspect of the process. Ferrer suggests how the imagination, going beyond mental fantasising, can also be used to enter what he describes as 'the isthmus between physical and spiritual realms'.[200] Here, he says, children are in a process of leaving their egoic selves in the course of a spiritual experience and are, yes, transformed. This is a generative potential, or, as Turner would have it, a 'subversive flicker', encapsulating the germ of future developments and even potentially, he says, societal change – such a hope-filled assertion, and not, as might be evident from the narratives, overreaching. We will read that some of the children, who described something like a liminal experience, seemed to understand on a deeper level that they may have encountered something that dwells behind or beyond the immediately obvious.[201] It would appear that they were able to perceive what anthropologist Burridge describes so vividly as a *mysterium*, 'a promissory note', which they may hold in their hearts all the years of their lives – a truth, an order to the universe, grasped intuitively.[202] Such a holding will be seen in this chapter.

Liminality implied for Victor Turner a range of aspects: a sense of transience, silence, sacredness, unselfishness, totality, humility, simplicity and an absence of, or change of, status. All of these stood and stand in relief against their antonyms, common in the social world. It also expresses enchantment, potentiality and potency and is full of experiment and play,[203] where the bizarre becomes normal, where ('a fructile') chaos intrudes into the normal structure of society. As a result, it can, he says, give rise to a striving for, and a gestation of, new forms and structures. It is unsettling and unsettled and rich in 'symbols' and 'metaphors'.[204]

Whilst Victor Turner tried to explain that a liminal state or process, in essence, represented the subjunctive mood of possibilities or 'what may be', Edith Turner also sought to capture its nature.[205] She described how difficult it was to explain the concept in logical terms (and readers might be sympathetic), given its strange 'out of this ordinary world character'. She labelled it 'a crack between worlds', where the normal does not apply, and after which one commonly hears an experiencer struggling to put it into words. Despite this, there is a sense of certainty about it. For her it is where the sacred and the secular entwine and where boundaries disappear.[206] Such a dissolution of boundaries was also noted by Victor Turner. This led to the ownership of our authentic self within which we take ourselves for our subject matter, distancing ourselves *from* ourselves to know ourselves better: 'the self is unmade in order to be remade.'[207] And thus, paradox was also a feature of liminality. So, liminality, for them both, is of great developmental importance. In it, Victor Turner poetically states, we may be in the presence of human ontological reality as an uncompleted being (or community of beings), still in process, still in evolution, a still open-ended and evanescent unformed clay, dying, as he says, to become a little child.[208]

Nor is it an unusual state to attain. June Boyce-Tillman asserts that liminal space is, in fact, a natural space for children to access, reached by, for example, the arts, taking them out of everyday consciousness. She describes the joy that can be engendered by entering the security of special places experienced during artistic performances or activities,[209] enabling, as Turner describes, the dissolution of the normal boundaries of 'I and not I', of Cartesian mind/body dualism. This, she notes, allows for a lifting of the burden of responsibility and the freedom to play, to take on a new persona and to take risks without fear of consequence.[210] Similarly, the harpist David Stang described to Edith Turner a time when for him time stood still, and he did not even know that he was playing, 'it's like the music is coming through you.' Careful readers might find, as I did, the resonances between this and the children's narratives notably powerful.

Furthermore, as these egoic boundaries are slackened and social boundaries and hierarchies are extinguished, different connections are created, however fleetingly, and it is in this new state of being that we see the arising of what Turner describes as *communitas*.

Communitas emerges, according to Victor Turner, in liminal contexts. That is, where there is no structure and where there is 'no social differentiation'.[211] It is not seen in the main organisational framework of society, therefore, but 'in the gaps', and has an existential rather than a cognitive quality. It thrives like Chinese philosopher Lao Tzu's clay pot[212] in the margins, the interstices, and occurs particularly (as with children) amongst the powerless and the dispossessed.

Turner suggests that *communitas* is actually needed by society, as it affords occasional release from everyday tensions and pressures and with a strong affective power on those involved.[213]

Edith Turner was equally impressed. Such experiences, she said, may lead people to stumble upon 'the best time they've ever had'.[214]As such, there is a link with joy. It may occur when there is a readiness to shed one's concern for status and may be seen in a group's sharing of a common pleasure. As with liminality, this is also an unbidden and essentially ephemeral experience, and, as we have seen, one that Boyce-Tillman sees as associated with the experience of music. Edith Turner explains this particular catalyst for *communitas* as deriving from the physical effect of music caused by sound waves, by-passing the cognitive mind, and that this goes further, providing a route to spirituality, a somatic link. We see sport, too, being a vehicle for *communitas,* particularly when a participant is in a team made up of disparate individuals and they come together as a single unit and a united cohesive force. Even large groups of spectators at a mass event may sense this coming together (though it is owned by some researchers that not all such experiences are positive). There are other contexts within which, according to Edith Turner, *communitas* may arise: moments of food-sharing (commensality), during the rhythm of work and, of course, during affinity with nature.

Sadly, neither liminal states nor *communitas* can be gained by seeking them, by a sheer act of will. Instead, Edith Turner advises us it is a 'kind of state of grace'.[215] We are simply the recipients of a gift as it were. Moreover, given the paucity of opportunities for most young people to engage with any rites of initiation, whether formal or informal, it seemed unlikely that our children would reach such conditions through these means. And yet, and yet ... so many of the children appeared to enter what I now deem to be liminal space, and beyond any socially or societally sanctioned context. This seemed to be a case of their unexpected stumbling across thresholds into liminal space via uncharted doorways. The space offers common characteristics, and it is these doorways and these characteristics, so familiar to us now, that we now consider.

Ideas crystallise

Very many of the children were providing clear evidence of spirituality and spiritual experiences outside of binary silence, and the contexts and experiences appeared to correlate with the concepts of liminality and *communitas* as already outlined. Children such as Christina and Jasmine when dancing, or Noah doing art, when they described a memorable spiritual moment, intimated the spontaneous crossing into a new space and one from which they emerged ineffably changed and newly content. Despite feeling perplexed, particularly due to temporal dislocation, many of them used the feelings and the potentialities that they remembered from the experience, to inform, positively, their subsequent lives. Beyond this many of them conveyed a sense of losing their 'normal' sense of self in such moments. They became something more expanded and whole, leading to an enduring memory of joy. These states were arising in nature, when alone, in groups, during creative pursuits, in silence, in noise and during already positive emotions such as wonder, and they were often felt physically. I was hearing of moments of spiritual engagement during intense social communion, during laughter or peak happiness, or even when the normal rules of their society or world appeared to be suspended. The correlation was compelling. The second interview question set was, therefore, amended to include questions relating to the new key concepts. The data analysis included, as you may remember, 34 aspects of liminality and/or *communitas* to be checked across all interviews.[216] In honesty, the extra questions did not prove particularly useful. They created an unnecessary cluttering of intent and took up valuable time. In retrospect, the continuation of a more open-ended interview style would have been more potent. Thankfully, and in any case, the children themselves largely determined the pace and the content of the interviews. What follows is a range of children talking about what eventually became clear to me were liminal states, within which were examples of *communitas*.

The children speak of liminality

Joshua is an example of a child who very much wanted to participate in the research, yet who was relatively taciturn during the first interview. During the second interview he was more forthcoming, leading, as we have read, to his outlining of what was for him, a Near Death Experience. Before he recounted this, however, he was asked whether he ever felt he was 'leaving himself behind'. You may remember that he described, with a sense of surprise, an increasingly occurring event when he suddenly felt 'weird' and he 'blurred out', almost going into a different world. This was a world where he could not hear anything (despite any background noise) and he just felt that there was 'silence, a lot of silence' and 'you are unaware of your surroundings'. On returning from this state, he found he could not remember anything at all about the experience: 'Like, I can't really *think* of what actually happens. It's like a dream almost. It's basically a dream.' This he found strange, though 'nice'. He then expanded on this, amidst some sheepish laughter, to say that if he were involved in a good story about, for example, birds (whether a book or a film, was unexplained), he would go there and actually *be with* the birds. At such a point he did not know where he, Joshua, was, as he was not using all his senses. He became unaware of time, having been 'frozen' and then he 'returned', not knowing what had happened: 'That's the thing. I don't know. I just see what my eyes see. I don't think of who I am, I don't think around, I just see.'

Joshua felt that he needed this 'silence', which he found within himself, 'every now and then'. He explained that he did not and *could* not do this 'on purpose' and that such experiences arose spontaneously, confusing him. Such perplexity about an experience and an apparent loss of self and any sense of time clearly find remarkable correspondence with the understanding of liminality as discussed earlier.

We now return to his classmate Jacob, who explained that he had had similar experiences, where returning to 'normal life' was like 'going through a portal back into the real world' and 'as if you're hallucinating or having a dream or something'. We have also read of the intensity of children's relationship with and tuning into nature. Jacob's conversation is a good example of this and here he told me how he liked to stand in his local wood in silence, seeing nature as alive:

J: When I'm in nature, I just feel very peaceful because there's like nothing hurting it and there's nothing disturbing it, that I know of.

V: You talk of the earth as though it's a being.

J: Well, yeah. I kind of think of it as like ... there's loads of different animals and plants and things, but when you think about it, they're all the same. They're all just nature. Like one thing.

V: So, do you see nature as something that's alive?

J: I do, yeah.

V: Do you? How does that work?

J: To be honest, I don't really know because ... when I walk through nature, like quietly, I just feel that it's kind of alive. I don't really feel like it's dead or anything.

V: You feel that ...

J: I feel that it's alive, yeah. [...] I just feel like a happiness inside of myself. That it's alive not dead.

Jacob did not understand why he felt such happiness in nature, when it was quiet, but it mattered to him. We see the happiness it brought when being within that space enabled him to feel the aliveness of a wood, allowing him, as it were, to 'tune into' nature. He does not aver that the wood *might* be alive, he feels it *is* alive and this brings him joy. Within this space he sensed, he *felt*, a comforting spiritual world that made him feel that he 'had company', and, when there, he is never alone. This is Jacob entering a highly affective space, neither of this world, nor that of death, but the 'betwixt and between' place of enchantment so characteristic of liminality.

For bee-loving Gracie such a place was a creative arena. She and her best friend, who was struggling with issues around sexuality, go into the woods to escape everyday pressures and to enjoy the natural sounds it affords. This is her 'happy place' where she can 'just be', away from all 'the horrible stuff'. Here she writes songs, the music of which simply comes when the lyrics are sung out loud:

> So, yeah. I guess it's just nice to like ... so, yeah, if you're thinking about that, then you've got no distractions. So, you just go and think of the lyrics and think of what is actually going on: write them down and then just *sing* ... I dunno ... the tune will just kind of come, if you just sing the words out loud. [...] I guess if you're like, if you're thinking of ... it just comes to you. It's like something, you don't think of it in your head, you just have to sing and see what comes, I guess.

In this space Gracie felt she had no problems, was calm and utterly 'focussed and centred' on a single thing and 'open to whatever's going to come'. As Victor Turner described: a space of liminal creativity.[217] She was unconcerned at this point about being judged by anyone, which released a feeling that *anything* could happen – a nice 'place' to be and very different from her normal, noisy life. Gracie later recalled other similar times of 'forgetting everything' and being 'in the moment', often precipitated by laughter. The memory of this triggered her very loud laughter as she described how, on one occasion, she and her best friend, Suzie, played tricks on another set of friends, hiding from them in the shops in the local town, running round the neighbourhood and being unusually free:

> And my other best friend – she's quite uptight – and she was sat like in *Costa* and on the phone to us, like, 'What are you doing?' And we was [*sic*] like hiding and I just remember running around town and everybody looking at us like 'What are you doing?' and we just didn't care. We were like, we just had this massive game, and we were like hiding in all these shops and stuff and it was just really fun. Like and, yeah, I remember we were just sitting down, and we were like, 'God, this is so funny!' and stuff. And she, like my other friend, was like 'Everybody's looking at you!' [mimicking a friend speaking critically] We were so cheerful, we were like, 'We don't care!' and stuff. [...] Because I was with her, and she was like, 'Oh my God, we're crazy!' And I was like, 'I know!' And then we just carried on [...].

Asked what was on her mind at this point she responded:

> Er, you don't ... you don't really think about anything else. You don't like ... you leave it all behind ... not like you're leaving your body behind, but you're like, you're leaving everything else behind. Nothing else is really important. Like I don't think about anything else. You're just kind of thinking about having fun and *that* thing at the time. You know, you're not like ... it's nice being in the moment and not having any of that stuff behind you.

Gracie valued this time for the way it brought her closer to Suzie and how it made her feel connected in some way to her. The sharing of laughter made her feel less 'weighed down' and happy. We see here an example of a process where Gracie embarked on a game with another person that was transgressive, albeit mildly. During the extended period of the game, she was somewhat nervous in case her other friends 'turned on' her for duping them, yet she was elated, as she felt, for a brief period, great freedom and license. This ended in a return to 'normal' life, with a deeper relationship with Suzie and a sense of future possibilities. The laughter enhanced the experience and also evinced a sense of *communitas*. We are reminded that Victor Turner informs us, that for his African tribe *Ndembu* laughter was deemed a 'white quality', representing the seamless web of connection, and with a mystical quality too.[218]

This was, therefore, a liminal experience for Gracie – a space where she briefly lost her historic and societal context, shedding her self-consciousness; it was also a space of paradox: the fear of doing potentially anti-social acts, incurring censure from her friends and the public, and the simultaneous joy of this activity as she sheds concerns about any such criticism. It was the space of 'anything might happen', of subjunctivity, potentiality, almost dangerous untouchability and a 'special kind of freedom'.[219] The events were clearly disorderly and ludic, as the girls ran about with no rules or restrictions in a context beyond their everyday world.[220] This culminated, as we have seen, in her return to her usual life, changed, more secure in her sense of the possibility of connectedness and joy, and feeling, as she later explained, that she might be able to return to this. This was, I suggest, a spiritual and liminal state.

Kay talked reflectively about times in her life when she went into another world entirely, often a world of the imagination. When asked whether this came naturally or whether she sought it, she spent some considerable time in silence considering how to respond: 'Erm, I think part of it is me trying to see what's around and stuff. But then some of it just comes and ... yeah.' I then tried to clarify whether she was imagining something that she hoped would happen, or whether it was just another world. She felt it was both. She later explained that, when she was in such a 'place', it was still Kay who was there, but somehow a deeper self.

For a self-declared shy young girl entering her teenage years, such moments of release and sense of potentiality created a joyful and memorable awareness of a powerful and integral personality, of being free to be fully oneself.[221] Losing any sense of her surroundings, whether environment, people or their possible judgements, and also of time, there was the feeling of freedom that we have seen evidenced by many of the children interviewed when describing liminal moments, and a loss of ego, often designated by them 'the old self'.

Catholic Isaac only prayed when it was a collective activity in school and felt that in any lengthy silence he would probably get bored. Nevertheless, one of his most memorable moments occurred when he was alone and in a different state. Here, as you may remember, he explained he felt a presence, though he didn't know what this might be, 'probably God' and he felt 'butterflies', 'weird' and it made him 'change' and 'you start to feel happy'. He was loath to share this with anyone, for example, his mum, as she wouldn't believe it and would feel he was making it up. In a quiet voice he murmured: 'I've never felt that before.' Isaac continued to describe similar disconcerting moments when he was thinking about the world ending and the future of the human race. He could not, he said, get his head around it as his brain was trying to think of different things that could happen:

> And there's just too many [...] and if you don't know the answer to something, your brain, like, just stops, 'cos

> you can't figure it out. [...] You're just ... you're thinking about something in your mind and you're that deep into thought, that's when you start to lose yourself. You start to lose yourself when you're really deep into thought.

Isaac talked of the way not having a sense of time was like a meditation: 'Yeah! Yeah. It's like that. With yourself, with no one around, silence and you're just in deep thought for about five minutes.' He also emerged from such a space changed:

> I: It could be any moment, any time. It's just if you're really deep into thought. Or let's say if you're really deep into a dream and you're asleep, it could happen then as well. So, let ... aw, I dunno, what kind of dream but...
> A really deep dream, or a really deep thought, and then you start to lose yourself. But when you come back to yourself, it feels a bit weird. [**Spoken fluently and confidently**] [...] It's just so, you've come out of this really big thought you're having, and you've come back and you're thinking to yourself – 'well that was a bit weird! How's that just happened? What a really deep thought.' And then you come back and I dunno, you feel really weird. And *different*.
> V: So, what's the difference between the person who is having the thought and the person who's come back?
> I: Well, the person who's having the thought is obviously in the thought. Er, erm, like it's special. But when you come out, you're kind of reflecting on it. So, let's say in a dream, you're there for the whole thing, but when you wake up, obviously you're not going to remember it. You're just going to reflect on, let's say, like the main points that have happened.
> V: And when you're in this space, this deep space, is it Isaac that's there?

I: Erm, no! 'cos [...] you lose yourself! So...
V: I want to know what that's like! Tell me what it's like! [**Enthusiastically**]
I: [**Really happily**] Your mind goes to a different place in your body!

This private experience was for Isaac special, and a place of happiness for him. Yet Isaac pointed out that spending such periods on this might cause him stress, as it would take time away from preparing for exams. These were all highly important, even at his age, as they determined setting arrangements, which, he explained, impacted on later success.[222] Once again, we see a child describing the entering of a liminal space, where a sense of time is changed, where there is a loss of self and then a return to normality. Here we see, unusually, that for Isaac this can be effected, he feels, by deep thought – in fact, attempting thoughts that are beyond human comprehension.[223]

Classmate Kaitlyn told of a similar experience that she felt she just couldn't describe. For her this was a feeling that happened only when she helped someone and for her it was a sense of 'making Jesus happy, because you are following in his footsteps':

> I'm not really sure. I can kind of describe it as if you're fulfilling everything that you've ever wanted, but it's only like in a few seconds. But then that's only how I can describe it. I can't really ... yeah. You've done like everything that you should do in life. In that one moment. And you only get a few of those moments.

As it did for Isaac, deep thought about matters incomprehensible prompted a liminal excursion for Kaitlyn and a return to normality, with an awareness of having been, as she said, 'somewhere else'. This is the state of liminality, typical of which is a sense of the return to normal life, a coming back from another place or way of being, that is also described by Jacob and will be by Kamal. It is redolent of the time, that Victor Turner has suggested, of knowing ourselves better through standing outside ourselves and becoming thereby closer to ourselves.

Alyssa appeared in the interviews very young in style and spoke initially in short and quiet bursts of sentences. Her syntax later shifted to much lengthier, confident utterances as she described, with some excitement, situations where, in an unusually sought silence (which she claimed she disliked), the world for her seemed to freeze and stop:

> A: I just feel that the air goes still [...] I don't know ... when I'm silent ... I think of nothing, and I speak of nothing obviously. My mind just goes blank in a way. And I don't think of anything. And that's one of the reasons why I think that the world stops. Obviously I know it hasn't, but I don't *think* that, I think of nothing. And like Alyssa hasn't gone, because obviously I can see myself and all that. And then, that would only be like for a few seconds for my brain to process and then when I just start talking and writing again, I just feel like ... well, not normal again, but like ... me again. Not that I haven't gone. [**Excited and speaking rapidly**] Like when I'm in the study, it's just like white, white, white paintings and all that, and I'm not daydreaming and I'm not thinking. It's just like my mind's gone blank, like actually white and it's only like two or three seconds and it's like the whole world's just stopped and I feel kind of odd – like different to what I am – Not completely different, but just different. Different like ... different. Just different!
>
> V: Yes. So, your mind goes blank and everything stops?
>
> A: Yeah, in a way, yeah. But it's only for a couple of seconds. It seems longer but I know it's not [...] [**Quietly and**

slowly] It seems like half a minute maybe. Not much longer. But I know it's only two or three seconds. But it just feels like [*sic*] little bit longer maybe.

V: And is it odd?

A: It *is* odd because obviously 24/7 I'm not going to be silent. Obviously I like to talk and all that, but ... I felt ... not different again but ... I just feel ... not ... I feel a bit odd [...] It's quite relaxing, as I've said, silence, but it only lasts like three seconds ... before my brain, like, returns to me.

This was clearly unsettling and perplexing for Alyssa and, in contrast to her peers, she did not suggest that she was particularly happy in this state, just that it was memorable. Within it she had an inchoate awareness of being somehow different from her normal self, with a new persona. Here her brain is temporarily 'absent', and time stops in 'an eternal now'.[224] In trying to describe these moments Alyssa employs a *via negativa* or the negative definitional style noted by Victor Turner as indicative of descriptions of liminal states: 'I don't think that; Alyssa hasn't gone; not normal again; not different again.' This was her attempt to describe the experience by saying what was *not* happening and it was important to her to get it right. This led to her questioning her own senses and judgements about time, qualifying her assessments with the familiar mood of subjunctivity, through the repeated use of 'maybe'. There is a sense of surprise here, as Alyssa stresses that she *does* like to talk and isn't going to be silent all the time, and yet this 'odd' situation was quite relaxing, albeit of short duration. As with others who have experienced liminal space, she returns, from a world beyond normal understanding, to her usual cognitive state.

This stepwise process was beautifully summarised by Kamal who had described his aural sensitivity and whose previous conversations had revolved around mundane aspects of his often-challenging daily life. It marks a period in his interviews of unusual eloquence. I had shown him a picture (as I had to others) of a young person looking out towards hills and his comment was part of the discussion that followed. Remarking that such an opportunity might be a pleasant escape from his noisy household, although possibly frightening and lonely, he explained that he didn't often go out into nature, nor would he seek silence or an opportunity to meditate. He did, however, sometimes sit on a bench and stare into the sky, particularly if the sky was blue, 'drifting off'. He could spend fifteen minutes on this, going into 'a different world'. He was asked where he went and whether this were a different space:

> Like dimension, probably. 'Cos once you start looking up and focussing your mind on just one thing. If you focus on a cloud then you think of, I dunno, like pop! I can't explain it. Basically, you just like drift off and think of something like out of the blue, like your family, whatever's happened to you just now and take your mind off it. And think about all the happy times you've had.

Kamal apparently spent up to fifteen minutes in such a state and was asked what happened to time then and how he felt afterwards:

> It just flies. Not fast like. If you were just sitting there ... and then ... like it could be two hours later ... But you're still sitting there. [...] It's like you're sleepwalking in another dimension. Like you're not ... it's not really real but you can picture it right in front of you. It feels like surreal. It feels like you're the same person, but you've come back from one dimension to another. But you're back in real life. Apparently. Yeah, it makes me feel differently of what's just been happening [*sic*].

This section of Kamal's interview was, as with Alyssa, a contrast in style and vocabulary from the remainder. That he used words such as 'sleepwalking', 'dimension' and 'surreal', unusual for him, alerted me to the particular significance of such events for him, and this was the only occasion in an hour's conversation where his commentary was abstract and hypothetical. Nevertheless, he intimated that the experience was something he found hard to explain and we have seen how he reverted to his more usual prosaic style, describing entering a new state as being sudden 'like pop!' As with so many of the other children, he could reach this state when listening to music, when 'everything was cancelled out of me'.

This largely positive state was also frequently enjoyed in nature, and we have already read of Dominic's 'zoned out' experience on visiting, alone, a harbour, untouched, he felt, by human hand. Here, too, Dominic described the sensation as magical and fascinating – he felt changed. Such moments made him question everything. It was purely the sounds of nature, the birds and the waves that were the crucible for the event.

Ravi, whom we have already met, a self-described work-driven, future- and achievement-focussed child, told me that 'we could learn a lot from nature' and that we had taken it for granted. It was here he found his peace:

> When I'm with nature I'm ... can I say peaceful again? I find it very peaceful. Take for instance the beach, the gentle swaying of the waves, coming in and out. Trees, the rustling of the wind. Basically, there's a clock to it. The waves they come in. I'd like to judge every 2 or 3 seconds. The rustling of the wind? I'm not quite sure. But it's always got its own natural rhythm. It's always got its own pattern that it follows ... mmm.

At this moment Ravi became lost in his memory of being by the sea and there was a shift in the rhythm of the interview, an interview which seemed to that point to have been carefully mentally edited by him. Now he allowed himself a moment of pause, of respite and reflection, even though his attempted calculations of wave frequency were a reminder of his usual emphasis on precision and certainty.

Ravi apparently sometimes returns to this memory where it was 'just me and the moment' and where 'time just became irrelevant'. Here Ravi tells of the hypnotic effects of grass and waves, both 'gentle and swaying'. In retrospect, and reverting to his self-proclaimed driven personality, he attempts a calculation of the frequency of movement, quickly followed by, however, by an apparent rehearing of the sounds of the wind. At this point in the interview, Ravi becomes lost for words and became dreamlike in tone, with a relishing 'Mmm'.

Many of the children's experiences shown in this chapter were redolent of flow. Yet, and as we will see in the following section on *Communitas*, they were autotelic, without purpose, arising spontaneously. They were so often ineffable, memorable and full of affect, that they were cited as key examples of 'losing themselves'. We are reminded that without affectivity there is no liminality and that this state is 'delicate, uncertain and malleable', possibly touching 'the core of one's being'.[225] The children here were certainly changed by the experience. Unsurprisingly, they were unable to say quite in what way, but they sought to return there like spiritual homing pigeons. In this we can see Victor Turner's earlier description of the self in liminality being 'lost in order to be remade, dismembered in order to be remembered'.[226] We can also see with these children's descriptions a common thread: they sense the loss of their old selves and in so doing experience joy, a lack of worldly cares, or the gaining of 'everything you've ever wanted', or, as with Alyssa, they emerge simply perplexed. These children have offered these moments as being meaningful for them, and they are spiritual experiences, corresponding to the definitions given earlier in the book and taking place in a liminal state. They were *all* recounted in a wondering tone, very different from their usual style, reflecting the importance of the event to them and accompanied by repeated, musing attempts to articulate it – sometimes reduced to a single dramatic ejaculation: 'Pop!', 'Mmm', 'Weird!' In many ways, the children, through the revisiting of the moment, recreated in the room a discernible sense of the experience itself and it was a privilege to be allowed to participate.

Nearly all of the children spoke of a distortion of time, of a perceptual transformation that suggested an altered state of consciousness, for some a dream-like condition. Such an altered state is for Edith Turner a key aspect of an experience that is for her 'a gift from liminality' –that of *communitas* – and we will now turn to this most delicious of presents.[227]

Communitas: The wind of which bloweth where it listeth[228]

Communitas, like liminality, is hard to define. Yet for the experiencer it is apodictic – the equivalent of 'You had to be there!' The term itself, though not its meaning, was borrowed by Victor Turner from the writer Paul Goodman (presumably from Paul Goodman's 1947 publication *Communitas*). The word immediately presents us with connotations of the familiar term 'community', though Turner stresses that there is an important difference between them. For him, *communitas* is not localised but stretches towards universalism. It is a spontaneous and levelling experience. It is also achievable by even a solitary person, for example, with nature. In general, though, it is a bond uniting people over and above any formal social bond. Moreover, it is not simply community where we are side-by-side, but a sense of being *with* one another in 'unmediated communication [...]

even communion'.[229] This powerful state sees a flowing from the 'I to Thou' identified by Martin Buber[230] and, according to the Turners, blossoms unexpectedly and particularly for the dispossessed and powerless. We are told that pre-industrial societies saw it as a 'charisma or grace'.[231]

Helping those of us without such an experience behind us to understand it more fully, Edith Turner turns to alternative concepts such as the sudden enlightenment of collective *sartori* or *unio mystica* and clarifies this yet further, here in reference to groups:

> It has to do with the sense felt by a group of people when their lives together take on full meaning ... when they rid themselves of their concern for dependence on structure and see their fellows as they are ... [...] It often comes in the driest moments of life [...] it knows no boundaries [...] It finds oneness in surprise. It comes unexpectedly like the wind, and it warms people towards their fellow human beings. [...] It happens when people rid themselves of their concern for status ... and see their fellows as they are.
>
> (Turner, 2012:2–4, xiii)

It is suggested by Victor Turner that in this space a person or a group reaches for the *Atman*[232] or root that is present in all people and beings, and in nature itself. It is, he says, and we will see this corroborated by the children, a highly affective event within the incubating framework of liminality. It is also ephemeral, essentially non-cognitive, and, as Edith reminds us, almost universally held by tribal societies to be holy or sacred.[233] It is not surprising, therefore, to see both Turners also designate *communitas* a sacred condition, or one in the making.[234] Again, the children's narratives will show us, as Edith Turner already knew, that such times also represent joy, it being unconditional love and in many ways sheer magic.[235] We are told by her, in addition, that it often arises in the contexts of disasters, in the moments between sufferer and comforter in a kind of entanglement. This is worth remembering.

We have also read of what she regarded as a 'failsafe bearer of *communitas*' – music, prompted by a physical effect, soundwaves, bypassing the mind. She is not alone in being aware of the power of this. Boyce-Tillman noting the effect of music and music-making and the liminal space within which it arises, refers to it as 'powerful medicine'.[236] There are, we are advised, many other freights of this potent experience, including the sharing of food, working together, illness, during an engagement with nature including both in landscape and with animals, both domestic and wild. But, and crucially, such *communitas* is spontaneous, unique and in fact can happen absolutely anywhere.

The *effects* of it are profound. We are presented with something utterly new: 'a new model of human society', homogenous and unstructured. Victor Turner regards it as 'the emptiness at the centre', bringing with it a sense of 'unprecedented potency ... revitalisation ... binding and bonding people'.[237] One's whole being is then reshaped, with a sense of there being no inequality, simply a shared essence, a *gnosis*[238] and it is undoubtedly epiphanic.[239] Turner points out that this glorious condition is reflected in the philosophies of many world religions, and he directs us to the Zen master Suzuki Daisetz Teitaro (1967) and his clarification of the Zen terms for awareness *prajna* and *vijnana,* where the latter sees division, whereas the former, being intuition, does not – seeing the whole rather than the parts.

As I have indicated, this is not to say that *communitas* and such experiences of merging are always positive. They can have negative outcomes and implications. 'Mob activities' and events at some (but certainly not all) sporting activities are cited by several researchers as examples of the expression of this collectivity, expressed then as violent destruction.[240] There is, therefore, a potential shadow side that should not be ignored. Nevertheless, the overwhelmingly positive impact of *communitas* on so many of the children in this research invites the consideration of this as an aspect of their spirituality.

The connection between flow and *communitas*

We have read in the children's conversations about spiritual experiences precipitated by 'flow' and, although at first glance there is an apparent similarity between *communitas* and flow, they are different. Viktor Turner suggests to us that *communitas* is the prime event, though it can be achieved through flow. In any case, he says, *communitas* at its inception is experienced as something *between* or *among* individuals (or, as we will see between an individual and nature). This is in contrast to flow, which is an experience *within* an individual, almost at times a technique. On the other hand, *communitas* is usually a shared experience that can happen anywhere. More than this there is in flow for Turner a voluntariness or 'a willingness to play', in contrast to the frequently unanticipated, extraordinary and often singular experience of *communitas.*

This certainly seems to be the key difference. When in a flow experience, a child may have sought a space or a situation (dance, sport or music, for example) within which they might 'lose themselves'. It concerns experiences of the self in relation to the self and is not necessarily unbidden. It is a repeatable experience, occasionally even (ask a musician or sportsperson) part of a performance technique. In *communitas,* though, the experience is that of merging with others or even nature, leading to a boundarylessness where the object, human or otherwise, becomes an integrated part of an undifferentiated whole. There is no immediate tangible benefit to the experiencer – no artistic inspiration, no faster run or enraptured dance – one is in flow certainly, but the benefits are simply those of incredulity and wonder and a broadened awareness of the nature of being itself. It *cannot* be sought. It is simply, as it were, we are told, gifted to us, and is unalloyed consciousness.

The children's experience of *communitas*

Some of the most significant and affective moments of the times spent with the children occurred during descriptions of events that led them to experience a form of love and unity that they struggled to express, but which remained with them as a joy-filled and lasting memory of something extraordinary that gave them an insight into a world that now held, for them, mysteries.

These arose so frequently that it became impossible to ignore them as a *leitmotif* of children's spirituality, and what follows is a selection of five illuminative examples taken both from those children who were highly articulate, sensitive and forthcoming, as well as those who were retiring and hesitant.

Harriet and Arianna: *Communitas* with one other person

What follows is an example of a highly articulate child whose powerful, almost breathless, account took up much of her two interviews. Harriet had told me in her questionnaire that she very much wanted to be interviewed, that she was a spiritual person, often thinking about the world, 'what's around us' and what that meant for her. In the final section of the questionnaire where the children were asked if they wanted to add anything in confidence, she completely filled the allocated space and then much of the blank back page with a brief description and reflections of momentous events on a holiday in Greece. This involved extreme weather and her cousin. Given the evident importance of this to her, I visited this in her first interview (and indeed the second), thus providing a deeper insight into its catalysts and the effects on her, both in the moment and subsequently.

This fast-talking, confident and bubbly child, when asked about this holiday, became suddenly quiet, and her voice tone changed. It was clear that she was remembering moments of great importance for her that had taken place at the age of nine or ten. Then, when asked to describe the events themselves, she became highly energised, spoke rapidly again and was full of very evident joy. Here she recounts this special time. Having spent 'a beautiful day' sightseeing with her extended family, she returned to their hilltop villa to a sudden change in the weather, and she stood alone with her younger cousin:

> And then, literally in a matter of seconds, like cloudless skies to black thunder, thunder, thunder. My cousin was terrified, and to be honest I was quite scared myself, because you could just see, the most crazy experience ever, you could just see the lightning ... in some ways the lightning was beautiful. It was like such an extraordinary experience at the time and my cousin ran towards me and I gave her a hug and I took my jumper off and I gave it to her [...] and then we ... it was chucking it down with rain, it was like such a surreal experience, even though people might say ... oh it's just weather ... and so we went to a café and we sat down and had hot chocolate and she had pineapple juice and we were talking about the experience. And oh! It was just lovely. [...] I don't think I've ever been so close to someone in my life! Like me and my cousin. Like we *are* close, but we don't see each other that much and I didn't really realise that I could feel that feeling with my cousin. We know each other, we obviously have known each other all our lives, but it was like me and my sister bond. Like it was *so* close, and we were hugging, we were laughing, we were petrified ... the most exciting thing ... [...] And it was just like, almost incredible in a way, because she was so scared, but it was

> amazing at the same time, because it was the first time all of us had experienced awful weather like that, and so it was almost like a magnet ... doosh! We were together and we were hugging the whole way; one of us had an arm in one sleeve and I had an arm in the other and we had to zip it up.
>
> Oh! It was lovely! It was because ... our families are so close and when they experienced that ... I'm not sure how she feels about the situation, or if she'd still remember it, **[Breathless with excitement]** I DUNNO. IT WAS SO INCREDIBLE **[With a loud voice, trying to convey how special this was]** ... Because I felt like ... I know that my family love me and I completely adore my family, but the hug that we felt, like ... I *felt* it.

I asked her to try to tell me why this was so special and to return to that moment to help her explain it, something she found very easy to do:

> Yeah ... ooh ... oh Lord, it's difficult to describe because I love her to pieces and for some reason I thought that the thunder was going to hit on us [...] I've experienced thunder and lightning but not as bad as this ... and then even worse things happened that night but ... **[Quiet and breathless. At this point there was a shift in atmosphere in the room]**. It was such an *incredible feeling* ... like there's love between two people that you don't know, then you meet, and there's love between family, and I feel that that part, that time there, it was just like ... like I was in a fantasy ... like a handsome prince came and saved me ... it was my little cousin and she had nothing to save, she just had to be there, and because she was there, if she wasn't there, if I was just there on my own, I probably might not have remembered it but because she took it in

> like such a mature way and she was scared ... it was like 'Oh, Kathy' ... it was kind of magical in a way.

Harriet went on to describe the whole time which she would remember with gratitude all of her life as 'surreal', 'amazing' and, also, a learning point:

> Like when you think you're alone, when you think no one's there for you, people still love you, even if they've passed away, even if they're on the other side of the world, you have someone that cares for you. And that people shouldn't feel alone, even like someone who feels they have no one, or they've been abandoned, there's always going to be someone. Even if that's God like they believe in, religion, or a family member.

This account was not simply that of a deepening relationship between a girl and her cousin under adverse circumstances; it was a moment of wonder, and a numinous state that Harriet conveyed as effectively in her body language as she attempted to do orally. Harriet talks here of a bond, the intensity of which took her by surprise, and of a closeness that she had never experienced before, of a feeling she never expected to have. This is, for me, a wonderful example of the unexpected experience of unity of which both Edith and Victor Turner speak, and a sharing of 'the vivid present' precipitated by an experiential sharing. It also exemplifies the gratitude which for Edith Turner is the response to true *communitas*.[241]

This is also a very clear example of the egalitarianism of *communitas*: the normal family hierarchy had been toppled as ten-year old Harriet became 'the protector' in a situation of perceived danger, and her even younger cousin became a peer, worthy of hugs and laughter. She explained earlier that she would have expected Kathy to seek out Harriet's elder sister or mother, but in this situation Harriet is elevated in status, as, ultimately, is Kathy. She then goes on to describe it all as 'surreal', and for her the intensity of the love and connection found no available analogue – the nearest simile she could find to express her experience was that of the arrival of 'a handsome prince'. This was fairy-tale, metaphorical vocabulary, otherworldly and evocative, and her visceral account of it had a powerful impact on us both.

Her graphic description of the two cousins coming together like a magnet intimates an unavoidability, a force of nature that existed and that became manifest without any effort on their parts – indeed effort cannot produce this. It reflects the charisma or grace alluded to by Victor Turner and is a flowing between two people – an identifying characteristic of communitas. It is, essentially, a *withness*. June Boyce-Tillman sees this liminal space as an opportunity for her to try on a 'new persona' and Harriet's understanding of the event was not a propositional or binary knowing but rather the 'both ... and knowing' – a relational knowing.[242] It was both an event that seemed to be redolent of normal family love, something to which she could relate, yet it also went beyond this to something greater, a pure experience that was almost beyond words and simply 'felt' by Harriet. This is understood in a range of disciplines: for anthropologist Arpad Szakolczai, here in the liminal space it is not the *I* that loves *you* but rather the *it*, the love itself, that emerges in the in-between of two humans, transforming them both; for Maggie Ross it is the heart speaking to heart that issues from silence and which happens in prayer.[243] A situation that might have been terror alone was transformed into something 'lovely', 'incredible', 'exciting' and also 'amazing', 'surreal', 'magical' and 'extraordinary' – like a fantasy. This was surely the unconditional love and the 'quick of human interrelatedness' identified by the Turners as such key facets of *communitas*.

It is particularly significant that throughout Harriet uses the pronoun 'we', almost staccato for emphasis: '*we* were hugging'; '*we* were laughing'; '*we* were petrified', expressing a unity and a common experience. The importance of the hug itself, the key moment, is explained in the interview through the immediacy of the [hug that] '*we* felt', followed immediately by '*I* felt it'. This was embodied and completely indisputable. For Victor Turner, the use of the pronoun '*we*' in the context of *communitas* has a liminal character and, importantly, it has perdurance. This is clearly emphasised by Harriet when she speaks gratefully of the lasting lesson of this event: never feeling alone, as whether from God or another human, living or dead, there is always love.

And there was laughter too. Such a signal feature of *communitas*, according to Edith Turner a kind of 'welcoming in', as well as a recognition of it being beyond description.[244]

The whole adventure took place in the context of an extreme of nature, recognised by the local authorities at the time as an impending disaster. Yet Harriet was very concerned to convey that there was something beyond the fear of dangerous weather conditions happening for her at this time, and that the context should not be dismissed lightly, as many might do, as 'Oh it's just weather!' She was aware that others might just reduce the whole event to her heightened emotions, and she was anxious to convey fully in the interviews the importance of an experience that she had safeguarded in her memory for several years. It resulted in joy, or returning to Edith Turner: 'a stumbling across the best time!'

In a different school, Arianna who liked to spend time daydreaming, was still grieving from a fairly recent death in her family. She reassured me, however, that she could find 'positivity in anything'. Asked to describe a particularly happy moment in her life, she described a recent camping trip with a group of family friends. She and another girl, who eventually became her best friend, sat together in a tent whilst the other girls congregated boisterously outside. Arianna and Polly were engaged in working on a scrapbook and playing *Minecraft*. Asked what was special about the time, she was almost mournful:

> Just the way that nothing ever seemed wrong. Everything that could have been bad just went! And I was happy. [**Sad voice**] Yeah. I just had nothing to worry about. Nothing in my brain was thinking about a little bad thing in the back of my head or something. Everything was just ... happy.

Asked if this were absolute happiness, she replied:

> A: Yeah. I'd say it was. And like leaving behind ... I always sort of imagine that there's a bit of my brain that is like evil [*sic*] ... what if there was maths homework?... and like that part of it just like went, and there was nothing that I could possibly have been worried about.
>
> V: So, Arianna, where does Arianna go when that happens?
>
> A: I guess I could say like into the clouds. Sort of like a glimpse of heaven. But I don't know if that's actually how I feel or not.[**Laughs**] It's just sort of what a lot of people say. Er, I don't know.
>
> V: Stay there. Because this is very beautiful. Right? You're in that moment. Here it was Polly and you in that moment, and you're saying – the bad stuff went, then homework went, all the ... that all went ... and where were you? What was happening?
>
> A: I was with her in like a special bit. It felt like nobody else could have a moment so good [**Tearful**] and, like, it was just for me.

Once again, we see very powerful emotions, beyond those that might be attributed to a particularly good afternoon of fun. Two girls separated, if only here by canvas, from the rest of the group, experiencing a moment of unexpected bonding and the familiar *withness*. All concerns and fears disappeared at this point and Arianne felt that she had entered a different space – a space that was just for her, full of joy, prompting an almost bashful use of simile and metaphor, with a memory of it so intense that it brought her to tears in its recall.

These are examples of *communitas* between individuals. What follows are examples of *communitas* arising in the context of larger groups. I was given many examples of this, but the two shown here are selected to show the diversity of those received.

Communitas within a group environment

Sophia came for a single interview only, due to her ill health, and she told me that she found silence with her cat quite 'cleansing', in the midst of her busy life that included a great deal of sport. She told me that she had grown up amongst people who were 'very spiritual'. Asked if she were spiritual herself, she responded:

S: It depends on what you mean by spiritual.
V: Well, you tell me what you mean.
S: Okay. Well, er ... **[Exhales loudly]** ... I quite enjoy silence and ... we ... go ... to ... a lot of things that ... so like if ... every year there's a gathering in the woods. My mum's friends Philippa and Rodger ... and we'll kind of sit around a fire and there's like everyone...

So, all like our family and our friends and like loads of us. There must be about 100 people there and we all just kind of sit round the fire and like in the summer, Summer Solstice and in the winter, that kind of thing, and we all sit together **[Very fast talking throughout]** and, I dunno, we just kind of ... it's not a party, it's like a gathering.

So, you ... there is like music but it's not like a party ... I dunno ... it's...

V: What does it feel like?

S: It's really nice because it's the one time in the year, two times in the year, when I get to see everyone, 'cos everyone lives in different places – like Angela and Steve or...

V: So, could you go back to this gathering; and you mentioned that in the context of spirituality ... what do you think is spiritual about it?

S: Humph ... it just feels ... it has that feeling about it? 'Cos for about 10 minutes we'll kind of sit silently round a fire ... together ... and it's really kind of nice and ... calm and ... I dunno [**Quietly**] ... just really harmonious. [...] There's loads of people there.

V: And you're saying ... 'Actually, I think that this a spiritual moment.'

S: Yeah [**Very quietly**].

V: [**Wonderingly**] What *is* it about it?

S: [**Exhales loudly**]

V: 'Cos it's obviously *very* special, isn't it?

S: It's just really ... I've never seen anywhere else 100 people just sitting silently around a fire ... and it just ... it's kind of ... It's really hard to explain ... it's just *really* ... nice? And ... there's just a feeling about it ... it's just really kind of ... I dunno ... [**Trails off into silence**]. [...] Because obviously that's quite unusual to have 100 people just sitting round a fire [...] but I think it's partly because it's who the people are as well. They've known me since I was born, most of them, and they know my mum for such a lot of years and...

V: So, you feel ... what ... with these people?

S: They kind of read me ... they kind of understand because ... they ... know everything.

At this point I asked several more questions to try to encourage her to articulate exactly what was special. She revealed aspects of her home life that intensified the contrast with this outdoor, relaxed space:

S: **[Long pause]** I dunno, I mean it's just … […] Er, they're just very laid back and calm people. So, [**Redacted**] … so, our whole house is like, well not in my own room necessarily, but downstairs – always completely spotless and it's completely tidy and, when she (her mum) goes *there*, because it's not in a house that you can make really tidy, it's different. It's like has a different personality which makes it a lot easier to kind of…
V: So, why is that spiritual?
S: There's just a feeling I can't…

I pursued this yet further (and, in case you were wondering, my 'inner power relationship critic' was alive and well … it seemed acceptable to do this). I asked her what she felt, and she replied that she was just 'really, really happy'. She explained that there was nothing more to add; it was just that event … 'that kind of just … yeah'.

In many ways this was a low-key event, without the drama of Harriet's impending danger, yet there are similarities. The unique feeling that Sophia described – 'that feeling' – using the word harmonious on several occasions, left her sensing that it had been a joyful spiritual moment, inexpressible and memorable. She told me later that *she had simply felt known*. She conveyed the bond that united people, its egalitarian nature and the contrast between her normal life and this scenario. This harmony (with a beautiful Greek etymology referencing the joining together of contrasted elements – a higher and a lower note, for example) represented for her a sense of being known and accepted for herself – indeed of the love that is a hallmark of *communitas*.

Such a unity and egalitarianism were also expressed by the silence-seeking and cheerfully entertaining Gavin. Asked about a moment of peak happiness he became particularly animated, and his excitement was palpable and contagious:

> When my dad ... my dad, who is probably the best dad in the world, he took me to see my favourite team in Manchester to play ... basically he took me to see Manchester United versus Sunderland which was my first ever Manchester United game and it was just astonishing. Like going into the crowd; like exploring Manchester; it was so nice. And just spending time with my dad in general. It was really nice.
>
> Well, first of all, it was when we were just walking up the stairs, like going to the seats. The view was just amazing. It was like unreal. It was probably the best thing I'm going to see for quite a while. Because it's stuck with me that image – the Manchester ground, because it was very dark. It was like 6.30. The floodlights were on; it was really dark. It looked like a wonderland in a way. But not the winter part! [**Laughs**] So, when I walked up the stairs and looked around, it just felt amazing, so I was just jumping up and down. Not literally, but inside I was jumping up and down! I just walked down the stairs towards where the grass was. I wasn't allowed to go on the grass, but I just looked, and it was so amazing, how close I was to that pitch. If I was on it, it would be even more special but ... it was *so* much fun! Just to see. Even though we drove, it was a very good experience because I was with my dad ... and really ... I'm just too excited...! [...] So basically, before the game, everyone was chanting like 'Whoah!!' the Man U thing. And then, when the game started, everyone was just chanting 'Come on you Reds' or something. Amazing!

Gavin was asked to explain why this was amazing:

G: I think like the commitment they have to watching their ... 'cos most of the people were from Manchester. So basically, it was just like people talking in like ... I don't want to offend ... slur their language, like what the way they speak. It's like Manchester. Like Manchester language. Basically, they were just saying that, and it was like hearing that language for the first time. It was like me understanding that different places speak differently. Because, before then, the only two languages I know were English and French. Or Cockney in England. And then when I heard *that* I was like – 'Oh wait, there can be different languages in England.' And then when they just chanted, it was like no matter what happened they just kept cheering on their team.

V: You said something about the fact that they were all together doing it?

G: Yeah. It was like ... because in a football stadium, well the one I went to anyway, basically you sat next to people. It was like row on row of seats. So, you can hear people just chant. You can look around and people would sometimes stand and just chant and sit down because they realise that the person behind wants to watch it. [**All of this related with great excitement and speed**]. And then there was this one, two people were behind my dad and they were offering sweets. [...]

V: So, was there a togetherness then?

G: Yeah! Like Manchester as a community is like one big club in my opinion. It's really nice. It was quite powerful. And it was like, when I ... stood up once, 'cos I was quite small then and not as high as I am now. Like the person behind me could still see.

V: Right. So that was Okay?

G: Yeah. Because I just sort of turned that way, because when I was standing, I was facing forward, and it was to the right, and the person was looking to the right. So, when I just stood up, no one minded at all.

V: So, wasn't the noise off-putting? You seemed to think that the noise was not off-putting?

G: It wasn't at all; it was like it went so well with the football. It was like, like the football, when they were passing the ball around just went with noise. It wasn't off-putting at all. It's like I was just too focussed on the game. But the noise came together perfectly with it.

Gavin had been taken on a special outing to Manchester with his father who often worked away during the week. Everything in this city ran counter to his cultural norms – he had been, as it were, transplanted into a strange environment. The Mancunian dialect was deemed to be a new language: 'Manchester language' and greatly contributed to his sense of pleasurable disorientation. The visual impact of the stadium at night and the juxtaposition of light and dark transformed it into a metaphoric 'wonderland', an unreal place that created the context for memorable joy. He was aware of the ceaseless chanting as background. Yet, as he later explained, he was so completely focussed on the game, it did not disturb this boy who had earlier described himself as a lover of peace. The noise merged with the action: 'it came together perfectly with it' and both of these instantiated the 'eternal now' of communitas that is a familiar trope.

Interestingly, food was also an important factor in Gavin's memorable day. He later commented on his appreciation of, what was to him, the different regional diet: 'chips and gravy', available at the stadium. The spontaneous sharing of sweets by strangers in the stadium was also of great significance for him, the commensality of which, as we have read, has been noted by anthropologists as being of particular importance in *communitas*. This prompted him to suggest that Manchester itself was 'one big club' and with its members having an awareness of each other, too, as the spectators sought to avoid impeding the view of others. This is a strongly suggestive experience of positive *communitas* and mirrors that of Sophie's story and many others not included here: that of unity, a sharing of the present, bonding, and above all, as sociologist Payne identifies, 'a dissolution of normative structures'.[245] It was also the heady, and for Gavin unique, sense of egalitarianism in a community where the weak and humble can have power and where a child may easily merge with adults who formerly have been seen as 'other'.[246] This experience was supported by a conscious break from normal life, a movement into the stadium 'sanctuary', the ritual of 'costume wearing' (team colours) and the temporal limitation of the game itself.[247] For both Gavin and Sophia, the time provided an indelible memory of a 'shared essence' and of the gnosis suggested by Victor Turner.

Gracie and Isaac: The *communitas* of nature

We have seen in the earlier part of this chapter that nature was often the precursor of a liminal experience. For some of the children this was particularly intense and an experience not between humans but in relationship with nature itself. Here we return, once again, to the self-proclaimed lover of daydreaming Gracie, who stated her belief that nature was 'innocent' and at the end of a busy day at school, she sought it out in the local fields and river, relishing the company of animals that were simply 'with you', not judging. Without this relationship to nature, with which she felt a palpable connection, Gracie explained that she would find life hard. Such *communitas* with the land and animals (presumably this included insects) is described by Edith Turner as an awareness of a presence 'that speaks'. We are reminded by her of this awareness of such presences in nature, whether sentient beings or natural forms, being a normal part of spirituality in the world: in Japanese Shinto and the concept of *kami*, *akishi* in Africa and *inua* in the Arctic.[248] Gracie certainly exemplified this in her interview, yet explained in her questionnaire that she just wasn't 'sure what to believe in ... yet!' Filling a whole blank page to expand on this, she told me that she believed in animal spirits, because nothing so beautiful and innocent could be just gone (at death), and, as we have seen in previous chapters, she went on to tell of her memorable connection with a bee that had found its way to her garden:

V: So, did you feel that you had a relationship with the bee?

G: Yeah! I was like really happy! I wouldn't say I was sad when I saw it go but ... just ... I wasn't like 'Oh, I'm going to miss it', 'cos, you know, I was kind of – Oh, I'm really happy.

V: What made you care for it?

G: I've *no* idea! [**Breathless**] I think I just ... once I saw it there and I saw that I was helping it, I guess I didn't have anything else to do and I was really tired, and I just lay there and just watched it and just tried to help it get back.

V: But for five hours!

G: Yeah! Strange [...] It just looked so helpless. One of its legs was all folded in and its wings were like all stuck together and I was like 'Oh no, that's really sad', and it was just like hobbling around and I was like 'Oh that's horrible'. I really didn't like seeing it like that.

V: Yeah. Well, that was a moment of joy, wasn't it?

G: Yeah!

V: How did that make you, Gracie, feel?

G: I was really happy. I guess I was really proud that I'd been able to help it and also really shocked that it actually like ... I'd seen it again and kind of unsure that it had been it. But I felt that there was definitely … I'd just really recognised it and I just kind of felt that wow that was actually … it actually came back and really surprised that I'd actually spent that long just trying to…

V: You'll remember it all your life!

G: Yes. It was crazy!

In those hours Gracie had entered a different space and an awareness of a change in the structure of time – a space she later described as being beyond normal thought ('not just sat there thinking'): 'You're somewhere else because otherwise how do you think all those thoughts that you don't normally think?' This was the state identified by Csikszentmihalyi as the 'centring of attention on a limited stimulus field',[249] but as we may be reminded, Victor Turner suggests that though *communitas is* a kind of flow, it can arise in both structured and unstructured situations. And here we see Gracie in a completely unstructured engagement with a bee, with evidence of a loss of self, as she, without even knowing why, lay supporting it, resulting in surprise that she had spent so long doing this and yet gaining great happiness from having done so. For her this was an act of power, once again the holy power of the weak and humble in *communitas* spoken of by Victor Turner and corroborated for her by the apparent miraculous and 'bizarre' return of the bee. Finally, there was the palpable unconditional love and autotelism so characteristic of *communitas* – Gracie wanted nothing from the bee, just the opportunity to lie by its side and to will it better.

Isaac, also, valued the sense of 'nature *communitas*' that he experienced when in a forest. As might be expected, he was unable to explain the feeling. He repeated, 'I don't know what it is', making tentative suggestions, but then feeling they were inadequate, and, finally, laughing at his own efforts. He did know that there was something about being 'in the moment':

I: Yeah. Like I said. I used the example of a forest. I don't know what it is. There's birds [*sic*] ... the sound of the birds as well. It's just ... I don't know what it is ... birds moving from tree to tree. Or something like that. The flapping. Don't know what it is [**Laughs**]. Just...

V: What is it? You like it?

I: I like it. Yeah. I don't know *what* it is. It's just 'cos it's...

V: What does it do?

I: I don't know. I really don't know. I just like being in that moment. Being in a forest by yourself. And just hearing the birds. 'Cos in the morning as well, when about 7 o'clock, the birds. I like the sound of the birds. Yeah. That's what I like.

Once again, we see the frustrated and bemused attempts to convey the ineffability of a valued moment in nature, where time is suspended and where there is, nevertheless, a certainty that something important is happening.

The *communitas* of ritual

In his major work *Dramas, Fields and Metaphors* Victor Turner explains the work of some religions in seeking to free individuals from their attachment to role-playing and personality, creating a 'release' or 'salvation' from their former self-identification – through *communitas.* This is achieved in pilgrimages, in formal communities (monasteries and convents, for example), and in rituals, and can be experienced, as we have read, with others or alone.

Millie, who we may remember, had suffered greatly during her life from severe and permanent medical conditions, provided a lucid, and of the children's interviews unique, example of a religious ritual leading to *communitas*. Here, we visit Millie's description of her memories in church during her Catholic confirmation with the local bishop. The description was given in a quiet and reverential manner:

> So, basically the altar is there [**Points**]. We're all standing in a semi-circle, all the people getting confirmed, and the people supporting us, or sponsors, people who say, 'We present this person to be confirmed', are all behind us, and my two parents. So, they're standing there [**Points again**] and I'm standing here. And the bishop confirms us, each one by one, and then he puts some, I can't remember which oil it is, it's a holy oil. It's not oil of chrism but oil of something, however, which oil, and he puts the sign of the cross on our forehead and ... and then he like ... places his hand on your head and then kind of blesses you. But it's almost like ... I almost felt like I was turning into another person ... As like this ache feeling went through me [**Questioning inflection, trying to convey and share it**] ... as it went through my head, and it went like into my arms and down to my feet.
>
> V: You actually felt something?
>
> M: Yes.
>
> V: What did you feel?
>
> M: It's hard to explain. It was like this erm ... like ... it's hard to explain. It's almost like relief, but then it was like a blessing? It was like God's blessing going through me. [...] [**Long Pause**] I'm quite proud of that moment [**Broken voice**]. It was a very big moment for me.

At this point her manner altered and she was clearly very moved as if reliving the experience. The mood in the whole room shifted as she sought, and was able to share, palpably, the change in her that day.

Though there is an extensive body of research relating to the symbolism of the sacrament of Confirmation in the Catholic church, this event is briefly presented here as evidence of another flavour of *communitas*. Few of the children interviewed described an engagement with formal ritual of any nature. Here, however, Millie was able to describe the ritual, and then its tripartite aspects, redolent of the tribal rituals witnessed in the fieldwork of the Turners. Firstly, she was removed from her 'normal' life to be in the church, standing in a semi-circle, sanctioned by 'elders' (her parents and sponsors). Such formal positioning, explained by her in detail through words and gestures, underlined the otherness of the occasion.

Secondly, following this 'extraction' from her 'old' world, Millie was exposed to a series of symbolic acts and artefacts that precipitated an embodied sense of a new Millie. The holy oil used to mark a sign of the cross, followed by a placing of the bishop's hands on her head, signify a cleansing of the old self.[250] She interpreted this within her cultural and religious expectations, but, and thirdly, emerged reaggregated and changed from the experience. As we know, Millie later confided that this 'new self' had a specific role to perform in life: to make the world a better place, and that because of her particular background disability and her life experience, she was well placed to fulfil this function. She also now wanted to travel to other countries to 'help the sick and stuff', and she explained that she now took her religion more seriously, as she understood it 'in some weird way'. She felt, following her confirmation, that she was now able to access new levels of understanding when, for example, singing in a church and reflecting on the ancient meanings of words. Thus, we see Millie enter a liminal space, and, briefly though memorably, touching during ritual a solitary *communitas* within which she released her former self-identification, accessing, I suggest, 'the root' deemed to be available to us all.

For some children, such as Millie, the experience of *communitas* engendered joy, whilst for others the experience of joy actually precipitated it. For yet others the two were intertwined and Isabel's account that follows shows this inextricable connection.

Isabel and the *communitas* of joy

When Isabel was asked to describe a moment of extreme joy that she would never forget, she went back in time to her experience in primary school of a swimming gala – the memory of which she suggested with some trepidation was a bit weird. Encouraged to be 'weird' if she so wanted, she laughed and went on to describe the event:

> [**Laughs**] Er, at my primary school I was a complete introvert. I didn't like talking and things. I was like an anxious person. I went to a swimming gala with my school, and it was quite a big one, against these other people. And I did my race. I didn't win but I did okay. But that day our school won the gold medal; like that feeling that you've accomplished a big thing. We won the overall. Not just our section. And it was just so happy to know that you've like helped to make your school have a bit ... of a voice? It's like saying, 'Yeah, I can do this. I'm a bit special really!' [**Laughs**] It's things like that. I just felt really, really happy!
>
> I was like floating. I was like where you just thought 'Wow. This is actually happening'. Just like people that you know and care about just like screaming and shouting and hugging each other. Just that moment of everybody being happy together [...] So, they're all like shouting, singing, hugging. You can tell ... not one person in there ... felt down, sad. Just that moment of like floating and happiness [...].

Isabel had kept this occasion to herself, not discussing her feelings about it with anyone.

V: So, you're there, and there's all these people and you said they were all happy too. And there was something very beautiful about the fact that *they* were happy? [...]

I: Yeah. You never usually get to see so many happy people around you that you care about. 'Cos if you're in a group at school, there's always one person who's feeling nervous, anxious sad – like angry. 'Cos there's always something going on, like no one knows about. And like I get that. But sometimes they, they like – you can tell that they are angry or sad. But sometimes it's the fact that they're not as loud or as funny as usual. You can sort of just tell that not everyone's going to be happy at the same time and it's just that moment when you can tell that everyone *was*! That was like really special.

I then asked Isabel to try to take me with her to the moment, to understand why this time was so special for her:

> So, you're less aware about other people around you. You don't feel any pressure on yourself. Like no one's going to care what you look like, what you sound like. 'Cos everyone's like ... the same. They're not caring about like if you're ... I don't know. If you don't feel comfortable – in *that* moment, you'll feel comfortable. Because I was like really self-conscious, hunched up ... and in that moment ... I stood up and I like – danced? **[Very animated and excited at this point]**
>
> I became ... I don't ... I was just ... myself. I let it out. The first time I was myself. 'Cos I am now, but at my primary school, I found it hard to do things like that.

Isabel felt very strongly that at that moment, somehow, she became fully herself, a bit like a butterfly coming out of a chrysalis. She went on to say that she had never had a similar experience, and, in the middle of laughter, stated that she was 'not really sure' what had released that personality change in her. In this narrative we see a normally shy child being taken with a group of peers out of her usual environment to share an unusual and joyful event. She describes becoming 'herself', following the group's success, and that this new 'self', the opposite of her normally self-conscious, hunched-up self, was *released.* As we have seen, Victor and Edith Turner suggest that other liminal events such as pilgrimages can have a similar effect in releasing the emergence of an integral person from multiple personae.[251] We note here Isabel becoming a more whole and multifaceted personality in a transformation, so typical of a liminal and *communitas* experience, shifting her future self-perception. We also hear, paradoxically, of her sense of losing herself and her self-consciousness, and then seeing herself as subject matter in the context of an egalitarian bond uniting her with others. This is the 'both this and that', not the propositional 'either/or' but the relational both/and.[252] Furthermore, Isabel stressed that it was 'in that moment' that this happened, a singular point and with an apparent shift in the structure of time.

We hear, too, that she felt as if she were floating in a context of universal happiness within which she shared in the joy of others, who are all at that point 'the same' – a further example of 'both/ and' thinking: being an inseparable part of the whole (swimming team) and yet also contemporaneously an expanded individual personality.[253] From this there arose a new freedom, with a sense of untouchability, as this hitherto shy and withdrawn girl, to her own amazement, danced with elation in public. Here is yet another child encountering a highly affective shift of perspective and sense of possibility, followed by a readmittance into the 'normal world' and bearing permanent effects. True to form, it was, inevitably, 'weird'.

And so...

You will remember that when I first set out to interview children, I was focussed on their opportunities for silence and how this affected their expression, if any, on spirituality. You may also remember that it became clear, very early on, that the majority of them had few chances of getting any solitude or silence in their lives. And yet there arose very many examples of children's spirituality arising as they stepped into another state, a 'betwixt and between' condition that was, as we have seen, highly affective and, for some, transformational. I recognise this as a liminal state and one which has resonances with a broader understanding of silence discussed earlier in the book. Others have pointed towards this power:

- Philosopher Picard speaks of silence as a catalysing phenomenon from which may arise other phenomena.
- Theologian Ross suggests the ever-present nature of silence as an available resource within which we might be transfigured, a 'deep mind' or apophatic consciousness, accessed for her through an emptying of the mind, or kenosis.
- Philosopher Dauenhauer speaks of silence as 'abiding', allowing a yielding into something different from the customary or the habitual.

We see in these thoughts echoes of the ideas of Victor Turner when he speaks of liminal space as being that of chaos and potentiality and an intrusion into our normal state. Silence as a non-binary and the concept of liminality have many congruities. In discussing this, I do not wish to diminish the relevance of binary silence and quiet for the spirituality of children. Chapter 7 has explored that already. But, and I think crucially, liminality with its spiritual sister *communitas* convincingly provides a catholic and integrative framework for an understanding of child spirituality, and one within which silence as non-sound is subsumed. It is a framework which accords with psychologist Ferrer's view of a participatory, creative spirituality, grounded in love, that has intuitive knowing at its heart.[254] It is an evanescent space, yet providing abiding memories. Brendan Hyde's view, that children's spirituality is concerned with ultimate unity and a transcendence of the ego, finds symphony and sympathy in the interviews of these children when they are in a liminal condition.

Whether liminal space and liminality are contexts for spirituality or *are* states of spirituality is a subject for other debates. What is apparent, though, is that liminality and its occasional corollary endowment of *communitas* were commonly experienced by these children. This provides us with a new way of seeing child spirituality, one that is neither fractured nor deconstructed, but, rather, coherent and holistic. Might this framework help us as adults to support and to understand children better? I believe it does. The final chapter will now take us back to the reasons for the investigation in the first place and how the outcomes provide an imperative for all of us involved with children.

Chapter 9

From Negation to Nurture

This book leaves questions, and these questions are pressing ones. It cannot only be of academic interest that, according to the UK newspaper *The Guardian*, referrals to emergency mental health care in England rose by 10% in a year (2024) with over 34,793 emergency, very urgent or urgent referrals to an adolescent mental health services crisis team between April and October 2024 – in seven months.[255] Nearly half a million children in the UK were in contact with mental health services from the beginning of 2024 to the end of November 2024, prompting the theme of the 2025 Children's Mental Health Week, organised annually by the UK Charity Place2be, to be 'Know Yourself to Grow Yourself'.[256]

We are told, alarmingly, that in the UK 50% of mental health problems are already established by the age of 14,[257] a statistic very precisely mirrored in Australia[258] and where 1 in 10 children aged 4–11 have a mental health disorder.[259] In 2023, 40% of high school students in the US felt so sad or hopeless almost every day for at least two weeks in a row, that they stopped doing their daily activities.[260] In China, the prevalence of mental health disorders among children and youth stands at 17.5% and is escalating further, prompting urgent government intervention.[261] These problems are widespread and not diminishing.

Can the outcome of an investigation into spirituality and silence amongst a mere 39 young people in England have any relevance at all to these seemingly overwhelming problems of child mental well-being? Are these children representative of other or all children in the UK, in Western nations, or even in the world? Is spirituality connected with mental health anyway? If so, are silence and liminality useful in understanding this connection better? And, even if they *were* relevant factors, is there anything at all that can be done?

Humbly yet insistently (and I do wonder whether they can go together), I think the answer is 'Yes'. In saying this I am not suggesting that the findings here suggest a panacea for the problems faced by our children. Clearly these issues are multi-faceted and complex. Yet I do propose that the conclusions might help, and although I cannot *generalise* from the limited number of young people interviewed, I suggest that their responses are certainly indicative. They represent a broad range of intellectual and physical abilities and (self-described) disabilities, introverts and extroverts, the articulate and halting, with different cultural, religious and sometimes linguistic backgrounds, from a range of social milieux, from urban and rural environments, and from both private and state-supported schools, and thus they provide a unique snapshot of children in England. And, as those who have worked with children throughout the world will probably tell you, children are children wherever they are.

Assumptions thwarted

The original intentions of the investigation were to discover whether silence and/or lack of it impacted on children's spirituality. I believed strongly that it might; a lifetime of (admittedly) sporadic meditation and an awareness of the importance of silence for many religions and spiritualities provided a seedbed of prejudice. Underlying all of this were assumptions that children were in fact spiritual beings. This was not, however, unreasonable given the extensive and convincing literature in the by now internationally established field of child spirituality. Nevertheless, this had to be the starting point.

Were the children spiritual?

Nearly all the children who took part in the study exhibited spirituality *in abundance*, corroborating the view that children's spirituality reflects a natural disposition.[262] Though each child's description of their spirituality was necessarily unique, similarities were evident. The opportunity presented by being able to speak to children from a range of social milieux in four very different schools, was helpful in gaining this perspective. Some similarities between the children within schools suggest that social, educational, cultural and environmental backgrounds inform these experiences and their description to a significant extent. Despite this, some of the children's framing beliefs differed (with an evident cognitive dissonance) from those that might have been expected from their social context: Catholic children asserting a belief in reincarnation, for example. Notably, few of them would have labelled their experiences or their 'being' as spiritual.

Having confirmed this, I was then able to move towards an exploration of the general contexts for these experiences, and they were wide indeed. Experiences arose, for example, in nature, during artistic and sporting endeavours, during deep thought or imaginative journeys, in the middle of laughter or other emotionally charged events, and also, in silence and solitude. The contexts reflected the importance of the body as a key hermeneutic and imagination and positive emotions, particularly wonder, as both conduits and expressions of child spirituality.

The children showed that they are actively engaged in theorising about the nature of reality, and that such theorising (often original and independent) matters to them and is chiefly derived from their personal experiences alone.

The children revealed how the senses functioned as multiple gateways to spirituality, through music, movement, sight and even smell. The verb 'to feel' was dominant in their interviews, as they sought to explain where some 'new knowledge' had arisen. Additionally, they often used somatic language that sometimes (and paradoxically) spoke of out-of-body experiences, where they left 'themselves'.

Whilst recounting these times, as we have read, the importance of non-verbal communication during its recollection and my awareness at this time of *my own* 'felt sense' were key. They helped to appreciate more fully and understand the child's story, and were an important valuing of their 'body knowing', rather than their cognitive knowing.[263]

The relevance of strong and positive emotions and feelings was highlighted, whether they were a prefiguring of or following a spiritual experience, or as sense of spirituality. Over half of the children reflected in their conversations radical amazement, wonder or joy that precipitated, accompanied or formed the expression of a spiritual state. Sadly, several of the children expressed, with some resignation, that opportunities for such emotions, particularly joy, had decreased with age and as they took on the mantle of 'adult' responsibilities. And we saw, once again, that descriptions of these experiences were often bracketed with expressions of either embarrassment about their believing them to be significant, or concern lest the listener saw them as odd.

This by now well-known trope of reticence about spiritual experiences is critical. Such experiences formed an important part of the children's sense of who they are (and an echo of the theme of the 2025 UK Children's Mental Health Week), and the memories of these are treasured, remembered and pondered on, sometimes for years. We see the children deny and suppress fundamental parts of themselves lest they be patronised as strange, or at worst, and paradoxically, lest they be deemed as having poor mental health.

A contextual thread

The children's conversations showed that though for some silence as non-sound was important and related to their spirituality or spiritual experiences, for very many others it was not the case, nor was it enjoyed or sought. Yet these children appeared to be accessing an ever-present state that erupted into their daily lives, one that resonated with Ross's comment that silence exists where self-consciousness is suspended, in the by now familiar '*excessus mentis*' – a departure of the mind.[264] We saw a wealth of examples of the loss of such self-consciousness and its positive outcomes, and these were peak, if sometimes perplexing and unsettling, experiences for the children. During this time, many of them were expressing becoming part of an undifferentiated whole. It was a malleable state, full of potential and one in which the children felt, as it were, as if they were returning to themselves, and it was a condition which they sought to re-experience.

This expanded and more nuanced understanding of silence led to a recognition that, in this form, it is an important and frequent category for the instigation, experience and expression of child spirituality. This was not categorised as 'silence' by the children, but it was a highly significant space, an interval, that they entered, usually accidentally, and from which they later emerged bearing fruits of wonder and amazement.

This space and altered state of consciousness fully echoes the concepts of liminality and *communitas* as developed by Victor and Edith Turner. Those so engaged are regarded by Victor Turner as being in an ambiguous state, a neither this nor that; neither here nor there, where the actual gives way to the possible.[265] For some of the children we saw examples of spontaneous, 'unmediated communication' and communion with others, in egalitarian, socially binding events, evoking memorable, often momentous shared essences – non- cognitive events, almost universally, we are told, regarded as sacred or holy by tribal societies.

So, the original hunch that silence was somehow important for children's spirituality was perhaps almost right after all – just not in the way usually conceived. Instead, the concept of liminality provides a hugely expansive embracement within which non-sound or silence might comfortably dwell, yet it is very much greater than these. It provides a coherent and overarching framework for the understanding of child spirituality and is a holistic lens and schema through which it might be identified and understood.[266] This understanding counters its often fragmented analysis, the subject of much recent criticism, and assists in its identification and recognition.[267] It highlights the importance of allowing children to articulate it openly and confidently, with broad societal implications, including for parents, educationalists, psychologists and all those concerned with child well-being. Beyond allowing its simple verbal expression, we (the adults who care about children) might now consider recognising the positive impact that such liminal experiences have for them.

The busyness of children

All but one of the children interviewed, whilst not necessarily expressing a desire for silence or solitude, indicated that their lives were full of commitments – whether school and homework, chores or scheduled activities. Many felt, as Ravi did, that it was necessary to be 'productive' and, for a few, sleep or, for example, waiting for a bus, were their only 'down times'. Nearly all spoke of the pressure of impending examinations, whether GCSEs[268] or termly tests that might determine, in the case of one school, setting arrangements. This was a noteworthy issue, given that the public GCSE examinations were, at the onset of the interview schedules, over three years away. Furthermore, and startlingly, many of the children spoke generally of 'pressure', being 'stressed out', 'worried', and constantly 'busy'. I had to remind myself frequently that these were young people between the ages of twelve and thirteen.

Fulfilling a promise

When, in the early days of the investigation, I sent out information to the school students, I stated in the letter that the results of it 'might be used to help influence those who are responsible for schools and education and also those interested in what young people need in order to develop into happy and fulfilled adults'. I ended it by expressing a hope that the results might help society understand the needs of children of their age.

It is with this implicit commitment in mind that I now address what I believe to be the main truths suggested by these children and how we, with power and influence (unlike they), of admittedly varying levels, might respond to their words:

- They told us that they are spiritual beings, yet they voice this in a different way from adults. They are usually loath to divulge events and states of spirituality to parents or other adults in case they are not taken seriously. They often use the adjective 'weird' to imply that *they* didn't understand what was occurring and perhaps that no one else would either. The word was used as a prophylactic against ridicule, as if to say 'Look, I've already said it was odd!'
- Many spoke of the value of nature, in its myriad forms, in providing a crucible for spiritual experience and showed a correspondingly intense concern, even distress, about its despoliation. A large number of children showed a numinous connection with animal and plant life, landscape, even weather, that points to their concerns going beyond current social and political impetuses. This was not a leap onto an adult ecological bandwagon, but rather they were voicing awe, wonder and joy, expressing a sacralisation of nature that has been lost for 'modern people'.[269]

- They described a very wide range of contexts within which their spirituality arose, only on rare occasions whilst in silence, for which they expressed a range of views. Instead, they entered a space commensurate with the concept of liminal space, and sometimes, and unexpectedly, experiencing *communitas*.

If their spirituality reflects, as we have seen suggested by other researchers, a *natural* disposition, then it is crucial that this is recognised and validated.[270] This runs counter to the suggestion by some who advocate a 'staged model' of spiritual development,[271] that children enter the world, as John Locke suggested, as a *tabula rasa* or blank slate, are morally neutral and develop as a result of the environment alone.[272] Indeed, the liminal state, simple, singular and often transformative, in which the children in this study often rest, points towards *a commonality of the space of spirituality*. This was regarded by Victor Turner, though not attributed by him to children, as 'a fact of everyone's existence'. We should now entertain the view that children, during their experiences, enter and return from the same liminal space *available to all*, though articulated and filtered through a child's perception and vocabulary.

We have seen a number of contexts within which children experienced their spirituality. In presenting them, I am not trying to give the idea that they are, as it were, reproducible triggers for child spirituality, nor, therefore, am I advocating that they be specifically sought or offered to young people. I am only suggesting that they point towards a more generalisable and repeatable set of circumstances that might help our nurturing of this important aspect of their being.

Such circumstances seem to coalesce around the importance of an offering of, or an opportunity for, non-structured time. Within this, a child, without the pressures of schedules or commitments, might be able to enter a mental and or physical space that is not 'everyday' and which allows the child to visit and experience aspects of their spiritual nature currently fettered. The word nurturing is carefully chosen.[273] It does not imply the development of their spirituality, but rather *the nourishing and cherishing of that which already exists.*

This is not without challenges. Much of the spirituality they described was embodied, and supporting the natural arising of this is currently problematic. Researchers in a range of academic fields are expressing concern of the modern pre-eminence in society (both Western and Eastern) accorded to the *visual* body over the *sensual* body.[274] This is illustrated by the often destructive emphasis on self-image and image and body manipulation. When a child is locked onto a form of digital technology, whether as part of schooling, leisure, or in the midst of an ever more loosely termed social activity, they are often separated from others, from their environment and from body awareness. They become observers rather than participants, passive rather than engaged, and certainly separate from the world of nature that *can* act (and *did* for so many of the children involved in this research) as source of wonder and a portal to spiritual experience. When children are engaged in, for example, physical activities, or are in nature or involved in the Arts, or in imaginative endeavour or reverie, they have, at least, an *opportunity* to experience their sensual bodies, perhaps at a deep level.

This suggests that the children need to be given time – if they are to flourish psychologically – to be able to use their imaginations and to engage with the world unconstrained by the mind – as Fuller suggests, 'in the depth of their flesh'.[275] It is the 'pathic knowing' identified by Hyde.[276] It also implies, given that they, too, are entering a space available to all of us, that we listen at times to children with the 'ears of peers', accepting that they may offer original and valuable insights into life. This is why an understanding of the significance of the liminal to children is so important. I suggest that it is not a space they find only on maturity, but one that often brings them great solace in their childhood. To them it is a completely natural shift in awareness, but one that seems (they say) to diminish with the pressures of adult life.

Helping a child who is suffering personally (as evidence given in this book suggests so many are) to become aware of their own spirit, allows them to rise above their own, often painful concerns.[277] Allowing more time – even, but not necessarily, stillness – in the lives of children for the respecting of this, could be hugely beneficial. An educational system and a society that focus on highly paced, highly structured, examinable curriculum content or activities contraindicate this. In contrast, we see the positive impact of spirituality and spiritual experience on many of the children. I have already highlighted the example of Millie, who found meaning and solace in her difficult life of disability, after a numinous experience during her Catholic confirmation. Suddenly making sense of her role in the world, and deeming it an honour to have it, helped her to move forward in her life.[278]

Several of the children were helped after bereavement by a spiritual experience. Christina, for example, grieving after her father's death, and becoming, she said, 'spiritual' during the time following it, found significance and comfort when his favourite song came on the radio, after she had made a plea for contact with him. Such an event took her, as it did Millie, into a sense that we are part of something meaningful, unfathomable – much more than we appear to be. We also read of the empathic Gabriel and Alexander, who both hated to see others' suffering and who gained relief only when they managed to help them in some way. Both boys carried this grieving for the world that they did not articulate to others, and they suffered privately. Similarly, and representative of over a fifth of the children, we read of Megan, who voiced distress at the depredation of the earth, becoming embarrassed about those feelings until she gained affirmation in the interview. As with Millie and Christina, they were all feeling that they were somehow a small part of a greater whole.

To affirm such anguish in children and to allow the expression of such concerns and feelings – all of which are aspects of their spirituality – is a socially necessary imperative, already identified and stressed by others from a range of disciplines,[279] and reiterated and reinforced *here* based on the homogeneity shown in the interviews across regions and schools.

Moreover, the children's stories illuminate both the facilitating qualities (as well as the modes of expression) of the positive emotions of wonder and awe, and *an actual cultivation* of that awe, and also wonder, gratitude and joy would be valuable, spiritually nurturing, gifts for children. It is this awe that can facilitate an opening for change, being 'the emotion of self-transcendence'.[280]

The imagination as a portal for spirituality is also underlined in these extracts, transcending daily experience, shifting a child into a transitional space, unencumbered by 'propositional knowing'.[281] Once again, the often heavily timetabled and circumscribed lifestyles of many of the children in the sample militates against this, as does a delivery model of education that focusses on those subjects (particularly STEM subjects: Science, Technology, Engineering and Mathematics) where imaginative engagement is often foresworn. In this respect, the potential importance of all forms of the Arts as opportunities for spiritual gateways is heavily indicated.

Whether children need silence to support them in their spirituality is an interesting question. The variety of attitudes towards silence as non-sound exhibited by the children, including some outright antipathy, has implications for our understanding of possible means of support (including mindfulness and meditation programmes). There is an urgency for an appreciation of the need for a *variety* of approaches, and by all of us involved with children.

Importantly, this is not a call for a knowledge-based, tick box taught addendum to children's lives, whether at home or at school. Job done. Nor is it a call for frameworks that will help them 'succeed in life',[282] information remembered and repeated. Our children do already *re-member* and they often have sometimes surprising things to tell us ... if we have the time. Failing to find such time to listen and to understand and validate the importance to them of spiritual experience and spirituality, the non-static ever-changing nature of it, and appreciating the way that they are utterly sure about its impact beyond all doubt, may prove a costly societal dereliction. As a returning favour they can point the way for *us*. Whilst psychologist Jorge Ferrer tells us that there exists a truth that transcends the domain of the scientific method,[283] wise twelve-year-old Katarina simply advises us: 'There is a truth in the earth that no one could ever know.'

Appendix 1: Schedule for Semi-Structured Interviews

All these were open-ended, not all were asked, and the emphasis was on a child's access to silence and any expressions of their spirituality.

Interview 1

A. *General questions and requests to put participants at ease (inter alia):*
   - Please describe yourself and your personality (prompts given). What is your average day like?
   - Please describe your use of social media/IT/digital technology.

B. *Questions triggered by questionnaire responses*

   How often do you experience silence or solitude? (explanation sometimes needed)

   What was this like? Did you enjoy the experience? What does the silence mean to you?

   Are you able to find this generally in your life? Why? Why not?

   Do you ever pray or meditate?

   Do you believe in a higher being or force? Have you ever had an experience that you might describe as religious or spiritual? If so, are you able to describe it? What was this like?

C. Please try to complete these sentences:

   I think what really matters in life is...

   I feel I am going beyond everyday things/going into another world when I...

   I believe the world exists because...

   I have had moments of peak happiness when...

Interview 2

General questions about the offered photo of a child in nature and their feelings about this.

A. If you were offered the chance to sit quietly by yourself each day, how would you feel? Is it scary for you? What is stopping this happening?
B. Thinking about any meaning or purpose to life – do you think there is one?
C. (Reprise) Have you ever had a religious or spiritual experience? Do any of your previous 'special' experiences impact on you even now What did you learn from them/if any, did it happen when alone?
D. Have you ever experienced anything you would describe as 'magic' or that could not be explained?
E. Have you ever been totally absorbed in something so that you felt different and lost yourself? What did it feel like?
F. When in connection with others, do you lose yourself, or are you still there?
G. How do you feel in nature?
H. Have you ever felt that you have had an unusual experience when doing something that you were not normally allowed to do? Or in music, dance, sport, singing etc.?
I. Have you ever had a wonderful, magical experience when playing games? (order/disorder)
J. (Where appropriate and in respect of paradox) Have you ever felt that something didn't make sense?

Appendix 2: Liminality and *Communitas*. Aspects of Identification/Coding

1.	Apodicticity/sense of absolute certainty	E. and V. Turner (2011)
2.	Paradox, perplexing, unsettling, affective. A sense of both/and not either or	Boyce-Tillman (2009); E. Turner (2012); V. Turner (1974,1992); Thomasson (2013)
3.	Loss of sense of time. The eternal now/unbounded time	V. Turner (1974b, 1982, 2007); Szakolczai (2009)
4.	Tripartite nature of experience	V. Turner (1974, 1992)
5.	Magical effect/enchantment	V. Turner (2007, 1979b)
6.	Rearrangement of thought after the experience	V. Turner (1974b, 1982, 2007)
7.	Use of symbols and metaphors to describe the experience	V. Turner (1992, 1974b. 1979b, 2007)
8.	Loss of self/ego and ourselves as subject	Boyce-Tillman (2009); Szakolczai (2009); V. Turner (1974a, 1992); Ross (2018)
9.	A dissolution of normative structures/a fructile chaos/ danger and new possibilities	Boyce-Tillman (2016); Payne (2001); E. Turner (2006); V. Turner (1974b, 1982,1986); Thomassen (2013)
10.	The sacred power of the weak and humble	V. Turner (2007, 1979b,)

11.	Ludic component; free from responsibilities and out of everyday world	Boyce-Tillman (2009, 2016); Iijima (1987); V. Turner (1982, 1992, 1974a, 2007)
12.	*Via negativa*/subjunctive mode	V. Turner (1982, 1992, 2007))
13.	Moral contradiction/ transgressive acts	Boyce-Tillman (2016); V. Turner (1982, 1992); van Gennep (1960)
14.	Liminal creativity	V. Turner (1992)
15.	Tuning into nature/land and animals	Neitz and Spickard (1990)
16.	Transformation on return/ reaggregation	Boyce-Tillman (2016); Szakolczai (2009); Thomassen (2013); V. Turner (1992)
17.	Liminality during the interview	Boyce-Tillman (2009)
18.	Liminality and joy	Boyce-Tillman (2016); V. Turner (2012)
19.	Laughter as precipitant	E. Turner (2012); V. Turner (1982, 2007)
20.	Awe when in places in everyday use	Iijima (1987)
21.	Music/art/sports as precipitants	Iannaccone (2013); Boyce-Tillman (2009, 2016); Neitz and Spickard (1990); E. Turner (2012); V. Turner (1992)
22.	The imagination leading to a liminal experience	Boyce-Tillman (2009)

23.	Rites of incorporation	Van Gennep (1960)
24.	Emergence of integral person from multiple personae	E. and V. Turner (2011)
25.	A special kind of freedom acquired. Untouchable/ dangerous	Boyce-Tillman (2009); V. Turner (1974a and 1974b)
26.	A playing with elements of the familiar to defamiliarize/ disorderliness	V. Turner (1982, 1974a))
27.	Forms of extensive flow	V. Turner (1982)
28.	Questioning of own senses	Thomassen (2013)
	Communitas Extensions	
29.	Experience of unity. I-thou. Bonding and egalitarianism. The essential 'we'	V. Turner (1974b, 1982, 1992, 2007)
30.	*Communitas* for a solitary person	V. Turner (1974b)
31.	Commensality (shared food)	E. Turner (2012); V. Turner (1974b)
32.	Unconditional love	E. Turner (2006)
33.	*Communitas* of disaster/ deculturalisation	E. Turner (2012); V. Turner (1982)
34.	*Communitas* with land	E. Turner (2012)

Endnotes

Preface

1. Turner, E. (2006)

Chapter 1

2. Julian of Norwich was an English anchoress and Christian mystic of the Middle Ages, remembered particularly for saying after several religious revelations 'All shall be well, and all shall be well, and all manner of things shall be well'. Over 200 'loose umbrella groups', secular and denominational gather, usually monthly, throughout the UK to hold sessions of silent contemplation and 'in her name'.
3. The Varkey foundation based in London is a not-for-profit organisation established to improve the standards of education for underprivileged children throughout the world.
4. The National Society for the Prevention of Cruelty to Children, established in London in 1884. https://www.nspcc.org.uk/keeping-children-safe/childrens-mental-health https://www.actionforchildren.org.uk/blog/supporting-children-through-mental-health-struggles
5. See: https://www.england.nhs.uk/2023/11/one-in-five-children-and-young-people-had-a-probable-mental-disorder-in-2023
6. *Hardwired to Connect* (2010).
7. Seden, J. (1998).
8. Fisher, J. (2009a); See also: Ivtzan *et al* (2013).
9. Hay, D. and Nye, R. (2006) [1998].
10. Scales, P. *et al* (2014).
11. Piaget, J. (1926) and Wilber, K. (2007).

12. Robinson, E. (1977).
13. Coles, R. (1977).
14. Hyde, B. (2008a).
15. See for example: Adams, K. (2010); Coles (1977); Erricker, C. *et al*, (1997); Hay and Nye (2006); Tamminen, K. (1994).
16. OCR 2017. OCR is one of the UK national examining bodies that set examination papers and produce the relevant curriculum. Level 3 is equivalent to an Advanced level examination, normally taken by school students at the age of 18 in the UK.
17. Fuller, R. (2001).
18. Puchalski, C. *et al* (2009).
19. Rankin, M. (2008).
20. Eaude, T. (2003).
21. Champagne, E. (2003)
22. Eaude, T. (2003, 2022).

Chapter 2

23. Elkind, D. and Elkind, S. (1962); Singleton, A. *et al* (2004); Tamminem, K. (1994).
24. Bosacki, S. and Ota, C. (2000); Coles, R. (1977); Hay, D. and Nye, R. (2006); Hyde, B. (2008a and 2008b, 2010); Lipscombe, A. and Gersch, I. (2012); Moriarty, M. (2011).
25. Cheek, J. and Krasnoperova, E. (1999); Zimbardo, P. (1977).
26. Some may, for example, have suffered a recent bereavement or be particularly shy. I needed to know this in advance so that I could make sure not to cause distress unwittingly.
27. Ezzy, D. (2002); Kozol, J. (2000); Pring, R. (2001); Risser, J. (1997).
28. Holder, M. *et al* (2010).
29. Houskamp, B. *et al* (2004).
30. Bussing, A. *et al* (2010).
31. Carter, N. *et al* (2014); Leech, N. and Onwuegbuzie, A. (2007); Terrell, S. (2011).

32. Coles and Hay and Nye all valued this method in their research with children, allowing children to convey meaning without words.
33. Bussing, A. *et al* (2010).
34. Lovelock, P. and Adams, K. (2017); Scott, D. (2004), Tisdall, E. *et al* (2010).
35. DiCicco-Bloom and Crabtree, B. (2006); Ratcliff, D. and Nye, R. (2006); Schlarb, C. (2007).
36. Ezzy, D. (2002); Farmer, L. (1992); Fielding, N. and Thomas, H. (2008); Holloway, I. and Wheeler, S. (2010); Houskamp, B. *et al* (2004); Lipscomb, A. and Gersch, I. (2012); Lovelock, P. and Adams, K. (2017); Moore, K. *et al* (2016).
37. See Appendix 1.
38. DiCicco-Bloom, B. and Crabtree, B. (2006); Rapley, T. (2001).
39. Hay, D. and Nye, R. (2006); Hyde, B. (2008a).
40. Champagne, E. (2003); Farmer, L. (1992); Hay, D. and Nye, R. (2006).
41. Best, R. (2011); van Cappellen, O. *et al* (2013); Fuller, R. (2007); Haidt, J. (2003); Nussbaum, M. (2008); Scheindlin, L. (2003); Vaillant, G. (2008a).
42. Adams, D. and Beauchamp, G. (2019); Boyce-Tillman, J. (2009); Broadbent, J. (2004); Csikszentmihalyi, M. (2002).
43. Adams, K. *et al* (2008); Best, R. (2011); Hyde, B. (2008a); Pearmain, R. (2007); Trousdale, A. (2013).
44. The 'Hardy Question', as it is now known, was posed by marine biologist Alister Hardy in 1969 to facilitate research into spirituality in the United Kingdom. Participants were asked to respond in writing to the question 'have you ever been aware or influenced by a presence or power, whether you call it God or not, which is different from your everyday self'. Over 6,600 responses are held in the Alister Hardy archives at the University of Wales, Trinity St. David, Lampeter.

45. Petitmengin, C. (2014).
46. Ogden, T. (2004).
47. Gadamer, H-G. (2013) A *Horizontverschmelzung*: giving the beautiful image of a melding or melting of perspectives.
48. Winnicott, D. and Winnicott, D.W. (1960).
49. Recognisable to researchers as hermeneutical phenomenology.
50. The identification and classifications of child spirituality largely started towards the end of the twentieth century and continued across the turn of the millennium. Key figures contributing to this particular work include: Adams, K. (2009, 2010, 2017, 2022); Armstrong, T. (1984); Best, R. (2011); Burrows, L. (2006, 2009, 2014); Champagne, E. (2003); Coles, R. (1977); de Souza, M. (2009, 2014); Eaude, T. (2003, 2008); Erricker, C. *et al* (1997); Farmer, L. (1992); Hart, T. (2003); Hay, D. and Nye, R. (2006); Hyde, B. (2008a and 2008b); Lipscomb, A. and Gersch, I. (2012); Moriarty, M. (2011); Pargament, K. (2011); Ratcliff, D. and Nye, R. (2006); Roehlkepartain, E. *et al* (2006); Schlarb, C. (2007); Scott, D. (2004); Tamminen, K. (1994); Zohar, D. and Marshall, I. (2001).
51. Bosacki, S. and Ota, C. (2000); Champagne, E. (2003); Eaude, T. (2003); Fuller, R. (2007); Hay, D. and Nye, R. (2006); Hyde, B. (2008a, 2011); Miller, L. (2015); Moriarty, M. (2011); Scheindlin, L. (2003); Scott, D. (2004); Stoyles, G. *et al* (2012); Trousdale, A. (2013).
52. As a visual learner I found such colour coding and highlighting indispensable, and efficient timewise.
53. This refers to deriving a code or heading from the data/information itself. In this case I was able to find what I deemed to be new types of spirituality and to search for these accordingly across all the interviews.
54. See Bryman, A. (2012); Corbin, J. and Strauss, A. (1990) and Ezzy, D. (2002) for definitions of axial coding and its uses.

In short, axial codes are larger themes that might emerge from data. They are particularly relevant to this piece of research.

55. The concepts of liminality and its partner *communitas* are thoroughly discussed in Chapter 8.
56. Grounded theory is an inductive approach which seeks to draw theory from data, rather than setting off with a hypothesis. See: Bryman, A. (2012); Ezzy, D. (2002); Glaser, B. and Strauss, A. (2017); Hodgkinson, P. (2008).
57. Harvey, G. (2003).
58. Hyde, B. (2011).
59. This 'mutual benefit' has been rightly emphasised by a range of researchers: Fahie, D. (2014); Head, G. (2020); Henderson, K. and Esposito, J. (2017); Kumashiro, K. (2014).

Chapter 3

60. National Aeronautics and Space Administration, 2003.
61. *The Chambers Dictionary* (1998).
62. *Cambridge Dictionary* (2018).
63. Picard, M. (2006).
64. Ross, M. (2014).
65. Sciacca, F. (1957).
66. Dauenhauer, B. (1979, 1980, 1983).
67. Fiumara, G. (1996).
68. Advices and Queries, 2008. This is the main guide to Quaker practice and derives from early epistles as well as current thinking.
69. This underlines the eschewal of all dogma, and the belief that the 'the deeper realities of our faith are beyond precise verbal formulation'.
70. In 2022.
71. Not all the children in these schools come from Quaker households.
72. Quaker Education in the UK and Ireland, 2020.

73. Ambler, R. (2013).
74. Brent Bill, J. (2016).
75. Amongst many other approaches, Steiner also set much store on artistic movement known as *eurythmy* which was an artistic kinaesthetic expression and a making of speech visible through gestures in a therapeutic harmonious whole. This is practised in all Waldorf schools.
76. Jarvis, P. *et al* (2017); Ulrich, H. (2014).
77. Steiner, R. (1994) [1947].
78. Harwood, A. (1992) [1958].
79. Steiner, R. (1988) [1923].
80. Steiner, R. (2012) [1923].
81. Petrash, J. (2014).
82. Steiner, R. (1994).
83. Montessori disliked any attribution of the word 'method' attached to her work, preferring that it was thought of as a 'help to life', that being much broader and deeper.
84. Montessori, M. (1949).
85. Standing, E. (1998).
86. Though Montessori does not define 'soul' in her work, her understanding of the term would appear to derive from a Christian understanding, as evident, for instance, in her description of the birth of a child: 'when the spirit enclosed in flesh comes to live in the world'. Montessori, M. (1966).
87. Standing, E. (1998).
88. Observing this at a Montessori school in Henley in Arden was an affecting experience as it was evident that the children found this both a fun and an earnest event, as well as having the effect of slowing down energy levels, the better to facilitate learning.
89. Montessori, M. (2014) [1912].
90. Bone, J. *et al* (2007).
91. The detrimental social and intellectual impact of auditory overload is well documented: Wohlwill, J. and Heft, H.

(2017); Cohen, S. *et al* (1988) cited by Lillard, A. (2005), and the contribution to improved cognitive function of silence or at least a *stimulus shelter*, similarly so – Wachs, T. (1986, 1992).

92. Haskins, C. (2011).
93. Standing, E. (1998).
94. This was particularly underlined during a personal conversation with musicologist and theologian June Boyce-Tillman in 2018 and, as will be seen, was strongly corroborated by the outcomes of the questionnaires and the interviews.
95. Hart, T. (2003).
96. Hyde, B. (2008a).
97. Stern, J. (2001) This term is related to Eliade's 'standing within'.
98. Thun, T. (1964).
99. Yust, K-M. (2008).
100. Taplin, M. (2011) Her work took place in 62 primary schools with no standard procedures and amongst teachers who determined the format of the silence, and with large groups of up to 60 children.
101. Kessler, R. (2000). The mission of the Passageways Institute in Boulder, US, is to motivate, prepare and support educators to implement its proven model for nurturing the inner lives of its students and teachers.
102. We will read extensive, moving, examples of this in future chapters. Elkind, D. (2001) [1981].
103. Australia: Burrows, L. (2009); Ireland: Keating, N. (2016); UK: de Kuyken, W. *et al* (2021).

Chapter 4

104. Because nearly every child interviewed had something important to contribute to this work (one was inhibited by language problems), I have tried to include as many of their

voices as possible. On some occasions I have mentioned their school type by way of interesting extra information. Sometimes this has been omitted, where it might lead to identification. Their voices are faithfully transcribed, even when this leads to repetition. At times bracketed ellipses indicate a merging of sentences. Pseudonyms have been used and place names changed.

105. Miller, L. (2015).
106. Vaillant, G. (2008).
107. Miller, L. (2015).
108. This is a familiar trope and can be seen, for example, in the work of Adams, K. (2009, 2010); Best, R. (2011); Champagne, E. (2003), Hay, D. and Nye, R. (2006); Hyde, B. (2008b); Lipscomb, A. and Gersch, I. (2012); Miller, L. (2015); Moriarty, M. (2011); Scott, D. (2004).
109. Hyde, B. (2008a).
110. Such spiritual questing and meaning making has been referred to by: Bosacki, S and Ota, C. (2000); Champagne, E. (2003); Eaude, T. (2003, 2008); Hay, D. and Nye, R. (2006); Hyde, B. (2008a); Moriarty, M. (2011); Scott, D. (2004).
111. For further examples of this and amongst others, see: Adams, K. (2010); Haidt, J. (2003); Fuller, R. (2007); Nussbaum, M. (2001).
112. Foster, R. and Armstrong, S. (2017) also found such descriptions.
113. Bosacki, S. and Ota, C. (2000); Bussing, A. *et al* (2010); Eaude, T. (2003, 2008); Hart, T. (2003); Moriarty, M. (2011).
114. Lipscomb, A. and Gersch, I. (2012); Miller, L. (2015).
115. Hyde, B. (2005).
116. Hay, D. and Nye, R. (2006); Bosacki, S. and Ota, C. (2000).
117. Vaillant, G. (2008a).
118. Hyde, B. (2008a).

119. For those unfamiliar with such vocabulary, 'corny' here means mawkishly sentimental.
120. Champagne, E. (2003); Cole, R. (1977); Hay, D. and Nye, R. (2006); Miller, L. (2015); Lipscomb, A. and Gersch, I. (2012) who said it was a 'core spiritual concept'.
121. Best, R. (2011); Coles, R. (1977).
122. See Ephesians 4:15 and also the Buddhist linking of truth and love, which are deemed to be deeply intertwined.
123. Miller, L. (2015).
124. Here we see examples of sympathy *symhedonia* where joy is taken in the happiness of others. It is during such an emotion that the self may be freed from the self, in a form of spirituality that draws others in and gives immeasurable pleasure to the giver. This reflects the deep psychobiological basis for altruism and love, posited by a wide range of researchers – neuroscientists, psychiatrists and educationalists, amongst others: Champagne, E. (2015); de Souza, M. (2014); Hyde, B. (2008a and b); Ramachandran, V. (2011); Vaillant, G. (2008a). It is also an example of 'relational consciousness', identified by Hay and Nye, 2006.
125. Ramachandran, V. (2011).
126. Hyde, B. (2008a); de Souza, M. (2014); Markstrom, C. *et al* (2010); McCreery, E. (2001); Schein, D. (2014); Watson, P. *et al* (1984).
127. De Souza, M. (2014); Vaillant, G. (2008b).
128. Hay, D. and Nye, R. (2006).
129. Miller, L. (2015).
130. Hossein Nasr, S. (1997).
131. Coles, R. (1977).
132. Fuller, R. (2001); Hay, D. and Nye, R. (2006).
133. Champagne, E. (2003).
134. Puchalski, C. *et al* (2009).

135. Bussing *et al* noted this in 2010. Berryman, J. (2013) suggested that this can be a sacred time and space.
136. Donaldson, M. (1993) refers to this as the 'point mode', whereas Hay and Nye describe it as the focussed awareness of the 'here and now'. Hyde (2008a) suggests that such a mode diminishes by adolescence – a decline noted by Gracie herself.
137. Referenced in Hossein Nasr, S. (1997).
138. Otto, R. (1958).
139. Moriarty, M. (2011).
140. Eaude sees this as a 'universal search for meaning' (2008), whereas Bosacki and Ota (2000) preferred to designate it the 'making sense of ourselves in the universe'. Bosacki and Ota confirmed (as did I) that children were keen to discuss existential and ontological issues. Bussing, de Souza, Hart, Hay and Nye, Hyde, Lipscomb and Gersch, Scott, Zohar and Marshall, similarly so.
141. Csikszentmihalyi (1990, 2002) defines flow as a state in which people are so involved in an activity that nothing else seems to matter. The experience is so enjoyable that people will continue to do it, even at great cost, for the sheer sake of doing it.
142. Boyce-Tillman, J. (2016); Hay, D. and Nye, R. (2006); Neitz, M. and Spickard, J.(1990); Turner, V. (1974a, 1992); Turner, E. (2012).
143. Moriarty, M. (2013).
144. Trousdale, A. (2013).
145. You will read much more about the nuances around the concept of flow in future chapters.
146. Vaillant, G. (2008a and 2008b).
147. Several researchers have noted this, including Bosacki, S. and Ota, C. (2000); Bussing, A. *et al*, (2010); Champagne, E. (2003); de Souza, M. (2014); Markstrom, C. *et al* (2010); Saroglou, V. *et al* (2005); Watson, P. *et al* (1984).
148. See also Hyde, B. *et al* (2013).

149. Hay and Nye suggested that children's individual personalities were *the* key determinant of their experiences.

Chapter 5

150. Fuller, R. (2006); Nussbaum, M. (2001).
151. Fuller, R. (2006).
152. Haidt, J. (2006) tells us that the emotion of wonder is a self-transcendent emotion prompting caring about others and catalysing change. He adds that it is always associated with 'fear and dread in the face of gigantic power'.
153. Fuller calls this an 'engagement with what lies beyond the limits of rational comprehension'.
154. Csikszentmihalyi, M. (2002).
155. Fuller, R. (2001).
156. William James (1909/1977) refers to possibilities in all of us that take our breath away and show us a world wider than either physics or 'philistine ethics' can imagine.
157. Heschel (1986) called this 'the hidden in the apparent'. Philosopher Dauenhauer (1980) identified such a silence as 'silence of the to-be-said' and an opening for hope, a yielding before a power that is beyond one's control.
158. Such fruits of positive emotions have been noted by a range of researchers: See Hyde, B. (2008a and 2008b); Nussbaum, M. (2008); Torevell, D. (2000); Watson, J. (2013a and 2013b).
159. States such as these have been identified by a very wide range of researchers including Adams, K. and Beauchamp, G. (2019); Best, R. (2011); Boyce-Tillman, J. (2009); Csikszentmihalyi, M. (1975a and 1975b); Ferrer, J. (2002); Hyde, B. (2008a); Torevell, D. (2000), Winston, J. (2003).
160. Feuerbach, L. (1967) [1851].
161. Adams comments that a child's imagination is 'not deserving of mistrust' (2010). See also Boyce-Tillman, J. (2016); Champagne, E. (2003); Hay, D. and Nye, R. (2006); Irwin, S. (2008); Kessler, R. (2000).

162. Philosopher Jorge Ferrer accords with Boyce-Tillman suggesting that imagination enables us to enter 'the isthmus between physical and spiritual realms'. Ideas of cocreation are central to his work. See: Ferrer, (2002, 2008, 2009).
163. Maslow, A. (1964).
164. Hyde, (2008b) regards this a key component of child spirituality. Hay and Nye (2006) named this 'reflective consciousness' and both Trousdale (2013) and Hart (2003) identified that sudden insights can arise from such transcendence.
165. Gendlin, E. (1981,1997).
166. Such near-death experiences are usually associated with adults, though several researchers into child spirituality note that they also occur in children: Adams, K. (2010); Fenwick, P. and E. (1996); Moody, R. (1998); Sartori, P. (2014) amongst others.
167. Todres, L. (2011) refers to this as a mystery, not reduced to thought.

Chapter 6

168. Kessler, R. (2000).
169. Elkind, D. (2001).

Chapter 7

170. Ross, M. (2014, 2018).
171. Williams, R. (2004).
172. Dauenhauer, B. (1979, 1980); Fiumara, G. (1996); Sciacca, F. (1957).
173. Berryman, J. (2006); Hart, T. (2003); Muldoon, M. (1996); Lees, H. (2012).
174. Berryman, J. (2013); Hart, T. (2003, 2008); Hyde, B. (2008a and 2008b, 2010); Keating, N. (2016); Kessler, R. (2000); Taplin, M. (2011); Zajonc, A. (2006).
175. Ross, M. (2014).

176. Recent meta-analysis of mindfulness programmes in 66 trials in the UK, involving 20,138 young people, suggests that enthusiasm for such programmes for youth has 'arguably run ahead of evidence' with inconclusive outcomes. See Dunning, D. *et al* (2022). Compare the research of De Kuyken *et al* (2021) in Chapter 3 that suggested a more positive impact.
177. Ross, M. (2014).
178. The fourth-century Christian monk Evagrius of Ponticus stressed that the goal of those seeking spirituality should be a relatively permanent state of deep calm of imperturbability or *apatheia*. For him this was a gift of healing from God.
179. Strawser, M. (2006).
180. Ross, M. (2014).
181. See Ross, M. (2014); Williams, R. (2004). Both writers emphasise the key role of the imagination and music in spiritual life.
182. Ross, M. (2014).
183. Berryman, J. (2013).
184. Weil, S. (1987).
185. There is a vast hinterland of work in respect of such active listening. Beyond those examples already given a further selection includes Ferrer, J. (2018); Fiumara, G. (1996); Lillard, A. (2005, 2011); Montessori, M. (2004, 2014) [1948]; Religious Society of Friends, (2017); Steiner, R. (1994, 2012); Strawser, M. (2006).
186. There was no interview-specific reason why these interviews were more lucid and intense than those from other schools: the weather and times were varied and there was a heatwave during one session making conditions for concentration less favourable than usual. The range of children here was similar to those from other schools – a mixture of the very willing and those who needed greater affirmation or encouragement. The children here,

though, did not wear uniform, and some came into the second session with faces brightly painted with glitter (a 'class craze') and in casual clothing suitable for outdoor activities. They seemed comfortable talking to adults. The class teacher (who was my link with the school) explained that in Waldorf schools the children are assigned the same class teacher from their early years up until about 14 years of age in order to provide continuity and to facilitate a deep mutual understanding and relationship between the adult in charge and the child.

187. On one occasion after I had missed a visit due to my illness, the whole class, under the guidance of their teacher (and my contact at the school), prayed for my well-being.
188. Ross, M. (2014).
189. Wood, M. and Tribe, R. (2016).
190. Lees (2012) refers to this as an 'inner realisation upon which a person might stumble'.

Chapter 8

191. Van Gennep, A. (1960/1909); Turner, E. (2006, 2009, 2012); Turner, V. (1974a and1974b, 1977,1979a and 1979b,1982, 1996, 1992, 2007).
192. Van Gennep, A. (1960) [1909]; Turner, E. (2006, 2009); Turner, V. 1974a and 1974b, 1977, 1979a and 1979b, 1982, 1986, 1992, 2007.
193. Thomassen, B. (2018).
194. Szakolczai, A. (2009).
195. Van Gennep, A. (1960) [1909].
196. Amongst many examples in his 1909 work, *The Rites of Passage,* van Gennep uses the Kunai tribe of South-East Australia as an exemplar of such a separation. A young boy (at around puberty) is taken from his mother, sometimes forcibly, into the bush and in seclusion. This symbolises

a complete break with his past. The child is considered 'dead' to be reborn as a man. He is then, during a liminal or transitional period, instructed in tribal law and lore. Only after this is he reintegrated into society following a religious ceremony.

197. Turner, V. (1982).
198. Edith Turner also suggested that the sick are also in a liminal state.
199. Turner, 2007:96.
200. Ferrer, J. (2008).
201. Turner, V. (1982).
202. Burridge, K. (1979).
203. Turner, V. (2011,1979).
204. Turner, V. (1974,1986,1973).
205. *Via Negativa* implies a focussing on what God is *not*, rather than what God *is*, the better to present what is essentially beyond direct description.
206. Turner, E. (2006).
207. Turner, V. (1992).
208. Turner, V. (1992, 1974).
209. Though the importance of the arts, sports and the imagination cannot be ignored as precipitants of liminal experience, I am reminded here of a mathematics examination in which I became utterly transported and shocked to be so (despite my fear and dislike of the subject at the time) and leaving myself entirely – and remembered for a lifetime.
210. Boyce-Tillman, J. (2009).
211. Turner, E. (2007).
212. *We shape clay into a pot, but it is the emptiness inside that holds whatever we want*. Lao Tzu (sixth century BCE).
213. Turner, E. (2007).
214. Turner, E. (2012).

215. The nature of this 'religious' language may be explained by the fact that both Turners converted to Catholicism later in life.
216. See Appendix 2.
217. Turner, V. (1992).
218. Turner, V. (2007).
219. Turner, V. (1974a).
220. Iijima, Y. (1987); Turner, V. (1992,1979b).
221. Turner, E. and Turner, V. (2011).
222. Setting is the separation of children, deemed to be of similar academic ability, into teaching groups or classes.
223. This is redolent of Zen Buddhism's 'breaking the thinking mind' during an unsolvable enigma.
224. Turner, V. (1992,1974b).
225. Thomassen, B. (2013); Szakolczai, A. (2009).
226. Turner, V. (1992).
227. Turner, E. (2012).
228. Turner, V. (1992) quoting the Bible (John 3:8 *KJV*).
229. Turner, V. (1992).
230. Buber, M. (2002) [1947].
231. Turner, V. (2007).
232. This is a basic concept in Hinduism from the Sanskrit 'self' or 'breath' referring to the universal self and the core of the personality that on death transmigrates to a new life or attains release from the bonds of existence. Victor Turner discusses this convincingly (1974).
233. Turner, E. (2007).
234. Interestingly, child spirituality researcher Elaine Champagne, when discussing the various modes of their spirituality, spoke of an 'existential mode' which relates to a sense of communion, in the theological sense (2003). 'Communion' as translated in the King James version of the Bible derives from the Greek *koinonia*: communion and a participative sharing in a common religious commitment

and spiritual community. Furthermore, Victor Turner identifies three types of *communitas*: spontaneous/existential; normative (for example, in religious communities); ideological where it is used as a 'utopian blueprint'. Obviously this book is focussing on the first of these.

235. Turner, V. (2006).
236. Boyce-Tillman, J. (2009). Adams, K. and Beauchamp, G. (2019) also clearly underline the *impact* of music on children's spirituality.
237. Turner, V. (1982,1977).
238. This is an esoteric knowledge of spiritual truth, held by the ancient Gnostics to be essential to salvation. Merriam Webster.
239. Turner, V. (1992).
240. Thomassen, B. (2018) in particular advises us of this, but it has not been ignored by others exploring liminality and communitas: Szakolczai, A. (2009); Turnbull, C. (1988) and Victor Turner, V. (1974,1982).
241. Turner, V. (1982, 2007) and Turner, E. (2012).
242. Boyce-Tillman, J. (2009).
243. Szakolczai, A. (2009); Ross, M. (2014). Ross terms this the *cor ad cor loquitur* where the heart speaks to the heart.
244. Turner, E. (2012).
245. Payne, F. (2001).
246. Turner, V. (1979a).
247. Iannacone, A. (2013).
248. Turner, E. (2012).
249. Csikszentmihalyi, M. (1975a and 1975b).
250. A historic analysis of the use of oil in the Catholic church by Austin suggests the importance of the biblical references to Jesus being the 'anointed one'. There is in oil, he says, a sense of cleansing, renewal and change. Austin, G. (2005).
251. Turner, E. and Turner, V. (2011).

252. Turner, V. (1992); Clarke, I. (2008).
253. Boyce-Tillman discusses such a state very clearly (2009).
254. Ferrer, J. (2002, 2008, 2009).

Chapter 9

255. *Urgent Referrals of Children in Mental Health Crisis.* https://www.theguardian.com>society.2025.jan
256. Place2be is a UK children's mental health charity established at the end of the twentieth century. They provide support on schools to pupils and their families.
257. *Children and Young People Statistics.* mental health.org.uk
258. In Australia, half of all adult mental health challenges emerge before the age of 14 and more than 50% of children experiencing mental health challenges are not receiving professional help. See https://www.mentalhealthcommission.gov.au/projects/childrens-strategy
259. Available at: https://www.healthdirect.gov.au/kids-mental-health
260. Available at: https://www.cdc.gov/yrbs/dstr/pdf/YRBS-2023-Data-Summary-Trend-Report.pdf
261. Available at: https://weekly:chinacdc.cn/fileC
262. For example: Adams, A. (2009); Adams, K. *et al,* 2008; Champagne, E. (2003); Eaude, T. (2003, 2009); Hay, D. and Nye, R. (2006); Hyde, B. (2008a and 2008b); Moriarty, M. (2011); Nye, R. (2009).
263. Berryman (2006) stresses the importance of adult respect for the spiritual *naivete* of children. Noticing and valorising these extra non-verbal contributions might assist in this.
264. Ross, M. (2014).
265. Turner, V. (1974b).
266. Liminality has not hitherto been attributed to or recognised as a *general* aspect of child spirituality. Some researchers have referenced the concept as being of relevance, but only

confined to specific contexts such as theatre, music-making or listening to music. Adams, K. and Beauchamp, G. (2019); Boyce-Tillman, J. (2009, 2016, 2018); Nortje, E. and van der Merwe, L. (2006); Turnbull, C.(1988).

267. Hyde, B. *et al* (2013); Moriarty, M. (2011).
268. A range of public examinations in the UK usually taken by 15–16-year-olds.
269. Hossein Nasr, S. (1997).
270. Many eastern traditions hold that children come into life with innate knowledge, which may reflect previous existences, and that experiences of going beyond the self can, and do, exist among children. E.g. Hinduism, Buddhism, Sikhism. See Armstrong, T. (1984).
271. As expounded, for example, by transpersonal psychologist Ken Wilber (2007) who suggested that transpersonal experiences are experienced only by very few children.
272. Locke, J. (2007) [1689].
273. Brendan Hyde notably chooses this word when he speaks of the support we might give to children in this respect. Its etymology from Latin *nutrire* has a horticultural resonance with an implication of preserving and looking after.
274. Carlson Jones, D. (2004); Morris, R. (2001); Rodgers, R. *et al* (2020).
275. Fuller, R. (2008).
276. Hyde, B. (2018, 2021) Pathic knowing is a 'non-cognitive knowing emanating from the body'.
277. See Stoyles, G. *et al* (2012) and their advocacy of this support.
278. See Hyde 2008a and his views on the importance of enabling children to find their place.
279. To note a few: Bone, J. *et al* (2007); Fisher, J. (2009); Harper, A. and Pargament, K. (2015); Hay, D. and Nye, R. (2006); Koenig, H. (2009a and 2009b); Pargament, K. (2011); Seden, J. (1998).

280. Haidt, J. (2003).
281. Adams, K. (2010); Boyce-Tillman, J. (2016); Champagne, E. (2003); Hay, D. and Nye, R. (2006); Irwin, S. (2008); Kessler, R. (2000); Johnson, M. (1990).
282. Following research into the Religious Education Curriculum in England in 2021, Ofsted refers to a curriculum that is designed 'to give learners the *knowledge* that they need to succeed in life'.They then suggest strategies for remembering that curriculum in the long term. Ofsted 2021.
283. Ferrer, J. (2002) referencing Gadamer and hermeneutics.

References

Adams, D. and Beauchamp, G. (2019) Spiritual Moments Making Music in Nature. A Study Exploring the Experiences of Children Making Music Outdoors, Surrounded by Nature. *The International Journal of Children's Spirituality (IJCS)*, 24, (3), 260–275.

Adams, K. (2009) The Rise of the Children's Voice; the Silencing of the Spiritual Voice. *Journal of Beliefs and Values*, 30, (2), 113–122. Available at: https://doi.org/10.1080/13617670903174991

(2010) *Unseen Worlds: Looking Through the Lens of Childhood.* London and Philadelphia: Jessica Kingsley Publishers.

(2017) The Concept of the Child Through a Spiritual Lens: Implications for Interdisciplinary Approaches and Religious Education. *Journal of Religious Education,65*, 81–93.

(2022) Religious Education, Children's Spirituality and the Problems of Academic Silos. *Journal of Religious Education, 70*, (2), 217–222.

Adams, K., Hyde, B. and Woolley, R. (2008) *The Spiritual Dimension of Childhood*. London and Philadelphia: Jessica Kingsley Publishers.

Advices and Queries, The Yearly Meeting of the Religious Society of Friends (Quakers) in Britain (2008). London: The Society of Friends.

Ambler, R. (2013) *The Quaker Way – A Rediscovery*. Winchester, Washington: Christian Alternative.

Armstrong, T. (1984) Transpersonal Experience in Childhood. *The Journal of Transpersonal Theory*, 16, (2), 207–230. Available at: http://citeseerx.ist.psu.edu/viewdoc/download?doi=10.1.1.472.1435&rep=rep1&type=pdf

Austin, G. (2005) *Anointing with the Spirit: The Rite of Confirmation. The Use of Oil and Chrism*. 2nd edition. Minnesota: Collegeville Press.

Berryman, J. (2006) Silence Is Stranger Than It Used to Be: Teaching Silence and The Future of Mankind. *Religious Education*, 94, (3), 256–272. Available at: DOI: 10.1080/0034408990940302

(2013) *The Search for a Theology of Childhood*. (ed. Hyde, B.) Ballarat: Modotti Press.

Best, R. (2011) Emotion, Spiritual Experience and Education: A Reflection. *IJCS*, 16, (4), 361–368.

Bone, J., Cullen J. and Loveridge, J. (2007) Everyday Spirituality: An Aspect of the Holistic Curriculum in Action. *Contemporary Issues in Early Childhood*, 8, (2), 344–351.

Bosacki, S. and Ota, C. (2000) Preadolescents' Voices: A Consideration of British and Canadian Children's Reflections on Religion, Spirituality, and their Sense of Self. *IJCS*, 5, (2), 203–219.

Boyce -Tillman, J. (2009) The Transformative Qualities of a Liminal Space created by Musicking. *Philosophy of Music Education Review*. Indiana University Press. 17, (2), 184–202. Available at: *https://www.jstor.org/stable/40495499*

(2016) Experiencing *Music – Restoring the Spiritual. Music as Well-Being*. Oxford, Berne, Berlin: Peter Lang.

(2018) Conversation with Valerie Duffy-Cross, 22 October.

Brent Bill, J. (2016) *Holy Silence: The Gift of Quaker Spirituality*. Michigan: Eerdmans Publishing.

Broadbent, J. (2004) Research Paper: Embodying the abstract: Enhancing Children's Spirituality Through Creative Dance. *IJCS*, 9, (1), 97–104. Available at: https://doi.org/10.1080/1364436042000200852

Bryman, A. (2012) *Social Research Methods*. 2nd edition. Oxford: Oxford University Press.

Buber, M. (2002) [1947] *Between Man and Man*. London and New York: Routledge.

Burridge, K. (1979) *Someone, No One: An Essay on Individuality*. Princeton, New Jersey: Princeton University Press.

Burrows, L. (2006) Does Spiritual Wellbeing Have a Place in Public Education? *Conference proceedings – AARE Annual Conference,* Adelaide, 2006. Australian Association for Research in Education. Available at: https://www.aare.edu.au/data/publications/2006/bur06182.pdf

(2009) Towards a Spirited Approach to Well-being for Children Who Challenge the System. *Curriculum Perspectives Journal*, 9, (2), 73–76.

(2014) Opening Pandora's Box: The Contribution of Mindfulness to the Inner World of Teaching in Steiner Education. Conference proceedings. *Mindfulness for Education, Health & Management*. Available at: https://www.researchgate.net/profile/Leigh_Burrows/publication/264418266

Bussing, A., Foller-Mancini, A., Gidley, J. and Heusser, P. (2010) Aspects of Spirituality in Adolescents. *IJCS*, 15, (1), 25-44. Available at: https://doi.org/10.1080/13644360903565524

Cambridge Dictionary *https://dictionary.cambridge.org/dictionary/english/*

Carlson Jones, D. (2004) Body Image Among Adolescent Boys and Girls. A Longitudinal Study. *Developmental Psychology*, 40, (5), 823–35.

Carter, N., Bryant-Lukosius, D., Di Censo, A., Blythe, J. and Neville, A. (2014) The Use of Triangulation in Qualitative Research. Oncology Nursing Forum, 41, (5), 545–7.

Champagne, E. (2003) Being a Child, A Spiritual Child. *IJCS*, 8, (1), 43–58. Available at: https://doi.org/10.1080/13644360304639

Charmaz, K. (2003) *Constructing Grounded Theory: A Practical Guide Through Qualitative Analysis.* Thousand Oaks, CA: Sage.

Cheek, J., Carpentieri, A., Smith, T., Rierdan, J. and Koff, E. (1986) Adolescent Shyness. In: Jones, W., Cheek, J. and Briggs, S. (eds.) *Shyness, Emotions, Personality, and Psychotherapy*. 224–250. Boston, MA: Springer. Available at: https://doi.org/10.1007/978-1-4899-0525-3_9

Cheek, J. and Krasnoperova, E. (1999). Varieties of Shyness in Adolescence and Adulthood. In: Schmidt, L. and Schulkin, J. (eds.), *Extreme Fear, Shyness, and Social Phobia: Origins, Biological Mechanisms, and Clinical Outcomes*. 224–250. Available at: https://doi.org/10.1093/acprof:oso/9780195118872.003.0013

Clarke, I. (2008) *Madness, Mystery and the Survival of God*. Ropley, Hants: O Books Press.

Cohen, L., Manion, L. and Morrison, K. (2000) *Research Methods in Education*: Fifth Edition. London: Routledge Falmer.

Coles, R. (1977) *The Spiritual Life of Children*. Boston: Houghton Mifflin Company.

Corbin, J. and Strauss, A. (1990) *Basics of Qualitative Research: Grounded Theory Procedures and Techniques*. Thousand Oaks, CA: Sage.

Csikszentmihalyi, M. (1975a) *Beyond Boredom and Anxiety: Experiencing Flow in Work and Play*. San Francisco: Jossey-Bass.

(1975b) Play and Intrinsic Rewards, *Journal of Humanistic Psychology*, 15, (3), 41–63. Available at: http://doi.org/10.1177/002216787501500306

(1990) Flow: The Psychology of Optimal Experience. *Journal of Leisure Research*, 24 (1), 93–94

(2002) [1992] *Flow*. London, Sydney, Auckland: Rider.

Dauenhauer, B. (1979) Discourse, Silence and Tradition. *The Review of Metaphysics*, 32, (3) 437–451. Available at: http://www.jstor.org/stable/20127222

(1980) *Silence, The Phenomenon and Its Ontological Significance*. Bloomington: Indiana University Press.

(1983) Authorial Words about Silence. *Philosophy Today*, 27, (2),147–153. Available at: https://philpapers.org/rec/DAUAWA

De Kuyken, W., Weare, K., Ukoumunne, O., Vicary, R., Motton, N., Burnett, R., Cullen, C., Hennelly, S. and Huppert, F. (2013) Effectiveness of the Mindfulness in Schools Programme:

Non-Randomised Controlled Feasibility Study. *The British Journal of Psychiatry,* 126–131. Available at: https://www.ncbi.nlm.nih.gov/pubmed/23787061

De Kuyken, W. *et al* (37 others) (2022) Effectiveness and cost-effectiveness of universal school-based mindfulness training compared with normal school provision in reducing risk of mental health problems and promoting well-being in adolescence: the MYRIAD cluster randomised controlled trial: *Evidence Based Mental Health* 2022,25. Available at: https://doi.org/10.1136/ebmental-2021-300396

De Souza, M. (2009) Promoting Wholeness and Wellbeing in Education: Exploring Aspects of the Spiritual Dimension. In: de Souza, M., Francis, L. J., O'Higgins-Norman, J. and Scott, D. (eds) *International Handbook of Education for Spirituality, Care and Wellbeing/International Handbook of Religion and Education, 3.* Dordrecht, Netherlands: Springer. 677–692.

(2014) The Empathetic Mind: The Essence of Human Spirituality, *ICJS* 19,1, 45–54.

DiCicco-Bloom, B. and Crabtree, B. (2006) The Qualitative Research Interview. *Medical Education,* 40, (4), 314–321. Available at: doi:10.1111/j.1365-2929.2006.02418x

Donaldson, M. (1987) *Children's Minds.* London: Fontana Press.

(1993) *Human Minds: An Exploration.* London, New York: Penguin.

Dunning, D., Tudor, K., Radley, L., Dalrymple, N., Funk, J., Vainre, M., Ford, T., Montero- Marin, J., Kuyken, W. and Dalgleish, T. (2022) Do Mindfulness Programmes Improve the Cognitive Skills, Behaviour and Mental Health of Children and Adolescents? An Updated Meta-analysis of Randomised Control Trials. *Evidence Based Mental Health,* (0), 1–8. Available at: doi:10.1136/ebmental-2022-300464

Eaude, T. (2003) Outshining Lights in Unexpected Corners; New Angles on Young Children's Development. *IJCS,* 8, (2), 151–162.

(2008) *Children's Social, Moral, Spiritual and Cultural Development in Primary and Early Years*. 2nd edition. Exeter, UK: Learning Matters Ltd.

(2009) Happiness, Emotional Well-being and Mental Health – What has Children's Spirituality to Offer? *IJCS, 14,* (3), 185–196.

(2022) What are the Barriers which Inhibit Children's Spiritual Development? Webinar paper 7.11.22. IACS Conference. Available at: https://drive.google.com/drive/folders/IPSM0051hM01B-LTS VeduUqPAxj4bUO

Elkind, D. (2001) [1981] *The Hurried Child*. Victoria, Canada: Abe Books.

Elkind, D. and Elkind, S. (1962) Varieties of Religious Experience in Young Adolescents. *Journal for the Scientific Study of Religion*, 2, 102–112.

Erricker, C., Erricker, J., Sullivan D., Ota, C. and Fletcher, M. (1997) *The Education of the Whole Child*. London: Cassell.

Ezzy, D. (2002) *Qualitative Analysis. Practice and Innovation*. New York and London: Routledge.

Fahie, D. (2014) Doing Sensitive Research Sensitively: Ethical and Methodological Issues in Researching Work-place Bullying. *International Journal of Qualitative Methods*, 8, (1), 54–63.

Farmer, L. (1992) Religious Experience in Childhood: A Study of Adult Perspectives on Early Spiritual Awareness. *Religious Education,* 87, (2), 259–68.

Fenwick, P. and Fenwick, E. (1995) *The Truth in the Light. An Investigation into Over 300 Near-Death Experiences*. London: Headline Press.

Ferrer, J. N. (2002) *Revisioning Transpersonal Theory. A Participatory Vision of Human Spirituality*. New York: State University of New York Press.

(2008) What Does It Mean to Live a Fully Embodied Spiritual Life? *International Journal of Transpersonal Studies (IJTS),* 27, 1–11.

Feuerbach, L. (1967) [1851] *Lectures on the Essence of Religion*. Translated by Ralph Mannheim. Available at: https://rowlandpasaribu.files.wordpress.com/2013/09/ludwig-feuerbach-lectures-on-the-essence-of-religion.pdf

Fielding, N. and Thomas, H. (2008) Qualitative Interviewing. *Researching Social Life*. 8, 123–144. Available at: https://openresearch.surrey.ac.uk/esploro/outputs/99512785702346

Fisher, J. (2009a) Understanding and Assessing Spiritual Health. In: De Souza, M., Francis L., O'Higgins, N. and Scott, D. (eds.). *International Handbook of Education for Spirituality, Care and Well-Being*. Springer: Dordrecht. 3, 69–88.

(2009b) Getting the Balance: Assessing Spiritual Well-being Among Children and Youth. *ICJS*, 14, 3,273–288. Available at: https://doi.org/10.1080/13644360903086547

Fiumara, G. (1996) *The Other Side of Language: A Philosophy of Listening*. Translated by C. Lambert. 2nd edition. London and New York: Routledge.

Fuller, R. (2001) *Spiritual but not Religious. Understanding Unchurched America*. London and New York: Oxford University Press.

(2007) Spirituality in the Flesh: The Role of Discrete Emotions in Religious Life. *Journal of the American Academy of Religion*, 7, (1), 25–51.

Gadamer, H-G. (2013) [1975] *Truth and Method*. Trans. by J. Weinsheimer and D. G. Marshall. London, New Delhi and New York: Bloomsbury.

Gendlin, E. (1997) [1962] *Experiencing and the Creation of Meaning*. Chicago: Northwestern University Press.

(1981) [1978] *Focusing*. New York, Toronto, London: Bantam Press.

Glaser, B. and Strauss, A. (2017) [1967] *The Discovery of Grounded Theory: Strategies for Qualitative Research*. London and New York: Taylor and Francis.

Haidt, J. (2003) The Moral Emotions. In: Davidson, R., Goldsmith, H., Scherer, K. (eds.) *Handbook of Effective Sciences.* Oxford: Oxford University Press. 852–870. Available at: https://www.overcominghateportal.org/uploads/5/4/1/5/5415260/the_moral_emotions

(2006) *The Happiness Hypothesis*. London: Arrow Books.

Hardwired to Connect, (2010). Available at: www.americanvalues.org.

Hart, T. (2003) *The Secret Spiritual World of Children*. California: New World Library.

(2008) Interiority and Education. Exploring the Neurophenomenology of Contemplation and its Potential Role in Learning. *Journal of Transformative Education*, 6, (4) 235–250.

Harvey, G. (2003) Guesthood as Ethical Decolonising Research Method. *Numen*, 50, (2) 125–146. Available at: http://www.jstor.org/stable/3270516

Harwood, A. (1992) [1958], *The Recovery of Man in Childhood. A Study in the Work of Rudolf Steiner*. New York: Myrin.

Haskins, C., (2011) The Gift of Silence. *Montessori Life, 23,* (2), 34.

Hay, D. and Nye, R. (2006) [1998] *The Spirit of the Child*. London and Philadelphia: Jessica Kingsley Publishers.

Head, G. (2020) Ethics in Educational Research: Review Boards, Ethical Issues and Research Development. *European Educational Research Journal,* 19, (1), 72–83. Available at: doi:10.1177/1474904118796315journals.sagepu.com/home/

Henderson, K. and Esposito, J. (2017) Using Others in the Nicest Way Possible: On Colonial and Academic Practice(s) and an Ethic of Humility. *Qualitative Enquiry*, 25, (9–10), 876–889. Available at: https://doi.org/10.1177/1077800417743528

Heschel, A., (1983) [1955] *God in Search of Man*. New York: Farrar, Straus and Giroux.

Hodkinson, P. (2008) Grounded Theory and Inductive Research. *Researching Social Life*. In: Gilbert, N. and Stoneman, P. (eds.)

Researching Social Life, 98–115. LA, London, New Delhi: Sage, University of Surrey.

Holder, M., Coleman, B. and Wallace, J. (2010) Spirituality, Religiousness, and Happiness in Children Aged 8–12 Years. *Journal of Happiness Studies*, 11, 131–150. Available at: https://doi.org/10.1007/s10902-008-9126-1

Holloway, I. and Wheeler, S. (2010) [1996], *Qualitative Research in Nursing and Healthcare*. Oxford and Iowa: Wiley-Blackwell.

Hossein Nasr, S. (1997) *Man and Nature, The Spiritual Crisis of Modern Man.* Chicago: ABC International Group.

Houskamp, B., Fisher, L. and Stuber, M. (2004) Spirituality in Children and Adolescents: Research Findings and Implications for Clinicians and Researchers. *Child and Adolescent Psychiatric Clinics of North America,* 13, (1), 221–30.

Hyde, B (2005) Beyond Logic – Entering the Realm of Mystery: Hermeneutic Phenomenology as a Tool for Reflecting on Children's Spirituality., *International Journal of Children's Spirituality,* 10, (1), 31–44. Available at: DOI: 10.1080/13644360500039477

(2008a) *Children and Spirituality: Searching for Meaning and Connectedness*. London and Philadelphia: Jessica Kingsley.

(2008b) The Identification of Four Characteristics of Children's Spirituality in Australian Catholic Primary Schools. *IJCS*, 13, (2), 117–127.

(2010) Silence, Agency and Children's Spirituality. *IJCS*, 15, (2), 97–99.

(2011) So, What Have We Learned. *IJCS,* 16, (2), 195–196.

(2013) *The Search for a Theology of Childhood. Essays by Jerome W. Berryman from 1978–2009*. Ballarat, Victoria: Modotti Press.

(2018) Pathic Knowing, Lived Sensibility and Phenomenological Reflections on Children's Spirituality. *ICJS*, 23, (4), 346–357.

(2021). Silenced by Performativity: The Child's Right to a Spiritual Voice in an Age of Neoliberal Educational Imperatives. *IJCS, 26,* (1–2), 9–23.

Hyde, B., Ota, K. and Yust, K-M. (2013) All the King's Horses and All the King's Men – Can You Put Spirituality Back Together Again Once it has been Deconstructed. *IJCS,* 18, (2), 233–234. Available at: https://doi.org/10.1080/1364436X.2013.850299

Iannaccone, A. (2013) Football: An Introduction to a Rite of Rites. *Italian Sociological Review* 3, (2), 121–129. Available at: http://dx.doi.org/10.13136/isr.v3i2.63

Iijima, Y. (1987) Folk Culture and the Liminality of Children. *Current Anthropology,* 28, (4), 47–48.

Ivtzan, I., Chan, C., Gardner, H. and Prashar, K. (2013) Linking Religion and Spirituality with Psychological Well-Being: Examining Self-Actualisation, Meaning in Life and Personal Growth Initiative. *Journal of Religion and Health* 52, (3), 915–929. Available at: https://doi.org/10.1007/s10943-011-9540-2

James, W. (1985) [1902] *The Varieties of Religious Experience: A Study in Human Nature.* London, New York: Penguin.

Jarvis, P., Swiniarski, L. and Holland, W. (2017) *Early Years Pioneers in Context.* London and New York: Routledge.

Johnson, M. (1990) [1987] *The Body in the Mind: The Bodily Basis of Meaning, Imagination and Reason.* Chicago and London: University of Chicago Press.

Keating, N. (2016) Children's Spirituality and the Practice of Meditation in Irish Primary Schools. *IJCS,* 0, (0), 1–23. Available at: https://www.tandfonline.com/doi/full/10.1080/1364436X.2016.126492

Kessler, R. (2000) *The Soul of Education.* Alexandria, VA, USA: Association for Supervision and Curriculum Development.

Kozol, J. (2000) *Ordinary Resurrections. Children and the Years of Hope.* New York: Crown Publishers.

Kumashiro, K. (2014) Troubling the Politics of Engagement, Ethics and Educational Research: Reframing Our Work. *Diaspora, Indigenous and Minority Education*, 8, (1), 44–54

Leech, N. and Onwuegbuzie, A. (2007) An Array of Qualitative Data Analysis Tools: A Call for Data Triangulation. *School Psychology Quarterly* 22, (4), 557–584.

Lees, H. (2012) *Silence in Schools*. Stoke-on-Trent, England: Trentham Books Ltd.

Lillard, A. (2005) *Montessori, the Science Behind the Genius.* Oxford, New York, Oxford University Press.

(2011) 'Mindfulness Practice in Education: Montessori's Approach', *Mindfulness*, 2, 78–85.

Lipscomb, A. and Gersch, I. (2012) Using a 'Spiritual Listening Tool'. *IJCS*, 17, (1), 5–23.

Locke, J. (2007) [1693] *Some Thoughts Concerning Education*. New York: Dover.

Lovelock, P. and Adams, K. (2017) From Darkness to Light. Children Speak of Divine Encounter. *IJCS*, 22, (1), 36–48.

Markstrom, C., Huey, E., Stiles, B. and Krause, A. (2010) Frameworks of Caring and Helping in Adolescence: Are Empathy, Religiosity, and Spirituality Related Constructs? *Youth & Society*, 42, (1), 59–80. Available at: doi:10.1177/0044118X09333644

Maslow, A. (1964) *Religions, Values and Peak Experiences*. Ohio: Ohio State University Press.

McCreery, E. (2001) Empathy, Experience and Spirituality. *International Journal of Children's Spirituality*, 6, (3), 363–364. Available at: doi: 10.1080/13644360120100513

Merriam Webster. Available at: https://wwww.merriam-webster.com

Miller, L. (2015) *The Spiritual Child.* London: Bluebird Books for Life.

Montessori, M. (1949) *The Absorbent Mind.* Adyar, Madras India: The Theosophical Publishing House.

(1966) [1936] *The Secret of Childhood*. Trans. by M. J. Costelloe. New York: Ballantine Books.

(2004) [1948] *The Discovery of the Child.* Delhi, India: Aakar Books.

(2014) *The Montessori Method.* (Not given, Amazon Press)

Moody, R. (1998). *The Light Beyond.* London: Random House.

Moore, K., Gomez-Garibello, C., Bosacki, S. and Talwar, V. (2016) Children's Spiritual Lives: The Development of a Children's Spirituality Measure. *Religions*, 7, (8), 95.

Moriarty, M. (2011) Conceptualisation of Children's Spirituality Arising Out of Recent Research. *IJCS*, 16, (3), 271–285.

(2013) Sport and Children's Spirituality: An Australian Perspective. *IJCS,* 18, (1). 103–117.

Mosher, R. (2001) Silence, Listening, Teaching and the Space of What is Not. *Language Arts*, 78, (4), 366–370.

NASA (2003) Interpreting the 'Song of a Distant Black Hole. Available at: http://www.nasa.gov./centers/goddard/universe/black_hole_sound.html

Neitz, M. and Spickard, J. (1990) Steps Towards a Sociology of Religious Experience: The Theories of Mihaly Csikszentmihalyi and Alfred Schutz. *Sociological Analysis*, 51, (1), 15–33. Available at: https://www.jstor.org/stable/3711338

Nortjé, E. and van der Merwe, L. (2016) Young Children and Spirituality: Understanding Children's Connectedness in a Group Music Class. *IJCS,* 31, (1), 3–18. Available at: https://doi.org/10.1080/1364436X.2016.1138932

Nussbaum, M. (2008) [2001] *Upheavals of Thought. The Intelligence of the Emotions*. Cambridge, New York, Melbourne: Cambridge University Press.

Nye, R. (2009) *Children's Spirituality: What it is and Why it Matters.* London: Church House Publishing.

OCR 2017, Level 3 Diploma in Practical Spirituality and Wellness. Available at: www.ocr.org.uk/images/201944-level3-unit-eol-304-support-the-spiritual-well-being-of-individuals.pdf

Ofsted, Research Review Series, Religious Education, 12. May 2021.

Ogden, T. (2004) On Holding and Containing, Being and Dreaming. *International Journal of Psychoanalysis*, 85, 1349–1364. Available at: On holding and containing, being and dreaming – OGDEN – 2004 – The International Journal of Psychoanalysis – Wiley Online Library

Otto, R. (1958) *The Idea of the Holy, An Inquiry into the Non-Rational Factor in the Idea of the Divine and its Relation to the Rational,* translated by John W. Harvey. Oxford: Oxford University Press.

Pargament, K. (2011) *Spiritually Integrated Psychotherapy: Understanding and Addressing the Scared.* New York: The Guildford Press.

Payne, F. (2001) Collective Effervescence and *Communitas*: Processual Models of Ritual and Society in Emile Durkheim and Victor Turner. *Dialectical Anthropology*, 26, 89–124.

Pearmain, R. (2007) Evocative Clues and Presence: Relational Consciousness within Qualitative Research. *IJCS*, 12, (1), 75–82.

Petitmengin, C. (2014) *Researching the Dynamics of Lived Experience.* Unpublished Paper at the Mind Science Conference 2014, Boston.

Petrash, J. (2014) *Understanding Waldorf Education. Teaching from the Inside Out*. Edinburgh: Floris Books.

Piaget, J. (1926) *The Language and Thought of the Child*. London: Routledge and Kegan Paul.

Picard, M. (2006) [1948] *The World of Silence.* Available at: https://herbertbaioco.files.wordpress.com/2017.../the-world-of-silence-max-picard.pdf

Pring, R. (2001) The Virtues and Vices of an Educational Researcher. *Journal of Philosophy of Education*, 35, (3), 407–421. Available at: https://doi.org/10.1111/1467-9752.00235

Puchalski, C., Ferrell, B., Virani, R., Otis-Green, S., Baird, P. and Bull, J. (2009) Improving the Quality of Spiritual Care as a Dimension of Palliative Care: The Report of the Consensus Conference. *Journal of Palliative Medicine*, 12, (10), 885–904.

Quaker Education in the UK and Ireland. Available at: www.aquakereducation.co.uk

Ramachandran, V. (2011) *The Tell-tale Brain: Unlocking the Mysteries of Human Nature*, London: William Heinemann.

Rankin, M. (2008) *An Introduction to Religious and Spiritual Experience.* London and New York: Continuum International Publishing Group.

Rapley, T. (2001) The Art(fulness) of Open-Ended Interviewing: Some Considerations of an Analysing Interview. *Qualitative Research*, 1 (3), 303–323. Available at https://doi.org/10.1177/146879410100100303

Ratcliff, D. and Nye, R. (2006) Childhood Spirituality: Strengthening the Research Foundation. In: Roehlkepartain, E., King, P., Wagener, P., and Benson, P. (eds.) *The Handbook of Spiritual Development in Childhood and Adolescence*. Thousand Oaks, CA: Sage. 473–84.

Religious Society of Friends (Quakers) (2017) Quakers in Britain. Available at: http://www.quaker.org.uk/.

Risser, J. (1997) *Hermeneutics and the Voice of the Other*. Albany: State University of New York Press.

Robinson, E. (1977) *Original Vision: A Study of the Religious Experience of Childhood.* Oxford: Manchester College Oxford, Religious Experience Research Unit.

Rodgers, R., Slater, A., Gordon, C., McLean S., Jarman, H. and Paxton, S. (2020) A Biopsychosocial Model of Social Media Use and Body Image Concerns, Disordered Eating, and Muscle Building Behaviors among Adolescent Girls and Boys. *Journal of Youth and Adolescence*, 49, (3). Available at: doi:10.1007/s10964-019-01190-0

Roehlkepartain, E., Benson, P., King, P. and Wagener, P. (2005) Spiritual Development in Childhood and Adolescence: Moving to the Scientific Mainstream. In: Roehlkepartain, E., King, P., Wagener, P. and Benson, P. (eds.) *The Handbook of Spiritual Development in Childhood and Adolescence*. Thousand Oaks, CA: Sage. 1–15.

Ross, M. (2014) *Silence: A User's Guide: Volume One: Process*. London: Darton, Longman and Todd.

(2018) *Silence: A User's Guide: Volume Two: Application*. London: Darton, Longman and Todd.

Saroglou, V., Pichon, I., Trompette, L., Verschueren, M. and Dernelle, R. (2005) Prosocial Behaviour and Religion: New Evidence Based on Projective Measures and Peer Ratings. *Journal for the Scientific Study of Religion*, 44, (3), 323–348. Available at: https://doi.ord/10.1111/j.1468-5906.2005.00289

Sartori, P. (2014) *The Wisdom of Near-Death Experiences*. London, New York: Watkins Publishing.

Scales, P., Syvertsen, A., Benson, P., Roehlkepartain, E. and Sesma, A. (2014) The Relationship of Spiritual Development to Youth Health and Well-Being: Evidence from a Global Study. In: Ben Arieh, A., Casas, F., Frones, I. and Korbin, J. (eds.). *Handbook of Child Well-Being*, 1101–1134. Springer: Dordrecht. Available at: https://doi.org/10.1007/978-90-481-9063-8_41

Schein, D. (2014). Nature's Role in Children's Spiritual Development. *Children, Youth and Environments*, 24, (2), 78–101. Available at: https://doi.org/10.7721/chilyoutenvi.24.2.0078

Scheindlin, L. (2003) Emotional Perception and Spiritual Development. *IJCS*, 8, (2), 179–193.

Schlarb, C. (2007) The Developmental Impact of Not Integrating Childhood Peak Experiences. *IJCS*, 12, (3), 249–262.

Sciacca, F. (1957) Meaningful Silence, *Giornale di Metafisica Philosophy Today*, 11, (4), 250-254. Available at: https://philpapers.org/rec/SCIMS

Scott, D. (2004) Retrospectives Spiritual Narratives: Exploring Recalled Childhood and Adolescent Spiritual Experiences. *IJCS*, 9, (1), 67–79.

Seden, J. (1998) The Spiritual Needs of Children, *Practice*, 10, (4), 57–67.

Singleton, A., Mason, M. and Webber, R. (2004) (On-line 2010), Spirituality in Adolescence and Young Adulthood: A Method for a Qualitative Study. *IJCS*, 9, (3), 247–262. Available at: http://dx.doi.org/10.1080/1364436042000292176

Standing, E. (1998) *Maria Montessori: Her Life and Work*. London and New York: Penguin.

Steiner, R. (1988) [1982] The *Child's Changing Consciousness and Waldorf Education*. (London: Rudolf Steiner Press).

(1994) *How to Know Higher Worlds. A Modern Path of Initiation*. Translated by Christopher Bamford. New York, Anthroposophic Press.

(2012) [1923]. *Knowledge of the Higher Worlds. How it is Achieved*. Volume 10 of collected works. Translation by Osmond, D.S. and Davy, C., Forest Row, East Sussex: Rudolf Steiner Press.

Stern, J. (2001) John MacMurray, Spirituality, Community and Real Schools. *IJCS*, 6, (1), 25–39.

Stoyles, G., Stanford, B., Caputi, P., Keating, A. and Hyde, B. (2012) A Measure of Spiritual Sensitivity in Children. *IJCS*, 17, (3), 203–15.

Strawser, M. (2006) Gifts of Silence from Kierkegaard and Derrida. *Soundings: An Interdisciplinary Journal*, 89, (1/2), 55–72.

Szakolczai, A. (2009) Liminality and Experience: Structuring Transitory Situations and Transformative Events. *International Political Anthropology*, 2, (1), 141–72. https://d1wqtxts1xzle7.cloudfront.net/34746291/ipa_journal_1_2009_szakolczai-with-cover-page.pdf

Tamminen, K. (1994) Religious Experience in Childhood and Adolescence: A Viewpoint of Religious Development between the Ages of 7 and 20. *The International Journal for the Psychology of Religion*, 4, (2), 61–85.

Taplin, M. (2011) Silent Sitting: A Cross-Curricular Tool to Promote Resilience. *IJCS*, 16, (2), 75–96. Available at: https://www.tanfonline.com/doi/abs/10.1080/1364436X.2011.

Terrell, S. (2011). Mixed-Methods Research Methodologies. *The Qualitative Report*, 17, (1), 254–280. Available at: http://www.nova.edu/ssss/QR/QR17-1/terrell.pdf

The Association of Social Anthropologists (1999) [updated 2021], *Ethical Guidelines for Good Research Practice*. Available at: https://www.theasa.org/ethics/

The Chambers Dictionary (1998) Edinburgh: Chambers Harrap.

Thomassen, B. (2013). *Affectivity in the Liminal: The Relevance of Arnold van Gennep and his Life-Work*. Paper presented at Affectivity and Liminality, Brighton, United Kingdom. Available at: http://www.open.ac.uk/ccig/dialogues/blogs/liminality-and-traces-of-affectivity-in-the-work-of-arnold-van-gennep-by-bjørnthomassen

(2018) *Liminality and the Modern. Living Through the In-Between*. London and New York: Routledge.

Thun, T. (1964) *Die Religion des Kindes: Eine Untersuchung nach Klassengespraechen mit Katholischen und Evangelischen Kindern der Grundschule*. Germany: E. Klett.

Tisdall, E., Davis, J. and Gallagher, M. (2010) *Researching with Children and Young People: Research Design, Methods and Analysis*. London: Sage.

Todres, L. (2011) *Embodied Enquiry: Phenomenological Touchstones for Research, Psychotherapy and Spirituality*. Basingstoke and New York: Palgrave Macmillan.

Torevell, D. (2000) Acting Out of Affections: Embodiment, Morality and (Post) Modernity. *IJCS* 5, (1), 27–36.

Trousdale, A. (2013) Embodied Spirituality. *IJCS*, 18, (1), 18–29.

Turnbull, C. (1988) Liminality: A Synthesis of Subjective and Objective Experience. Intercultural Studies of Theatre and

Ritual. In: Schechner, R. and Willa Appel, W. (eds.) *By Means of Performance*. New York and Melbourne: University of Cambridge Press. 50–81.

Turner, E. (2006) [2005] *The Heart of Lightness. The Life Story of an Anthropologist*. New York, Oxford: Berghahn Books.

(2009) Interview with Edith Turner. In: Rodriguez, L.(ed.) *AIBR Revista de Antropologia Iberoamericana* 4, (3), Available at: https://www.aibr.org/antroplogia/04v03/entrevistas/0403016.pdf

(2012) *The Anthropology of Collective Joy*. New York: Palgrave Macmillan.

Turner, V. (1974a) Liminal to Liminoid in Play, Flow and Ritual. *Rice University Studies* (54-92). Available at: https://sc/bitstream/handle/1911/63159/article_RIP603_part4.pdf

(1974b) *Dramas, Fields and Metaphor: Symbolic Action in Human Society*. Ithaca and London: Cornell University Press.

(1977) Variations on a Theme of Liminality. In: Moore, S. and Myerhoff, B. (eds.) *Secular Rituals*. Amsterdam: Van Gorcum. 36–52.

(1979a) *Process, Performance and Pilgrimage; A Study in Comparative Symbology*. New Delhi: Concept Publishing Company.

(1979b) Frame, Flow and Reflection: Ritual and Drama as Public Liminality. *Japanese Journal of Religious Studies*. 6, (4), 465–499. https://www.jstor.org/stable/30233219

1982) *From Ritual to Theatre. The Human Seriousness of Play*. New York: PAJ Publications.

(1986) Dewey, Dilthey and Drama: An Essay in the Anthropology of Experience. In: Turner, V. and Bruner E. (eds.) *The Anthropology of Experience*. Urbana and Chicago: University of Illinois Press. 33–44.

(1992) *Blazing the Trail: Waymarks in the Exploration of Symbols*. Tucson and London: University of Arizona Press.

(2007) *The Ritual Process. Structure and Antistructure*. New Brunswick and London: Aldine Transaction.

Ulrich, H. (2014) *Rudolf Steiner*, translated by Duke, J. and Balestrini, D. London, New Delhi, New York, Sydney, Bloomsbury: Bloomsbury Library of Educational Thought Series.

Vaillant, G. (2008a) Positive Emotions, Spirituality and the Practice of Psychiatry. In: Singh, A. and Singh, S. (eds.), *Medicine, Mental Health, Science, Religion and Well-Being*. 48–62.

(2008b) *Spiritual Evolution. A Scientific Defence of Faith*. New York: Broadway Books.

Varkey Report, Generation Z: The Global Citizenship Survey. Available at: https://www.varkeyfoundation.org/sites

Van Cappellen, O., Saraoglou, P., Iweins, C., Piovesana, M. and Frederickson, B. (2013) Self-Transcendent Positive Emotions Increase Spirituality Through Basic World Assumptions. *Cognition and Emotion*, 27, (8), 1378–1394. Available at: https://doi.org/10.1080/02699931.787395

Van Gennep, A. (1960) [1909] *The Rites of Passage*. Translated by Vizedom, M. and Caffee, G. Chicago: University of Chicago Press.

Wachs, T. (1986) Noise in the Nursery: Ambient Background Noise and Early Development. *Children's Environments Quarterly*, 3, (1), 22–33.

(1992) *The Nature of Nurture. Individual Differences and Development Series*. London and New Delhi: Sage Publications.

Watson, J. (2013a) Spirituality and Physicality: Crossing Thresholds. *IJCS*, 18, (1), 1–3.

(2013b) Knowing Through the Felt Sense: A Gesture of Openness to the Other. *IJCS*, 18, (1), 118–130.

Watson, P., Hood, R., Morris, R. and Hall, J. (1984) Empathy, Religious Orientation, and Social Desirability.

The Journal of Psychology, 117, (2), 211–216, DOI: 10.1080/00223980.1984.9923679

Weil, S. (1987) *Gravity and Grace.* New York: Ark.

Wilber, K. (2007) *Integral Spirituality: A Startling New Role for Religion in the Modern and Postmodern World.* Boston and London: Integral Books.

Williams, R. (2004) *Silence and Honey Cakes: The Wisdom of the Desert.* Oxford: Lion Books.

Wilson, J. (2001) The Spiritual and the Earthly. *IJCS,* 6, (2), 147–157.

Winnicott, D. and Winnicott, D.W. (1960). The Theory of the Parent-Infant Relationship. *International Journal of Psychoanalysis,* 41, 585–595.

Winston, J. (2003) Drama, Spirituality and the Curriculum, *IJCS* 7, (3), 241–255. Available at: https://doi.org/10.1080/1364436022000023248

Wohlwill, J. and Heft, H. (1977). Environments Fit for the Developing Child. In: McGurk, H. (ed.) *Ecological Factors in Human Development.* Amsterdam: North Holland Publishing. 125-138. Wolverton, M. (2009) Research Design, Hypothesis Testing and Sampling. *Appraisal Journal,* 70, (74), 370–382.

Wood, M. and Tribe, R. (2016) In a Silent Way: Student Perceptions of Silence in Community. *Pastoral Care in Education: An International Journal of Personal, Social and Emotional Development,* 34, (2), 144–155. Available at: https://ray.yorksj.ac.uk/id/eprint/1695/1/In%20a%20Silent%20Way%20main%20doc%20Revised%20May%2016.pdf

Yust, K. (2008) Let Those Who Have Ears to Hear, Listen. Silence with Children. *Lifelong Faith,* 2, (4). Available at: https://www.lifelongfaith.com/uploads/5/1/6/4/5164069/lifelong_faith_journal_2.4.pdf

Zazonc, A. (2006) Love and Knowledge: Recovering the Heart of Learning Through Contemplation. *Teachers College Record,* 108, (9), 1742–1759.

Zimbardo, P. (1977). *Shyness: What it is, what to do About it.* Reading, MA: Addison-Wesley.

Zohar, D. and Marshall, I. (2001) *Spiritual Intelligence, the Ultimate Intelligence.* London: Bloomsbury.

Author Biography

Val Duffy-Cross worked with teenagers for over 38 years in the UK and also in a German state school and was the headteacher of two large secondary schools. She became increasingly alarmed by the obvious deterioration in children's mental health since the mid-1980s – a notable change. Though her teaching subjects were History and German, her PhD research, catalysed by conversations with many groups of children in her schools, focussed on child spirituality, believing that a recognition and appreciation of this, might in some way help to alleviate the psychological distress so evident amongst our young. A former feminist activist, she has retained the optimism from the 1960s, and the view that it is possible to make positive societal change through the raising of consciousness.

She is a member of The Alister Hardy Trust, The Scientific and Medical Network and several meditation groups. She loves the company of young people, and cooking.

ESSENTIA

Essentia Books, a collaboration between Collective Ink Ltd. and Essentia Foundation, publishes rigorous scholarly work relevant to metaphysical idealism, the notion that reality is essentially mental in nature. For more information on modern idealism, please visit www.essentiafoundation.org.

Recent Bestsellers from Essentia Books Are:

Irreducible
Federico Faggin
The inventor of the microprocessor explores the fundamental nature of consciousness.
Paperback: 978-1-80341-509-3 ebook: 978-1-80341-510-9

The Sapient Cosmos
James B. Glattfelder
Novel paradigms in physics and philosophy are uncovering radical new visions for the ultimate nature of reality and consciousness.
Paperback: 978-1-80341-404-1 ebook: 978-1-80341-405-8

Children's Unexplained Experiences in a Post Materialist World
Donna Maria Thomas
Paperback: 978-1-80341-084-5 ebook: 978-1-80341-085-2

Mind, Matter and Life
Massimiliano Sorrentino and Daniela Panighetti
Why the mind-matter problem could invalidate the neo-Darwinian materialist conception of the world.
Paperback: 978-1-80341-530-7 ebook: 978-1-80341-613-7

What Lies Beyond
Matt Colborn
Paranormal experiences — why they matter and how they can help make a better tomorrow.
Paperback: 978-1-80341-829-2 ebook: 978-1-80341-836-0

In Pursuit of the Inconceivable

Peter Guy Jones

A comprehensive explanation of the relationship between formal scholastic metaphysics and the philosophical foundation of mysticism and the Perennial philosophy.

Paperback: 978-1-80341-906-0 ebook: 978-1-80341-921-3

Find more titles at

www.collectiveinkbooks.com/essentia-books